COPYRIGHT 2001

ALL RIGHTS RESERVED

Library of Congress Control Number: 2001098384
ISBN: 09676602-5-4

Reflections

From

a Flying Falcon

Ahmad H. Sakr, Ph.D.

Published by:
Foundation for Islamic Knowledge
P.O. Box 665
Lombard, Illinois 60148 (USA)
Telephone: (630) 495-4817
FAX: (630) 627-8894
Tax I.D #36-352-8916

NOTE: Your generous contribution to this **Foundation** will enable us to publish more valuable literature and to render more services to all. The **Foundation** has a tax-exempt status with the IRS. Your donations are tax-deductible.

DEDICATION

    This book is dedicated to Allah Ta'ala (Almighty) for all the favors He has bestowed upon me in creating and bringing me to this world. His Love, His Mercy, His Compassion, His Forgiveness, His Graciousness, His Kindness and His Bountifulness are above any humble person like me, to be able to thank Him enough and to praise Him.

O Allah !   I am humbly dedicating this work **to You.**

O Allah !   Accept my humble work and help me disseminate the information to those who need it.

O Allah !   Make this humble work worthy **of You.**

O Allah !   Forgive my shortcomings.

O Allah !   Help me live as a Muslim and die as a Mu'min (Believer).

O Allah !   Let me be summoned on the Day of Judgment with Prophet Muhammad (pbuh), with the other Prophets, the martyrs and the noble believers. Ameen.

Reflections From A Flying Falcon

TABLE OF CONTENTS

*	Dedication	ii
*	Table of Contents	iii
*	Acknowledgements	vi
*	Special Prayers	viii
*	Supplications	x

	Introduction	1
1.	Introducing Islam	6
2.	Graduation	9
3.	Air Trip Unfulfilled	11
4.	Air Trip Fulfilled	17
5.	Reading Qur'an In The Plane	22
6.	Listening To The Qur'an After Death	24
7.	Wrong Expectations	29
8.	Rewards From Allah (Swt)	34
9.	I Had No Choice	38
10.	They Claim Results	44
11.	Las Vegas Visits	48
12.	Going To Canada	51
13.	Trip To Peoria	56
14.	We Need You ... But	58
15.	Parasites	64
16.	Tell Us When You Are Around	68
17.	Gorgeous But Scary	71
18.	Air Tickets Are Expensive	77
19.	I Wish I Was Never Created	82
20.	Use Me!	85
21.	Homeless In Paradise	89
22.	A Catalyst	93
23.	A Mosque Or A Castle?!	95
24.	Wanted As Honored Guest	99
25.	Post Mortem	106
26.	Empty Buildings	110

27.	A Wall In The Masjid	114
28.	Trying To Take-Over	117
29.	Sleeping In The Same Bed	123
30.	I Don't Want To Die	126
31.	Green And Dry Leaves	129
32.	A Child In The Hospital	131
33.	Shoveling Snow	134
34.	'Ilm And 'Ulama'	137
35.	A Visit To The Vatican	140
36.	Muslims And Catholics Dialogue	143
37.	Visits To Trinidad	153
38.	Unexpected Experiences	161
39.	Ugly… Ugly … Ugly	169
40.	Shame … Shame … Shame	174
41.	Dirty … Dirty … Dirty	180
42.	Deposition	183
43.	I Don't Know	192
44.	Money … Money…Money	195
45.	Rush… Rush…Rush … Wait… Wait.. Wait	200
46.	We Did Not Come To Listen To You	204
47.	Happiness Through Miseries	208
48.	A Plane Of My Own	213
49.	Blank… Blank.. Blank	215
50.	Islamic Vs. Public Schools	217
51.	Living By Islam	220
52.	At The Age Of Forty	224
53.	Retirement	234
54.	Happy… Happy…Happy	237
55.	Final Remarks	240

- Addendum A. …………… Countries Visited   243
- Addendum B ………Supplications Of Traveling   245
- Addendum C ………….. Qur'anic Supplications   248
- Addendum D ……………………Invocation   253
- Addendum E ……Reflections On The 4th of July   257

Table Of Content

- Addendum F ....Legal Statements   264
- Addendum G ....Social Support in Healing   270
- Addendum H .... Synopses   272
- Foundation For Islamic Knowledge   280
- Publications   285
- Books To Be Published   288

بسـم الله الرّحمن الرّحيم

In the name of Allah whose Mercy is maximum and infinite.

ACKNOWLEDGEMENTS

The author wishes to thank all those friends who helped in making this book available to the readers. Special thanks go to Dr. Yusuf Kamaluddin (Yao-Keng) Chang and his wife, Audrey, for their tremendous help and moral support during the last few years.

Thanks and appreciation go to the Vakil families (Abu Bakr, Usman, Farouq, Ishaq, Iqbal, and Akhtar) for their support to the author and the Foundation. May Allah bless them and bless their late parents (Umar and Amina).

Moreover, the author wishes to thank all the respected brothers and sisters who have helped previously and are still helping. Among the many are Mr. Asad Khan and his wife, Sister Azma Khan; Dr. and Mrs. Mohammed Shafi; Mr. & Mrs. Javed Habib; Mr. & Mrs. Abdul Wahab; Mr. & Mrs. Saghir Aslam; Dr. & Mrs. Nadim Daouk; Mr. Refat M. Abo Elela; Dr. & Mrs. Zeyd A. Merenkov; Dr. and Mrs. Daudur Rahman; Mr. and Mrs. Shakeel Syed; Dr. and Mrs. Maqbool Ahmad; Mr. Zia Khan and his wife Tina Khan; Dr. and Mrs. Syed A. Zahir; Dr. and Mrs. Muhammad K. Zaman; Dr. and Mrs. Mostapha Arafa; Dr. & Mrs. Samir Arafeh; Dr. M. Munir Chaudry and family; Dr. Dani Doueiri; Late Dr. F.R. Khan and his respected wife Sister Farhat Khan, may Allah (swt) bless his soul, and many more.

Special thanks and appreciations go to Sister Fawzia Akalal; Sister Sajeda Sultani and her family members; Sister Houyda Najjar Mertaban and her family members; Brother Mohammed Bilal Khan; and Brother Waseem Najmi and his wife Yasmeen; for their kind help in many areas. Also our thanks and appreciations are extended to sister Azizah Abdul Rahman of Singapore, on behalf of her late parents Aminah Bint Ahmad and Abdul Rahman bin Mohamed. May Allah (swt) be pleased with her and her late parents. Ameen.

Acknowledgements

Special thanks and appreciation to Sister Shadia Hassan and her children for their help, advice, and contributions for the love of Allah. Our prayers of Maghfirah for her husband Mr. Samir Hassan. May Allah (swt) bless his soul and make his final stay in Paradise. Ameen.

We are thankful and grateful to Mr. Muhammad El-Bdeiwi and his family for their generosity in helping this Foundation for Da'wah purposes. Our thanks also go to Mr. & Mrs. Abu Ramy Assaf.

Our thanks and appreciations go to Mr. Ammar Charani and his brother Samer Charani of MEF for their help. May Allah bless them.

Thanks and appreciations go to Mr. Khaled Obagi for his support to the Foundation on behalf of his late father and mother Aref Obagi and Nabila Al-Beik. Our thanks and appreciations also go to Mr. Ahmad Al-Khatib for his support to the Foundation on behalf of his mother Soraya, and his late father Adel Baheej Al-Khatib. Thanks and appreciations also go to Dr. Osama Haikal on behalf of his late father, Mr. Omar Haikal. May Allah be pleased with them and may Allah keep their relatives in Paradise. Ameen.

Our thanks and affections are to Brother Fathy Haggag and his family for their tremendous support to the author for all the years in California. It is only Allah (swt) Who will reward them.

Last but not least, my thanks, appreciation and love are to my wife, Zuhar Barhumi Sakr and our loving children, Sara, Hussein, his wife Dania, and their daughter Aya, Jihad and Basil as well as to my grandchildren Nada, Abdur Rahman, Ibrahim, Jenna and Hena from our daughter Sara, and their father Muhammad Nasser.

We pray to Allah (swt) to open the hearts of other friends to invest with Allah in a Sadaqah Jariyah (endowment fund) on behalf of their loving parents before it is too late. Ameen

SPECIAL PRAYERS

The author prays to Allah (swt[1]) to bless Prophet Muhammad and the family of Prophet Muhammad, (pbuh[2]) in as much as He blessed Prophet Ibrahim and the family of Prophet Ibrahim. The author also prays to Allah (swt) to bless the Khulafaa' Rashidoon (Rightly guided) and the Sahaba (Companions) of the Prophet as well as the Tabi`oon (Followers) and the Followers of the Followers till the Day of Judgment.

The author prays to Allah (swt) to reward all the `Ulama', who carried the Message of Allah and His Prophet, and who transmitted it to the new generations.

The author prays to Allah (swt) to reward his parents: his late father Al-Hajj Hussain Mustafa Sakr and his late mother Al-Hajjah Sara Ramadan Sakr for their sacrifices to their twelve children in general and to this author in specific. The author prays to Allah (swt) to reward the late brother of the author, Mr. Muhammad H. Sakr, for helping the author to get his academic education, and his late brothers Mahmood H. Sakr, and Mustafa H. Sakr for taking care of the author's responsibilities overseas.

Special prayers go to the Shaikh of the author who taught him Islam, and trained him from childhood to practice its teaching: Shaikh Muhammad `Umar Da`ooq. May Allah be pleased with him.

Special Du`a' goes to Al-Shaheed Shaikh Hassan Khalid, the late Grand Mufti of Lebanon, who had also great impact on the author's knowledge of Islam. May Allah bless his soul and make him stay in Paradise.

---

[1] swt: Subhanahu Wa Ta'ala (Glory be to Allah, and He is The High).

[2] pbuh: Peace Be Upon Him (The Prophet).

Special prayers and Du`a' go to the many teachers, scholars and `Ulamaa' who were directly tutoring this author at the time of his youth. Through the efforts of Shaikh Muhammad `Umar Da'ooq, the following is a partial list of the teachers who taught this author: Dr. Mustafa Siba`ee; Shaikh Muhammad M. Al-Sawwaf; Dr. Muhammad Al-Zo`by; Shaikh Muhammad `Itani; Shaikh Muhammad M. Da`ooq; Shaikh Al-Fudail Al-Wartalani; Shaikh Muhammad `Abdel Kareem Al-Khattabi; Shaikh Malik Bennabi; Shaikh Faheem Abu`Ubeyh; Shaikh Muhammad Al-Shaal; Dr. Sa`eed Ramadan; Atty. `Abdel Hakeem `Abideen; Dr. Tawfic Houri; Shaikh Abu Salih Itani; Shaikh Hashim Daftardar Al-Madani; and the late Shaikh Abdul Badee` Sakr. May Allah bless them and reward them.

A final prayer is to the readers who took the time to read this book. May Allah (swt) bless them all.

Allahumma Ameen.

الله اكبر.   الله اكبر.

ALLAHU AKBAR   ALLAHU AKBAR

SUPPLICATIONS

DU`A'

O Allah ! I seek refuge in You from anxiety and grief; I seek refuge in You from incapacity and laziness; and I seek refuge in You from the overcoming burden of debts and the overpowering of people.

O Allah ! I seek refuge in You from poverty except to You, from humiliation except for You, and from fear except from You.

O Allah ! I seek refuge in You from stating a false testimony, or committing immorality, or provoking You; and I seek refuge in You from the malice of the enemies, and from enigmatic disease, and from the despair of hope.

O Allah ! I seek refuge in You from the wicked people, from the worries of the livelihood, and from the ill-nature such as from bad attitude.

O Allah ! You are the Mercy of the mercies, and You are the Lord of the universe.

O Allah
Allahumma Ameen

Supplications

بسم الله الرحمن الرحيم

اللهم

اللَّهُمَّ إِنِّي أَعُوذُ بِكَ مِنَ الْهَمِّ وَالْحَزَنِ
وَأَعُوذُ بِكَ مِنَ الْعَجْزِ وَالْكَسَلِ
وَأَعُوذُ بِكَ مِنْ غَلَبَةِ الدَّيْنِ وَقَهْرِ الرِّجَالِ
اللَّهُمَّ إِنِّي أَعُوذُ بِكَ مِنَ الْفَقْرِ إِلَّا إِلَيْكَ
وَمِنَ الذُّلِّ إِلَّا لَكَ وَمِنَ الْخَوْفِ إِلَّا مِنْكَ
وَأَعُوذُ بِكَ أَنْ أَقُولَ زُورًا أَوْ أَغْشَى فُجُورًا
أَوْ أَكُونَ بِكَ مَغْرُورًا وَأَعُوذُ بِكَ
مِنْ شَمَاتَةِ الْأَعْدَاءِ وَعُضَالِ الدَّاءِ
وَخَيْبَةِ الرَّجَاءِ اللَّهُمَّ إِنِّي أَعُوذُ بِكَ
مِنْ شَرِّ الْخَلْقِ وَهَمِّ الرِّزْقِ وَسُوءِ الْخُلُقِ
يَا أَرْحَمَ الرَّاحِمِينَ وَيَا رَبَّ الْعَالَمِينَ

INTRODUCTION

There is a large variety of birds in the society: different colors, sizes and habits. All of them fly and settle down on earth in different houses, cages, nests or caves. Some of them fly very low while others do insist to fly high in the sky above all other birds. Some of the birds are herbivorous, while others are carnivorous. Some insist to live in the mountains away from people while others want to be close to human beings. Some eat other birds to survive, while others eat cereals and leaves.

Eagles, Falcons and Hawks are among the big birds that have to fly high above others in the sky. They desire to live in mountains hiding themselves or even in deserts away from mankind as much as possible. They want to stay free to do whatever they want without being attacked, hunted, or shot down. However some are being caught during hunting, others are being caught and put in the cages for display in animal zoos.

The bird Falcon has being selected from all other birds for many reasons:

1. He is one of the flying birds regularly.
2. He insists to fly high in the sky above many other varieties of birds.
3. He hates to be caught and to be put in a cage. He enjoys Freedom instead of being enslaved.
4. He does not need people to help him or to guide him. He knows where to go and find foods without the help of people.
5. He lives longer than many other birds.

Introduction

The family name of the author of this book is SAQR. *(Flying Falcon)*. Historically, there was a young man during the Umayyad period whose name was Abder Rahman Al-Daakhil. He was living in Damascus. He did not agree with the policies of the Umayyad Caliphate. He left Damascus and went all the way to Andalus (Spain) where he established the Umayyad Caliphate in the Western Hemisphere. It was not easy for anyone to do so. At that time there were no cars or planes, but horses, camels and mules. There were boats, but not as big as we have now. People were astonished how a courageous person he was to do such travel in a short period of time. The only way a person might be able to do so, is by flying. Therefore, he was given the name of a Flying Falcon SAQR or AL-SAQR.

The best falcons at that time were those of Arabian Peninsula. The Quraish Tribe was famous in hunting SAQR and raising them better than any other tribe. They knew how to go to deep deserts and get the best quality of SAQR, NISSR, UQAAB, SHAAHEEN, etc. Hence, they nicknamed him as SAQR of Quraish. This Book is called **REFLECTIONS FROM A FLYING FALCON**. The author's name is SAQR; however, his name was misspelled as Sakr. This is a wrong spelling, but he is stuck with it.

This Flying Falcon (Sakr) [The Author himself] has to fly and travel to a good number of countries to give lectures, speeches, dialogues, and to attend and participate in workshops, seminars, conferences and camps. Addendum A is a partial list of countries that he has visited.

Flying for the bird Falcon is normal. This is his life style. He has to fly to survive and to nourish himself. It is not easy for human beings to fly: it is safe but dangerous; it is exciting but scary; it is fine when the plane is flying smooth, but when it is bumpy, breath is shortened. Life seems over.

I had no choice but to fly. Da'wah necessitates traveling from place to place days and nights. One gets headache, jetlag, lack of sleep, ear pressure, scared, and high blood pressure, looking for the Angel of Death through the windows of the planes as if he is approaching me to take out my soul from my body.

I don't know how to say NO to the local communities! I don't know how they got my name, my phone number, my fax and E-mail. They invite me with sweet invitation. They make me feel ashamed of myself to say NO..I cannot lie or pretend that I am busy. All what I try to do is to prorate one after the other, week after week, and within the same week also.

This Book contains a series of articles and a varieties of experiences during traveling and during flying. No one article is similar to the other. Each and every article is different from the other. As one expects, each trip has different taste, experience, reflections, mood, etc. Some of these articles were written while flying in a plane reflecting by looking at the sky, clouds, mountains, rivers, seas, oceans, etc. Other articles were written while isolated in a room overnight in one hotel or the other accordingly.

The author believes that traveling is part of his faith. Allah (swt) praised the faithful believers who travel from place to place so that they will be among those who reflect about the past and the previous nations. In so doing, they take a lesson for the present and the future. In Surah Al-Tawbah (Repentance), Allah (swt) says about the travelers the following:

$$\text{ٱلتَّٰٓئِبُونَ ٱلۡعَٰبِدُونَ ٱلۡحَٰمِدُونَ ٱلسَّٰٓئِحُونَ ٱلرَّٰكِعُونَ ٱلسَّٰجِدُونَ ٱلۡءَامِرُونَ بِٱلۡمَعۡرُوفِ وَٱلنَّاهُونَ عَنِ ٱلۡمُنكَرِ وَٱلۡحَٰفِظُونَ لِحُدُودِ ٱللَّهِۗ وَبَشِّرِ ٱلۡمُؤۡمِنِينَ ۝}$$

Those that turn (to Allah) in repentance; that serve Him, and praise Him; that wander (Travelers) in devotion to the Cause of Allah; That bow down and prostrate themselves in prayer; that enjoin good and forbid evil; and observe the limits set by Allah,-(Those do rejoice). So proclaim the glad tidings to the Believers. (9:112)

Also, Allah (swt) praised those who reflect, contemplate, and remember Allah with the creation of the whole universe. In Surah Al-'Imran, Allah (swt) says the following:

$$\text{إِنَّ فِى خَلۡقِ ٱلسَّمَٰوَٰتِ وَٱلۡأَرۡضِ وَٱخۡتِلَٰفِ ٱلَّيۡلِ وَٱلنَّهَارِ لَءَايَٰتٍ لِّأُو۟لِى ٱلۡأَلۡبَٰبِ ۝ ٱلَّذِينَ يَذۡكُرُونَ ٱللَّهَ قِيَٰمًا وَقُعُودًا وَعَلَىٰ جُنُوبِهِمۡ وَيَتَفَكَّرُونَ فِى خَلۡقِ ٱلسَّمَٰوَٰتِ وَٱلۡأَرۡضِ رَبَّنَا مَا خَلَقۡتَ هَٰذَا بَٰطِلًا سُبۡحَٰنَكَ فَقِنَا عَذَابَ ٱلنَّارِ ۝}$$

> ***Behold! In the creation of the heavens and the earth, and the alteration of Night and Day-There are indeed Signs for men of understanding- men who remember Allah standing, sitting, and lying down on their sides, and contemplate the (wonders of) creation in the heavens and the earth, (with the saying) " Our Lord not for naught have You created (all) this glory to You! Give us salvation from the Chastisement of the fire. (3:190-191)***

Finally, I do recommend that Muslims should try their best to offer their services to Muslims and non-Muslims. They should travel all over the world and have different experiences. In so doing they will appreciate what Allah has bestowed His Blessings on them. Most of the Prophets had to go from place to place to deliver the Message of Allah. Through their experiences we learn how to behave and how to act and react. Similarly, if our humble experience can be of some use to the new generations, we should be happy and satisfied. Ameen

*   In the Name of Allah, the Most Merciful, and the Forever Merciful. *   Praise Be to Allah, Lord of the worlds.

I. INTRODUCING ISLAM

The theme of a talk given to Christian students at Wheaton College on April 15, 1983 was an introduction of Islam.

* Islam is a total way of life. It embraces all aspects and systems of life. Muslims believe in the oneness of God, oneness of prophethood and their messages, oneness of mankind, and finally the belief in the oneness of this life with the hereafter. The true God in Islam is Allah. He is the Creator of the whole universe. He has ninety-nine beautiful names through which we will be able to recognize Him. He is neither male nor female. We are not in His image. Among other names He is the Most Merciful, the Most Generous, The Source of Peace, and the Most Forgiver. He has no son nor partner. He is the First and the Last. The main sources of legislation to Muslims are the Qur'an, Hadith and Sirah. Muslims believe in the unification of religion with politics, and indeed all are to be derived from the sources of legislation. Islam is an ideology, whoever believes in it, transcends himself above all barriers. There is no race difference in Islam, no color, and no geographic barriers. All are equal and whoever does better to mankind is to be rewarded by God.

* Muslims believe that every person is born free of sin, and whoever commits a mistake will be forgiven if he asks for it. There is no intercession, no proselytization, or priesthood.

Muslims pray five times a day, fast the month of Ramadan, pay Zakat and perform Hajj. The Muslims in the world are more than one billion, and in America eight (8) millions, and in Chicago half a million. They are a peaceful community, and they establish a peaceful society wherever they move to. They have contributed to the American Society:

They are highly educated, family oriented and morally committed. They live peacefully wherever they go. They also practice the teachings of the religion of Islam. They integrated themselves as Muslims from every corner of the world. They don't isolate themselves, but integrate themselves with the American Society. At the same time, they do not assimilate themselves or dissolve their religion and their family values with others.

The early Muslims have already contributed to the success of present civilization. They were the ones who brought about European Renaissance. The early Muslims were pioneers in science, technology, math, social sciences, arts, geography, algebra, physics, medicines, navigation, astronomy, and spiritually. They invented all these specialties because of their religion. The driving force behind them was the religion of Islam. They wanted to practice the teachings of their religion, and accordingly they ended up in pioneering in those fields.

Muslims have dietary rules and regulations. They do not eat pork or drink alcohol. They use both lunar and solar calendars for practicing their religion. They have two feasts: Eidul Fitr, and Eidul Adha. They have three very important mosques in the world: Ka'aba in Makkah, the Mosque of the Prophet in Madinah, and Masjid Al-Aqsa in Jerusalem.

As far as the Qur'an is concerned, it is the only Book, Revealed and preserved by Allah (swt). In Surah Al-Hijr (The Rocky Tract), Allah (swt) says the following:

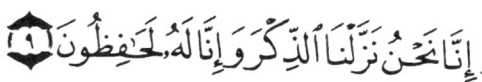

We have, without doubt, sent down the Message; and We will assuredly guard it (from corruption). (15:9)

The Qur'an is also the only Book that has been protected by Allah from corruption, distortion or any change. Allah (swt) says in Surah Al-Waaqi`ah (The Inevitable Event) the following:

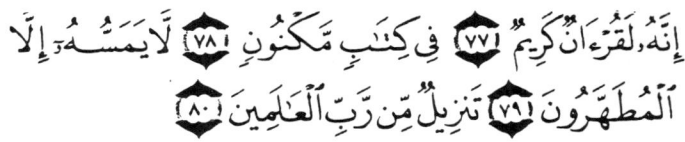

That is indeed a Qur'an most honorable, in a Book well-guarded, which none shall touch but those who are clean: A revelation from the Lord of the Worlds. (56:77-80)

There is not a single book in the history of mankind that has been memorized by millions of people with love and fervency as much as the Qur'an. Thousands of books have been written about the Qur'an. Thousands of people tried to explain the Qur'an. Hundreds of scholars, Muslims and non-Muslims translated the Qur'an to different languages. None of those translations is perfect, because the translator is a human being, while the author of the Qur'an is Allah (swt) Himself.

Finally, we invite every sincere person to come and study Islam with an open mind. We do not convert, proselytize, baptize, debate, preach or convince anyone. The door is open for dialogue with the hope to discuss commonalities rather than differences. Then and only then we will be able to live in peace and harmony. Ameen.

II. GRADUATION

On Friday evening, May 20, 1985 there was a graduation party for a Muslim family at Lombard Park District. It included a dinner and a speech. The speaker was the author of this book. He congratulated the university graduated student and his parents.

The speaker reminded the audience that a person should seek knowledge to it maximum from the cradle to the grave. A Muslim should look for the inherent characteristics of the things, and find out the innate information to bring him closer to Allah (swt). A Muslim should not be satisfied with secular education. He should have simultaneously Islamic education as well. The more a Muslim gets higher education, the more humble he should be. The speaker narrated the stories of the Prophet Sulaiman (being highly knowledgeable and humble), and the story of Qaroon (being knowledgeable but haughty and arrogant).

The speaker reminded the audience that the graduation certificates are not the ones that allow a person to enter paradise. The only certificate (Shahada) that allows a person to enter paradise is that of "Shahadat an la ilaha illal-Laah, wa shahadat anna Muhammadan rassoolullah", i.e., that there is no one worthy of worship except Allah (swt), and that Prophet Muhammad is the Messenger of Allah (swt). This type of declaration of such Shahadah if applied properly in the life of a person, he will be on Allah's chosen list of honors. Graduating from a university does not make a person 'Alim or highly knowledgeable. The knowledge that he got is basic. He needs time, efforts, energy, and experience so that he will be equipped with some types of knowledge. At that time, he hopes to make use of it, and to benefit from it.

It should be stated here that knowledge cannot be acquired by reading books. One has to have several teachers to educate, to inform and to correct any misunderstanding that a person might have acquired. Moreover, one has to recognize the following: Not every teacher is knowledgeable enough. The same thing is applied for all other professors, scholars, etc. For that reason, every student who is seeking knowledge should have series of those people who are considered scholars. In so doing, one will complement the other, and the student will benefit from their wisdom, knowledge, and experience. The knowledge about this life is not enough, one has to seek knowledge about the hereafter. It is understood that life on this planet earth is very short, while the life-after is an eternal one. Accordingly one should make sure to benefit from this life for the sake of the eternal one.

Moreover, knowledge by itself is not enough. Shaitan is very knowledgeable, but he is devil and demon. He abuses his expertise to guide people to immorality so that they will go with him to hell. Therefore, everyone of us should have a direct Ustaz who acts as a supervisor on us. He will act as a Murabbee. He will make sure to train us how to be humble, modest, wise and at the same time knowledgeable. One has to remember that the first few verses revealed to Prophet Muhammad were about Reading in the Name of Allah. Read through the unseen so as to appreciate what Allah has created. Even the name of the Second Chapter in the Qur'an is The Pen. One has to recognize that he has no right to write anything unless it is for the sake of Allah and for the benefits of mankind. Finally, one has to recognize that the source of knowledge is from Allah (swt). We should pray daily and request Allah (swt) to enrich us with the true knowledge that will bring us closer to Him. We hope and pray that our children will be the future leaders of the world. May Allah bless us all. Ameen.

* * *

III. AIR TRIP UNFULFILLED

I was invited to go to Denver and Boulder Colorado, on April 20-23, 1984, (Friday through Sunday) to give Khutbah on Friday and a series of lectures, training program and to be a speaker for a fund raising dinner. Reservation was made for me at odd times, hence I had to rearrange my schedules and paid airlines penalties.

The plane (Continental Airline) was delayed and instead of leaving at 10:00 a.m. we left Chicago at 10:50 a.m. to Denver on its way to Los Angeles. Instead of arriving 11:20 a.m. at Denver Airport, the plane stayed in the air for one extra hour. At 12:30 p.m., we were informed that the plane can't land because the Denver Airport was closed with four inches of snow. We were told the plane is to be diverted to Kansas City. At 1:30 p.m., we finally landed safely. The weather between Chicago and Denver was bad and most of the trip, the air turbulence was the norm rather than the exception.

We had to stay inside the plane till 2:00 p.m. without any information. Later we were told, we may get out for a few minutes to stretch our tired legs and to make phone calls. No one knows what is going to happen including the pilot. I stayed for a few more minutes and performed my Zuhr Salat.

At 3:30 p.m., we were informed that we may have to go to Houston and from there we may board another plane to Denver on the same night or we may have to stay there overnight. Kansas Airport is not equipped to handle us. There is no lounge to sit and wait either. "Please stay close to the gate for more information" we were told.

Air Trip Unfulfilled

At 4:15 p.m., we were told that the plane is going to Los Angeles, California. Passengers of Denver will go to Los Angeles. Any time there was a flight back from Los Angeles to Denver, they will put us on it. We may have to stay in Los Angeles till the following day, Saturday. The weather at Denver Airport was very bad, the runways were closed, and snow was still falling. They didn't know, when they would be able to open it. Hence, I made my Asr prayer momentarily before doing anything else.

It is good to remember at this time my engagement and my schedule.

- 11:20 a.m. -Arrival at Denver Airport and driving to Boulder.
- 12:10 p.m. - Khutbah for Friday prayer in Boulder
- 01:30 p.m. - Lecture at the University of Colorado about "Crisis in Lebanon."
- 4:00 p.m. - Talk to Muslim sisters in Arabic about "Role of Muslim Women in the Society"
- 7:00 p.m. - Talk at Mosque about Food, Health and Behavior.

After midnight, we were to sleep at the Masjid, and we were planning to wake up one hour before first twilight (dawn) for Tahajjud (praying, zikr, and reading from the Qur'an). We were to have dawn prayer (Fajr Salat) and a speech of Tafseer after that. At 9:00 a.m. Saturday we were planning to have a talk in English to all Muslim sisters. After lunch we were planning to drive back to Denver to attend a fund raising dinner for the Muslim community there. All these ideas were crossing my mind while I was still in the plane and also when we landed at Kansas City airport. I was boiling to death, but I could not do anything except to submit myself to Allah (swt) and to accept whatever comes.

I was also thinking of my good friends the organizers of the program, the publicity and the arrangement. I was trying to live the feelings of those at the University in Boulder, what they are doing, and how they were thinking. The lecture might have been cancelled because of the weather or because of me being not there. I could not call anyone at all to pacify myself or to pacify them.

At Kansas airport, I called my family and informed them about the situation. Of course, my wife was worried and annoyed, but she could not do anything to solve the problem. While at the airport, I was thinking of the alternatives on hand:

1. Stay in Kansas and proceed to Denver the second day.
2. Go to Los Angeles, California and catch another flight After midnight, just to be there early in the morning without sleeping and exhausted.
3. To go back to Chicago without fulfilling my mission.

At Kansas airport, I remembered our daughter was not feeling well the night before. I left house in the morning when she was not feeling well. While talking to my family from Kansas airport, I was informed that our daughter is sick, and she had fever of 102F. I was also informed that three of our children had to go to the dentist for their check-up.

I had to make a decision while at Kansas airport. Friday programs at Boulder were over of course. If I had to arrive Saturday morning, I am sure I will be physically tired and exhausted to do much of the work planned for me. I realized that the Windsor Islamic Community is visiting the American Islamic college on Friday, and Saturday and Sunday in the Chicago area. I realized that Islamic Society of North America (ISNA) dinner is to take place on Saturday in Chicago.

I realized that Midway Airline has a plane to leave to Chicago at 5:30 p.m. I made the decision to go back to Chicago Midway Airport. However, my luggage (suitcase and a box of books and literature) can't be taken from the plane. The facilities of the airport are not equipped for the DC 10 planes . I requested the airline to ship them back from Kansas City to Chicago with the assumption that I will have to pick them up from O'Hare airport after a day of two.

The weather at Kansas was horrible. It was foggy, heavy rain and the visibility was minimum. Even to leave this airport at 5:30 p.m. was not possible as the plane of the Midway Airline never arrive on time. I was informed that the plane may arrive at 6:00 p.m. and then we will depart for Chicago.

Now, it is 5:45 p.m. and I am watching the heavy rain with lighting and thunderstorms. My heart is full of worries and anxieties. What can I do? It is a Good Friday for the Christians, which has no significance to the Muslims. Every Friday is a holy and sacred day for the Muslims.

I called my wife and requested her to call Denver and Boulder, and to inform our good friends about the situation. I also requested her to call the Islamic College and to request brother Shamsi and brother Madi, if they can pick me up from the airport on their way home. I realized that they left the college early for the day. My wife had to make arrangement to pick me up, while she was to take care of our sick daughter.

Here is the plane arriving at 6:00 p.m. to take me back to Chicago. Yes, I am going back full of worries. I spent the whole day without any result. Going back to Chicago gave me the feeling of not fulfilling my mission. I failed my mission.

I got into the plane. Here is the pilot speaking to us that we were number 28 to leave. Too many are coming here to Kansas, because Denver airport is closed. We can't leave now because the weather is bad and heavy winds prevent us from flying.

It is now 6:30 p.m. and we are still taxed at the gate. I had no appetite to eat, and for this reason I did not have lunch in the plane on the way to Denver. Here too, the flight attendant distributed food and I had no desire to eat. While reading this information, you may be thinking that I am disturbed. However, I have peace in my heart and mind, because I have submitted myself to Allah (swt).

At 7:10 p.m. we were ready to depart Kansas City airport to Chicago. My family is supposed to be waiting for me at 6:40 p.m. at Midway airport, and we are hoping now to arrive at 7:30 p.m. My friends in Boulder, Colorado, might have been waiting and wondering what is happening. I don't know really what was the wisdom of all of this. As long as Allah (swt) is happy, I am most certainly happy.

We left the airport with Du`a', Zikr, and reading Qur'an back to Chicago. Throughout the air trip, we were regularly disturbed with air turbulence. Are we going to crash now before reaching Chicago? Or are we going to arrive safe? If we have an air crash next to St. Louis would they find our bodies? What will happen to my wife and children who are waiting at Midway airport in Chicago? I prayed Maghrib prayer in the plane and I submitted myself to Allah.

When we got closer to Chicago, the weather was fine, no clouds, no turbulence, and one can see the bright city. Some good feelings started flooding my mind. Finally, the plane landed safely, Al-Hamdu Lillah. Here are my children waiting for me at the gate. I saw Jihad, Basil and Hussein. Then I saw my wife and my daughter Sarah. My sons Jihad and Basil jumped on me and I hugged them with many kisses, Al-Hamdu Lillah.

I had to reflect on this trip. There is a general proverb: I want ... you want ... and Allah does what He wants. Our intention therefore, should be good, and our efforts should be right. Allah (swt) will give credits based on good intention (Niyyah) followed by right efforts (Sa'y). Results are in the Hands of Allah (swt). He knows what is the best for all of us. All what we should do is to submit to Him, and pray so that He will reward us for our deeds and efforts. We also pray requesting Allah to forgive us for our shortcomings. Ameen.

God (Allah) Almighty says the Truth.

IV. AIR TRIP FULFILLED

In the late eighties and through the nineties too many invitations have been proposed. Sometimes I have to travel within the state and out of state on weekends or even in one day. Some of these trips are driving, while others are by planes. During the weekdays I have to accept local and regional invitations. However, I do insist that I have to be back early morning Sundays so that I will be able to take care of my local community by giving them Qur'an Tafseer and/or a lecture. This means that I have to be on the freeway by 5:00 A.M. Saturday to catch my plane at 6:00 or 6:30 A.M. The same thing is to be said while coming back Sunday. One has to think twice and to reflect. At 5:A.M. in the East Coast of U.S.A. means 2:00 A.M. at the West Coast. I feel obliged to do so in order to please Allah by helping others. It is very difficult to do so, but it is a spiritual happiness indeed.

One time I was invited by two groups in the same weekend. On Friday October 3, 1997, I had to give a Friday Khutbah at the Islamic Center of Hawthorne, next to Los Angeles Airport (LAX). On October 4th I had to go to St. Louis, Missouri. The invitation came to me by the American Muslim Alliance (AMA). I went through Dallas, Texas Airport from Ontario Airport, California then changed plane. I arrived in St. Louis safely Al-Hamdu Lillah. I participated in the conference. On Sunday October 5, 1997, I had to come back to California through Dallas, Texas. After arriving to Ontario Airport, I drove my car to our Community Center in Walnut. I gave a talk to the youth, and then gave Qur'anic Tafseer to the adult.

In the same day I had to go to Sacramento to help the local Muslims in Yuba City to raise money for rebuilding their Masjid. Unfortunately, it was burned after it was built. The Zuhr prayer was at one o'clock. Being a community, sometimes it takes them time to finish on time. I had to be at the Airport about 1:30 P.M. to catch my plane. So my wife and myself prayed Zuhr in my office. I was in a hurry! One friend asked me if I need a ride. I thanked him and I preferred not to trouble anyone. I was tired and exhausted, but for the love of Allah, everything should be easy.

I drove my car in a hurry. The moment I started driving, I predicted a trouble is to happen. I don't know why. However, I read Du`a' of travel along with Ayatul Kursi and I requested Allah (swt) to protect me. While driving from the city of Walnut to Ontario Airport, I used to hear a strange noise in the engine of the car. I was worried, but I left it up to Allah (swt); and I prayed to Him to protect me.

Click-click-click…noise started while I was on Grove St. about four miles away from the airport. Then I saw a light that said: Service! I reduced my speed and I drove to the right-lane as a safety measure. I tried to put the gear on neutral and pushed my foot on the gas pedal so that the car will not stop. Before turning right to the Airport road, the engine stopped completely. I could not stop the car. I wanted to turn right at the stoplight. The car could not turn right enough to enter the street. I was to hit two cars on the other side of the street. The steering wheel was solid. I had to force my hands on it to turn right. It turned little enough to avoid hitting the other cars. Here my car stopped completely in the middle of the street.

I came out of it immediately. I put the gear on neutral. I pushed my car by myself to the extreme right. It hit the curb. It stayed diagonal rather than parallel to curb of the street. I was Al-Hamdu Lillah safe from any accident!

I was alone and too far away to make phone call for my family to help me. I had to think twice: How should I continue my trip? I was not at the airport. I could not call the friends in Sacramento to inform them of my problem. Even if I wanted to call them, I didn't have their phone number at the Mosque in Sacramento. I had their phone number in Yuba City. Any movement needs more than one person and more than one brain to function. However, I was by myself. Wild ideas crossed my mind and I wished I had a friend to drop me at the airport. I wished I had a cellular phone to call my family. But where is my family. Some of them are still at the Islamic Education Center, while others could be at the house. I said La Hawla Wa La Quwata Illa Billah! I said: Ya Allah! I need your help and Your guidance.

I pulled my brief case and my file case from the car and locked it. I put a piece of paper on the antenna saying: Out of Order, giving my name and my phone number. I started walking toward the airport. But I don't have time to catch my plane even if I have to walk. If I walk it will take me one hour or more if my hands are free. But both of my hands were full. While walking for few minutes, I saw a shuttle bus coming out of the parking area. I waved for the driver and he was very helpful. He stopped and I went with him to the airport. I arrived at the airport safe and on time! Al-Hamdu Lillah! I took my boarding pass! But how about the car!

I called home. My son Jihad picked up the phone. I told him the story. I repeated myself several times to make sure he understood the problem. I requested him to convey the message to his mother when she comes home. Yes! Dad! Yes! While talking to my son, he informed me that our friend Tamer was at home. I talked to him and explained the situation. I requested him to buy transmission fluid to be used because it was low for sometimes. That was my assumption. Then I requested my son to let me speak to my wife who was still at the Islamic Center. He put me in a conference call, and I talked to her in depth and explained the situation. I requested three of them (my wife, Jihad, and Tamer) to drive from home to the airport (20 miles) and find out the problem. I took my plane to Sacramento.

They came! They checked it. They added the transmission fluid; but it did not start. They had to go to the parking area of the airport. They requested if there is any gas station with towing facilities. Luckily, they found a nearby station. The car was towed away. They found out that it was the alternator. They will take care of it Monday. They left the car and drove away home. Meanwhile I took my plane to Sacramento. I helped the local community to raise some $20,000 for their Masjid to be rebuilt. I finished my role and came back home in that same night by 11:00 P.M. My family came again to the airport to pick me and took me home. They informed me what went wrong with the car.

The second day after the incident the car was finally fixed. We had to go again to the airport area to pick up the car and pay for the cost of repair. However, the trip was over; it was successful; it was full of excitement; it was full of difficulties! The two air trips to St. Louis and Sacramento were fulfilled in the same weekend (Saturday-Sunday) along with the community programs.

If one loves Allah and puts his trust in Him, Allah will send angels to make his trip successful. The more I reflect upon such an air trip, the more I become humble, and the more I put my trust in Allah to use me to the fullest extent. Al-Hamdu Lillah.

I remember that whatever I wish is still a wish. Whatever Allah (swt) decides it will be executed. I recognize the Ayah in Surah Al-Takweer (The Folding Up) when Allah says the following:

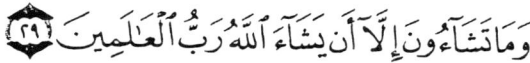

But you shall not will except as Allah wills,-the Cherisher of the Worlds. (81: 29)

A final remark: One has to be honest and sincere with Allah. When we pray we should ask Him humbly to use us in the right direction for His love and for the sake of humanity at large. None has to brag about the services that he/she renders to others. On the contrary, one has to be thankful and grateful to Allah for all the Blessings and Favors that He bestowed upon us. Ameen

V. READING QUR'AN IN THE PLANE

I am a frequent traveler in the U.S.A. I have to visit Muslim Students Association (MSA) Chapters and Islamic communities. I have to attend seminars, conferences, workshops and conventions. I have to attend fund raising dinners for building masajid and to attend inaugurations of some masajid. I have to recruit students and to present lectures on food, health and behavior and other lectures on Islam.

Most of the travelling I have to make by plane, some by car or public ground transportation. Travelling by plane is frightening to me for reasons that I don't know up till now.

While in the plane being frightened, I do enjoy reading the noble readings, i.e. the Qur'an. I keep the Qur'an with me ready all the time. I read most of the time while in the plane. I look around me and see people enjoying their time, while I am frightened. I look through the window and I enjoy the clouds, the sky, the stars and the moon (because most of my travelling are at dark).

Any time there is air turbulence the plane shakes, and my heart beats very fast. My face is pale and blood pressure is very high. I shiver and tremble and I put my hands on my chest and especially on my heart. I start reading Ayatul Kursi seven times, followed by Surah Al-Ikhlas, Surah Al-Falaq, and An-Nas.

While the drama is going on, my imagination goes with me further than my situation. I imagine that the plane falls down on earth; an air crash is to take place; I am to see my death in front of my eyes; I am to suffer all the pre-death sufferings and pain; and I am going to be burned with plane fire before dying.

My heart continues to beat high, my lips become dry; my tongue stuttered; my readings in the Qur'an is interrupted with the fear; my reading of Ayatul Kursi and others are also interrupted; and my Tasbeeh and Zikr are also interrupted by the stuttered tongue and the shaky body. There is nothing that I can do except reading Al-Fatiha on my soul by myself before it is taken away as there may not be anyone to read it for me later. I start reading Shahada (Kalimah); I make Talqeen to myself and I catch the Qur'an with my hands and put it on my chest. If I die, I pray that the Qur'an will be a witness to me when I will meet Allah. I remembered an Ayah in the Qur'an that if people remember Allah, He will give them peace of mind. It is in Surah Al-Ra'd (Thunder). It goes as follows:

ٱلَّذِينَ ءَامَنُواْ وَتَطۡمَئِنُّ قُلُوبُهُم بِذِكۡرِ ٱللَّهِۗ أَلَا بِذِكۡرِ ٱللَّهِ تَطۡمَئِنُّ ٱلۡقُلُوبُ ۝

Those who believe, and whose hearts find satisfaction in the remembrance of Allah: for without doubt in the remembrance of Allah do hearts find satisfaction. (13:28)

Finally, we have to keep ourselves with Allah (swt) all the time, whether we are in the plane or on the ground. Whether we are traveling or at home. The more we keep our hearts, mind and tongues remembering Allah (swt), the more we will live in peace and harmony.

O Allah! Give me peace and mercy of Yours always all the time. Ameen.

VI. LISTENING TO THE QUR'AN AFTER DEATH

I am blessed by Allah (swt) that I enjoy reading from Qur'an on a daily basis. I still remember that at the age of 12, I made an effort to read the whole Qur'an by myself. It became a habit for me to read from the Qur'an on a daily basis, Al-Hamdu Lillah. This habit continued even more when I left my birthplace Beirut, to the United States. As I grew older, I made the effort that I should read the whole Qur'an every lunar month. This means that I read one Juzu' (volume) every day.

At the same time, I recognized that reading by itself is not enough. One has to listen to the recitation of Qur'an on a daily basis. Al-Hamdu Lillah, I made it as an effort to listen to the recitation of Qur'an from other people as well as from radio, TV, audio, and video. I really enjoy both methods tremendously. It became a habit that I read Qur'an in the morning, and I listen to Qur'anic recitation when I am driving a car. I also enjoy listening to it at bedtime. I reach a stage that if I don't read or listen to Qur'an daily, I feel I am lost, I am dishonest, and my life that day was miserable. Therefore, I say to myself: I should be considered dishonest and hypocrite. Then I ask myself: How could you dare to forget or to delay reading and reciting Qur'an? My inner heart tells me: I am ashamed of you! You were told a long time ago: If you wish to talk to Allah(swt) you are to read from the Qur'an. If you want Allah, Himself to talk to you, you are to recite from Qur'an. It is He Himself Who is talking to you personally.

Therefore, I made it clear that I prefer to read Qur'an before I listen to any speaker, or even the international news. To me the TV and radios are no more essential in my personal life. Al-Hamdu Lillah...I love to read Qur'an and listen to its beautiful melodic recitation, much more than eating.

Listening To The Qur'an After Death

Some reflections passed over my mind while I was flying in an airplane. I was enjoying reading and listening to Qur'an. In a few minutes the Qur'an touched my heart. I wanted to cry! Why?! I did not know! I looked at the sky...clouds...sun...I looked up and down! I saw houses, cars, birds, lakes, sailing boats, etc. I was neither up nor down! Yes! I was sandwiched in between inside an airplane. But! The most striking ideas crossed my mind were the following:

1. After I die, how can I talk to Allah, and how will Allah talk to me on a daily basis? My body will be catabolized, hydrolyzed, and metabolized into essential ingredients and components. My soul will be taken to Isthmus. It will visit my grave daily. Therefore, none of my biological organs and systems will be able to read and listen to Qur'an! I started crying!

2. I started thinking: would my soul be able to read and listen to recitation of Qur'an!? I had no answer, because I don't know. I felt unhappy.

3. Does this mean that I have to wait millions of years till the Day of Judgement. Am I going to be deprived from the beautiful melodic voices of the reciters who used to recite Qur'an for us?!

4. If my soul cannot talk and cannot listen, would it be possible that some angels will recite Qur'an for me while I am in the grave?! It is a possibility...We were told and we read that souls of different people meet one another and talk to each other. Then I asked myself: Why not the angels will talk to us and we talk to them. We read that the two angels Munkar and Nakeer will talk to us after we are buried. They will ask us many questions.

My heart started shivering and my whole body started trembling! It was an emotional moment of positive feeling. My heart started crying: Ya Allah! Please Ya Allah! Don't leave me alone! Don't let my soul wait millions of years aside without hearing the echo, the melodic voice of the recitation of Qur'an. Since at that time I cannot read, but please Ya Allah, make me hear and listen! Please Ya Allah! Send me special angels to read Qur'an for me while I am in the grave, and while my soul will be in the grave and in Isthmus! Please Ya Allah! Don't let me down! I love You so much! I don't want myself to be denied that happiness.

I do appreciate all what You have done for me Ya Allah. I am grateful to you because You created me as a human being without my knowledge. You put Iman in my heart. You put in my heart how to love You and how to Obey You! I am indeed grateful to You Ya Allah! You helped me all my life. You helped me to get my Ph.D. in Biological Sciences, but You guided me to devote my life in the field of Da'wah for Your love Ya Allah!

This is my wish and my prayer to You Ya Allah! You informed us to call upon You and You promised to listen to our crying hearts! You told us in Surah Al-Baqarah:

$$\text{وَإِذَا سَأَلَكَ عِبَادِى عَنِّى فَإِنِّى قَرِيبٌ أُجِيبُ دَعْوَةَ ٱلدَّاعِ إِذَا دَعَانِ فَلْيَسْتَجِيبُوا لِى وَلْيُؤْمِنُوا بِى لَعَلَّهُمْ يَرْشُدُونَ ﴿١٨٦﴾}$$

When My servants ask you concerning Me, I am indeed close (to them): I respond to the prayer of every suppliant when he calls on Me: Let them also, with a will, listen to My call, and believe in Me, that they may walk in the right way. (2:186)

I do know that You, ya Allah informed us in Qur'an in Surah Qaaf that You are closer to us than our jugular veins. The Ayah goes as follows:

$$\text{وَلَقَدْ خَلَقْنَا الْإِنسَانَ وَنَعْلَمُ مَا تُوَسْوِسُ بِهِ نَفْسُهُ وَنَحْنُ أَقْرَبُ إِلَيْهِ مِنْ حَبْلِ الْوَرِيدِ ﴿١٦﴾}$$

It was We Who created man, and We know what suggestions his soul makes to him: for We are nearer to him than (his) jugular vein. (50:16)

I know that our prayers and our Du`a' go to You immediately. They are being recorded by Your angels. Therefore, I leave my wish, my prayer, and my Du`a' in Your Hands Ya Allah!

Finally, I enjoy the following Ayah in Surah Ghafir or Mu'min (The Forgiver / The Believer) whereby Allah (swt) says, the following:

$$\text{الَّذِينَ يَحْمِلُونَ الْعَرْشَ وَمَنْ حَوْلَهُ يُسَبِّحُونَ بِحَمْدِ رَبِّهِمْ وَيُؤْمِنُونَ بِهِ وَيَسْتَغْفِرُونَ لِلَّذِينَ ءَامَنُوا رَبَّنَا وَسِعْتَ كُلَّ شَيْءٍ رَحْمَةً وَعِلْمًا فَاغْفِرْ لِلَّذِينَ تَابُوا وَاتَّبَعُوا سَبِيلَكَ وَقِهِمْ عَذَابَ الْجَحِيمِ ﴿٧﴾}$$

Those who bear the Throne (of Allah) and those around it sing Glory and Praise to their Lord; believe in Him; and implore Forgiveness for those who believe; "Our Lord! You embraces all things, in Mercy and Knowledge. Forgive, then, those who turn in Repentance, and follow Your Path; and preserve them from the Chastisement of the Blazing Fire! (40:7)

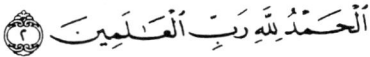

Praise Be to Allah, the Lord of the Universe

Surah Al-Fatiha or (the Opening Chapter);
Chapter I in the Qur'an

VII. WRONG EXPECTATIONS

I. Introduction

As a frequent flier, I get tired, exhausted and jet-lagged. Imagine yourself traveling every week, from state to state, city to city, by plane and car in order to reach your destination, and come back either in the same day or the next day. Imagine also that you have to give lectures in different cities not less than 30-50 miles apart on the same day, and you have to drive your own car. You have to take with you friends to be exposed to the process and techniques of Da'wah. And you have to prepare the material for your lectures and come back very late or midnight.

While you are to do all of these, still you have to attend to the needs of your office on a daily basis. Among the many services you have to do are: family counseling, officiate marriage, bury the dead, prepare the material for the series of lectures-- duplicate it, prepare the taping of the audio and the video. You also participate in different activities with the Board of Education, Sheriff Department, Operation Safe Community, Citizen's Academy and Interfaith Council. Then there are still the very many calls that come to you for questions and answers that are related to many issues.

The following section is some information for those who are in the field of Da'wah. I want them to prepare themselves for the challenges that they will face while they are assuming the responsibility of Da'wah to Muslims and non-Muslims. It is better to expose them to the negative experiences that many of us had already faced without being prepared and without expecting them. In so doing, they will do a better job and have more successful activities.

We pray to Allah (swt) to bless all those who want to work in the field of Da'wah. May Allah (swt) give them wisdom, patience, endurance, and the knowledge of making Da'wah. They have to realize that being involved in Da'wah, they have to spend money, time and effort for the love of Allah (swt). They should not complain if anything goes wrong against them. Ameen.

II. Don't Expect

1. To be informed about the program/function in advance.
2. To be given and informed of advanced accommodations according to your choice: -Airline, Airport, Time, Seat Assignment, Choice of Food, Frequent Flier Number
3. To be welcomed at airport
4. To be put in hotel overnight
5. To be taken back to the airport…to go back home
6. To be given food
7. To be given your expenses you rendered during the trip
8. To be appreciated for your help
9. To be Imam! Lead Salat
10. To help financially from your pocket
11. To give them your books free
12. To sell your books!… They take them.
13. To receive any honorarium….gift….thanks

Many Muslims do expect to receive the best in this world and the hereafter. Speakers do travel from place to place to give lectures, participate in panel discussions, seminars, workshops, etc. Some are invited to give Friday Khutbah and lead salat. A good number do expect some thing good to come or to happen to them. In this section, the author wishes to write the wrong expectations rather than the good ones. In so doing, the speakers would be immune against all types of odds or strange expectations. Then and only then, they will accept these abnormalities and make Ihtisab (anticipation and expectations from Allah).

1. When you are invited you may have to pay your travel expenses, and to give even donation to the local society. Don't expect otherwise.
2. If you travel by plane, you should expect to be left stranded at the airport for sometime. You have to manage yourself.
3. You may have to expect that there is another speaker with you or to replace you from one session to another.
4. The local community may change the time of your speaking in the program as well as the title of your speech the very last minute.
5. In a Muslim gathering, you may expect a crazy and ignorant person who will challenge you publicly or blame you and criticize you. Try to absorb him. Be calm and cool.
6. For no reason, during Friday Khutbah, someone may challenge you without any respect to the Khutbah or prayer.
7. Someone may request you to lead salat, but you should expect that another person may shout at you by saying: you cannot be Imam because you are a traveler.
8. Don't expect anyone to thank you for the lecture you gave, or the participation you were involved in.
9. Do don't expect any Muslim to give you a gift or a souvenir or a letter of thanks or even to welcome you with a smile.
10. You may have to expect some type of a rumor to be spread against you without any reason.
11. If an honorarium is to be given to you, the local Muslims may feel jealous. You might be accused as to how you accept

such a thing when you are making Da'wah for the sake of Allah (swt)

12. After receiving an honorarium from a university through the local student body, the Muslims may request you to sign the check and pass it over to them. They ask you in public to embarrass you. Don't worry!
13. You were told that the local people would put you in a local hotel or motel. In order to save money you end up staying with a family you don't know.
14. After the function is over, you find yourself lonely. They were excited and happy. They got what they wanted from you. You will be stranded! No one is willing to take you to a hotel, house, or anywhere. You should know how to handle yourself.
15. You may find yourself stranded at the hotel and you have to take a taxi to get to the airport. At the same time you may have to pay the hotel for the night you stayed there. Don't worry! This is your account with Allah (swt).
16. Sometimes you may find out that the local people like you very much. Accordingly each wants you to stay with them in their local houses. You end up that your coat is in one house, your suite case is in another house, your brief case is in a third house, and you yourself in a fourth house. When you want to leave the town the second day, you have to collect your items from different places. Please don't complain!
17. After being invited by the host family, one member from the guests comes to you and say: we did not come here to listen to you!. We are here for something else. The host was not aware of such thing. So don't worry! It happens to all of us.
18. You are invited to deliver Friday Khutbah, and to lead Salat. Just before the Khutbah, someone comes to you and says: Are you the Khatib Today?! You answer him politely: Yes! He

says I am not going to listen to you. I am going to pray in another Masjid because you are from the people who make Bid'ah. You don't know that person at all. I looked at him and smiled. I had to absorb what he said without affecting me in delivering the Friday Khutbah, as if nothing happened.

III. Final Remarks

A Da`iyah is a Da`iyah . Before assuming Da'wah one has to read the stories of the Prophets and Messengers as narrated in the Qur'an. None was treated well, and none asked any compensation or favor. Some were tortured, persecuted, insulted, and defamed. Others were killed. Moreover, one has to study Islam and Da'wah through the scholars who are involved in delivering the Message of Islam. We pray to Allah that the number of the Da'iyah will be increased, as well as their qualities will be magnified.

Allah is the Greatest!

VIII. REWARDS FROM ALLAH (swt)

The theme of Khutbah in Lombard Park district on April 15, 1985 was the "Rewards From Allah (swt)". Allah (swt) made many avenues for us to be rewarded. For every good act, He will reward us double, ten times, seven hundred times or beyond any account. Some of the major rewards are the following:

- Whoever gives a loan without interest, Allah (swt) will multiply his/her reward.
- Whoever does a good deed he will be rewarded ten times.
- Whoever reads Qur'an, he will be rewarded ten times for every letter.
- Whoever spends money in the way of Allah (swt) will be rewarded seven hundred times. Allah (swt) will multiply this percentage for whoever He wishes depending upon the good intention and the hard striving.
- Whoever is patient for any difficulty, any problem or catastrophe his reward is beyond count.
- Whoever fasts the month of Ramadan with good intention, his reward is beyond count of any measure.
- Whoever commits a mistake, then realizes his fault and asks Allah (swt) forgiveness, he will be forgiven. Allah (swt) will wipe off his mistakes and substitute them with equal rewards.
- Whoever reads Qur'an while it is difficult for him, he will be rewarded twenty (20) times for every letter.
- Whoever fasts Ramadan and follow it with six more days in the month of Shawwal, he will be rewarded as if he has fasted the whole year.
- Whoever fasts the Day of Arafa (outside Hajj), he will be rewarded with a credit of one year of fasting. Moreover, he will be rewarded forgiveness of two years. One year in the past and another year to come.

- Whoever fasts the Day of `Ashura, will be rewarded one year of forgiveness.
- Whoever prays Salatul Duha, as if he got rewards equal to 360 sadaqa (charity) or more.
- Whoever attends Salatul Jumu`ah: week after week, he will be credited forgiveness for the whole week, plus three more days to come from the coming week.
- Whoever makes Wudoo' (ablution) his rewards are: For every drop of water that comes out of the body, Allah will erase a mistake for him. For every one-milliliter (there are 20- drops in a milliliter). One has to figure out how many milliliter have been used during the process of wudoo'.
- Going to the Masjid is a blessing from Allah. For every footstep up he will get a credit (hasana). Also for every footstep down, Allah will erase a mistake (Saiy-ah) for him. One has to figure out how many footsteps it takes to come to the Masjid.
- Reading Surah Al-Kahf (The Cave) on Friday is of great blessing. One will get forgiveness for the whole week. Moreover, in the Day of Judgement, he will have light, a light from heaven down to his feet, showing him his way to paradise.
- Those who leave their houses and come to the House of Allah to read the Qur'an and to study its meaning, will get the following rewards:

1. The Mercy of Allah will fall upon them.
2. Peace, tranquility and relief come down to them
3. Angels come down to encircle them, to protect them, to make Istighfar for them, to make records for each person, and to be blessed with their blessings.

4. Allah will mention their names, and put them on the honor list.

We hope to benefit from these occasions and varieties of situations. At the same time, we Muslims should encourage one another to do the Fard at the very least. Whoever wish to do the extras, it will be in their credits in this world and in the hereafter. We should encourage everyone to come close to Allah (swt). We should refrain from accusing or blaming anyone.

P.S. (1)

The Islamic Foundation of Villa Park, Illinois, did not have at that time a Masjid and a school of their own. So we used the author's house, and then the Lombard Park District.

P.S. (2)

A General Advice to all those who assume the responsibility of delivering a speech or Friday khutba are to encourage the Muslims. They should refrain from scarring and blaming Muslims. There are some who are not scholars, but stand at pulpit of the Masjid and tell the Muslims: Haram, Haram, and Haram. They add: Bid'ah, Shirk, Kufr, Mushbooh, Makrooh, and so on. It seems they don't know anything about Halal in Islam. They think everything in this world is Haram. Such type of individuals have to go back and study Qur'an, Hadith, Sunnah, Sirah, Fiqh, Shariah, etc. They should study these under the supervision of Muslims scholars. Those who try to read books by themselves and assume such responsibilities without teachers supervising them, their teachers would be devils, satans and `Afareet. The role of shaitan is to possess such ignorant speakers, and accordingly such speakers will create commotion and disturbance in the society.

Our beloved Prophet was sent as a Bashir before he was sent as a Nazir. May Allah (swt) guide all of us. Ameen.

P.S. (3)

No one person is safe from being tested with Trials and Turmoil. The more a person is faithful believer, the more he is to be tested by Allah. He will be tested with what he likes or with what he hates. The rewards are for him on both cases. Therefore let us pray to Allah (swt) to keep us faithful believers till we meet Him in the Day of Judgement. Ameen.

Do they not observe the birds above them, spreading their wings and folding them in? None can uphold them except (Allah) Most Gracious: Truly it is He that watches over all things. (67:19)

IX. I HAD NO CHOICE

I accept invitations many times to different places. I get tired and exhausted from these trips: lack of sleep, jet lag, headache, physically tired, muscle spasm and losing my voice. Moreover I get scared with each flying trip, I think that I am going to die by having plane crash. Therefore, I make a series of Du`a', I do pray in the plane and I do make Istighfar. I plead my case to Allah (swt) to let me arrive safe, and then to bring me back to my family safe and rich with blessings.

Many times I ask myself as to why I accept weekly invitations, and I had to go through these agonies. I had no reply except I am doing these services to win the blessings of Allah (swt). These ideas cross my mind: Don't you know how to say No!?? I reply to myself by saying: Yes, I do know how to say No; but I feel I have no choice, but to accept such invitations. I love to help others. In order to do so, I have to sacrifice my time, effort, energy, knowledge, leisure, and money for the love and the pleasure of Allah (swt). All these ideas and many more cross my mind when I am flying, and at the same time I am scared. One time an idea crossed my mind, and I recognized that I HAD NO CHOICE !...I found out that it is true that I had no choice. The following are some of the Reflections about this subject:

1. I had no choice to be created or not. Allah (swt) did not give me the choice. He did not discuss it with me at all. He did what He wanted, and I had to accept what He decided for me; and I am grateful to Him.
2. I had no choice to choose my parents.
3. I had no choice to choose whether I wanted to come as a boy or as a girl.
4. I had no choice whereabouts I should be born. Allah (swt) made the decision. I was born in Beirut, Lebanon.
5. I had no choice to come as black or white or any other color.

He decided for me my color and my appearance.
6. I had no choice to be born in a hospital, a house or on the street. But I was born in my parents' house.
7. I had no choice to come healthy or with deformities. But, Al-Hamdulillah I came healthy, and from a good family.
8. I had no choice to come from a poor or a wealthy family. But I am happy that I came from a poor family. I do appreciate life, and I do know the value of one dollar or even a penny. I do appreciate the food that did not contain meat because we could not afford it. If we had one pound of meat in a pot of food for twelve children and two parents, we feel we are rich that day!!
9. I did not have the choice to come as number one or the last child in the family. I came as number three, in a family of (8) eight boys and (4) four girls. All from one father and one mother. I really appreciate what they had done for us. May Allah (swt) bless their souls, and may Allah make them in paradise. Ameen.

In as much I had no choice in what I said before, I recognized the following:

1. I had no choice <u>when</u> I am supposed to die.
2. I also had no choice to decide for myself <u>where</u> I am to die. Although I wish and pray to die in Makkah and/or Madina very close to the Prophet, his family and his sahabah (companions). I wish to be buried in Jannat Al-Baqee',
3. I recognized that I had no choice as to <u>how</u> I am going to die. I wish I will die when I am praying, and while I am in a state of Sajdah. I wish, I die in Ka'bah in Makkah, in the month of Ramadan, in the last ten days, and especially in Lailatul Qadr, while I am in a state of fasting. I wish to meet Allah in a position of Sujood.

I hate to die in America or in any kufr country. I hate the system of coroner who enjoys doing autopsy. I don't want anyone to touch my body and to play with its parts haphazardly. I wish to be buried immediately without any delay. I don't want them to put me in a freezer for few days. I don't like them to expose my face to anyone. I wish to go to Allah peacefully as soon as possible without any delay. This is only a wish; I hope and pray that Allah (swt) with His Ultimate Mercy will not let me down with my hopes, wishes and aspirations. I do believe that He sees, He hears, and He gives better than what we wish and hope. He is the Creator and He is the Most Merciful, Al-Hamdu Lillah. In as much as I had no choice in the topics discussed above, I found myself I had no choice in many aspects of life. The following is a partial list of items that I found out that I have no choice, no decision or even no time to plan my daily and weekly schedules:

1. Someone dies and his family calls on me. They need me immediately to help them, to guide them and to render the funeral services.
2. Someone wants to get married. He calls and he wants me to go to his house in the same day to perform the marriage.
3. Someone calls midnight. He has a problem. He divorced his wife, but he did not mean it. He was mad. He wants to know what to do.
4. Some people have family problems. They want someone to counsel them. I give them appointment. They refuse because they are working. They want to decide the day and the time. I have no choice. I do it free but still it is them who have to decide when to come.
5. I accept to go and help different communities. I found out many times that I have no choice as to the airline, the time of departure, the airport, and the number of days they want me

to do so. They think that I have nothing to do in life. I am totally free for them alone. They have rights on me and I have obligations toward them.
6. I had no choice as to the topic to speak about. They may change the subject or even the time and the room during their conferences. They may cancel the session without having the courtesy to inform me.
7. If I do agree to visit a particular community, another one demands me to cancel my commitment and go to the second one. They think I am a slave. I should listen to their demands and cancel the previous agreement. They tell me: don't worry! Just tell them that you have more important function!.. They want me to lie, to break my commitment, and to lose my face with other. They did not care for me to be discredited with the Book of Allah, as long as they are happy!...
8. I recognized in my travelling that I had no choice as to where I should stay overnight. They don't tell me. Although the Speaker Bureau Administrator informs the local community that I should stay in a hotel, so as to have privacy. I find out that they insist to keep me with someone's house. One time I ended up having: my suit-case in one house, my winter coat in another house, my brief case in a third house, and myself in a fourth house! Masha-Allah!...They liked me so much!... The second day I had to rush to the airport, but I needed my belongings!..

Finally, as a Da'iyah I had to convince myself that as long as I am rendering services for the love of Allah, I should not mind anything. I should Not complain, otherwise I will lose my credibility with Allah (swt). Please Ya Allah! Accept what I do. Direct me to the right services, and bless me with your Mercy. Ameen.

I remember the Ayah in Surah Luqman which goes as follows:

$$إِنَّ ٱللَّهَ عِندَهُۥ عِلْمُ ٱلسَّاعَةِ وَيُنَزِّلُ ٱلْغَيْثَ وَيَعْلَمُ مَا فِى ٱلْأَرْحَامِ وَمَا تَدْرِى نَفْسٌ مَّاذَا تَكْسِبُ غَدًا وَمَا تَدْرِى نَفْسٌ بِأَىِّ أَرْضٍ تَمُوتُ إِنَّ ٱللَّهَ عَلِيمٌ خَبِيرٌ ۝$$

Verily the knowledge of the Hour is with Allah (alone). It is He Who sends down rain, and He Who knows what is in the wombs. Nor does any one know what it is that he will earn on the morrow. Nor does any one know in what land he is to die. Verily with Allah is full knowledge and He is acquainted (with all things). (31:34)

One has to recognize that life on this planet earth is very short. X / over infinity reaches zero. This means that the Duration, the Value, the Happiness or the Sorrows on this planet earth are X. If one would like to compare these items with life in the hereafter means zero. Therefore, a good faithful believer will try his best to make use of this life, and plan for the permanent life, i.e., hereafter.

I will continue to accept things as they are for the love of Allah. Life is a life of tests and examination by Allah for all of us. Either we should be patient or we should be grateful. We pray to accept from all of us. If we are tested with what we like we should be grateful to Allah (swt). We should make Sujood of Shukr, and give donations for the good things that we had and we received from Allah. However, if we are tested with what we hate, we should be patient. The more people are patient, the more they receive credits and rewards from Allah (swt). Moreover, they will receive Mercy and Guidance from Allah too. Ameen.

As a final remark: I had to convince myself that I should accept whatever has been decided by others for me. I don't mind at all. For that reason, I used to say to the friends the following: Please! Use me.. Abuse me.. Don't lose me ... and Reuse me... You may try even to clone me if you wish. All my hopes that Allah (swt) will accept whatever we do for His Love. Ameen.

It was Our power that made the hills and the birds celebrate Our praises, with David: it was We Who did (all these things). (21:79)

X. THEY CLAIM RESULTS

This is a strange subject to talk about, but the real life is that I work hard and someone else claims the results. In my life span, I learned how to take initiatives and how to be among pioneers. I learned how to establish things for the Muslims to help them practice the teachings of Islam. I learned how to open doors for jobs and positions so that members of the Islamic Community may be able to enjoy life even in a non-Muslim society.

I learned for the last thirty years or more in America, that I should continue to take initiatives and to establish many more Islamic institutions. However, in every case I worked hard: days and nights for a number of years. My hope is always that Allah (swt) may accept my humble efforts. In many cases, someone else who carries a Muslim name or some groups who carry Muslim titles, come forward and take over the responsibility. They never were up to the expectations, and in many times they ruin the reputation of that effort, or that project.

I trained a good number of them how to be Khateeb, speakers and leaders. I helped many of them and I introduced them to the public with respect. I had to spend time, effort, knowledge and money on a good number of them. Many of them turned to be honest, sincere and hard working people. However some were dishonest. They did their best to harass me, nickname me and spread rumors against me. Others have accused me and my family. While being a professor I was a regular host and a private chauffeur to the students. My wife was a good host, a servant and a cook for them. Some were guests in our place and after dinner they blame me for no reason, and accused my wife. After eating her prepared dinner they disgraced her and demanded her to get out far from them. All this took place in our own house. Others wrote letters of accusation: cheating, stealing, immorality, and many cheap ideas.

Those people were insignificant and were looking for fame and reputation. They grasped the opportunity to portray themselves as heroes, and leaders. They claimed themselves to be not among the pioneers but the pioneers themselves. They never mentioned even the names of the pioneers in any good feeling.

However, in my life span I learned that I should continue to take the initiative, to establish new needed establishments for the love of Allah (swt) and for the help of the Muslim community. In most of the projects that I initiated, I found out that I was never present during the happy occasions of the results, but I was among the accused. Those people are among the ones that Allah (swt) had warned them, otherwise they will go to Hell. In Surah Al-Imran (The Family of Imran), Allah (swt) says the following:

لَا تَحْسَبَنَّ ٱلَّذِينَ يَفْرَحُونَ بِمَآ أَتَوا۟ وَيُحِبُّونَ أَن يُحْمَدُوا۟ بِمَا لَمْ يَفْعَلُوا۟ فَلَا تَحْسَبَنَّهُم بِمَفَازَةٍ مِّنَ ٱلْعَذَابِ وَلَهُمْ عَذَابٌ أَلِيمٌ ﴿١٨٨﴾

Think not that those who exult in what they have brought about, and love to be praised for what they have not done, think not that they can escape the Chastisement. For them is a Chastisement grievous indeed. (3:188)

For those who are looking for credits, positions, titles, fames, reputation and money in this world, I say to them take it. This life is a temporary one. After they die, would they take anything with them? The answer is No. Therefore, all of us should remember the following Ayah in the Qur'an in Surah Al-Dukhan (The Smoke):

How many were the gardens and springs they left behind, and corn- fields and noble buildings, and pleasant things wherein they had taken such a delight! Thus (was their end)! And We made other people inherit (those things)! And neither heaven nor earth shed a tear. Over them: nor were they given a respite (again). (44:25-29)

For the pleasure of Allah, I will do my utmost best to continue to work and help everyone. I will help Muslims and non-Muslims as well. I am not looking for titles, positions or money, none of these attract me at all. When we read Qur'an, we find out that all the Prophets have done marvelous jobs in delivering the Message of Allah. However, they were accused, blamed, harassed, prosecuted, tortured, and some Prophets were killed as well. So one has to be patient, and at the same time, should pray to Allah to reward us for all what we do. The more I read the Qur'an, the more I realize that we have to be tested. The unfortunate thing is that we are being tested from within each other. Muslims are the ones who cause trouble to one another much more than the non-Muslims. I feel sorry for those trouble makers. Most likely those who are failures in their professional life are the very same ones who come to the Masajid and Islamic Centers to make troubles, commotions and Fitna. A'oozu Billahi Minash Shaitanir Rajeem.

Finally, I recognized that I am not doing good to anyone for the sake of worldly affairs. I believe (Allah knows the best) I am doing all these services for the love of Allah. I submit my case to Allah so that He will judge all of us in the Day of Judgement with justice and Mercy. Ameen.

There is no deity except Allah, and Muhammad is the messenger of Allah.

XI. LAS VEGAS VISITS

I travel quite often from place to place. I hate traveling by plane because I get scared all of the time due to air turbulence. However, I travel for the love of Allah (swt) in order to render my humble services to Muslims and non-Muslims. Therefore, I have no choice but to fly regularly. Then I do remember that Allah gave me the name Saqr which means flying falcon. Accordingly, I have to continue to fly in order to fulfill my obligations as long as I live. Meanwhile, I pray to Allah (swt) to accept my contributions to the success of the Muslim Ummah. As far as the city of Las Vegas is concerned, I was invited so many times by the local Muslims living there. I used to say to myself as to why these noble Muslims had to go to the sin city and live there. The whole world is opened for every person to go, live, and work there. Why these Muslims could not go outside the sin city and live anywhere else!

Las Vegas is the city of gambling, the city of committing all varieties of haram. People come to the city from all corners of the world to gamble, to lose their money, to lose their jobs, to lose their families, and be homeless. Sometimes we used to drive by car from California to Las Vegas. While coming back, we stop at a gas station and we see handsome individuals stranded and requesting few dollars to put gas in their cars because they lost their money. You feel sorry for them! You feel the agony for not helping them, but if I help them, this means that I am encouraging them to continue this habit of gambling again and again. As a Muslim, I should help the poor, the needy, and the wayfarer, i.e., the one outside his home town to reach his place; but these people did not lose their money accidentally, they lost the money by their own choice. One would say instead of helping these people, I better help those innocent people in the so-called third world countries or what they have been given the title as the developing nations. Yes! Indeed!. There are millions of people who are refugees because they were invaded by strong nations for no reason except to take over them and enslave them. Others are dying out of hunger, diseases, and natural catastrophes. They are indeed the ones who should be helped in every capacity and in any form. More reflections come to our minds. Most of the immigrant Muslims have their relatives still overseas. They do need all types of help. Every dollar counts. The purchasing power of a dollar is very high. Therefore, one feels that he should help his poor relatives overseas instead of helping those addicted to gambling...At least some say: if we help our relatives, they will make Du`a' for us. Even if we help other poor Muslims in the Muslim world, they will make Du`a' also.

As far as the city of Las Vegas is concerned, it has all varieties of buildings. It is the city of sun and hot weather. It is the city of sins due to gambling, drinking of alcohol, dancing, topless shows, etc. It is also the city of churches! I was shocked to find out that Christian ministers and priests do officiate religious marriages to those who want it to be so; and they officiate secular marriages as long as they get money. I found that it is the city of noise all throughout the days and the nights. There is no peace and no silence. Anywhere you go it is noisy, even in the washrooms, airport, and the boarding areas of the airport. So many people go there for one reason or the other. A large number of them go for gambling or for the fun of trying their fortune. Most of them go there with a big hope, but they come back with gloomy faces. It seems many people are not convinced yet that gambling is a losing venture. They try their fortune week after week till they lose all their income. Then they lose their jobs, their houses, their families, and any other assets till they become single and homeless.

Anytime I go to Las Vegas, a series of reflections cross my mind. The more I think of those people, the more I see the miseries on their faces. I really appreciate that I am a Muslim who is abiding by the teachings of Islam. I really feel very happy by abstaining from gambling. I always remember what Allah (swt) says in the Qur'an in Surah Al-Ma-idah (The Table Spread):

يَٰٓأَيُّهَا ٱلَّذِينَ ءَامَنُوٓا۟ إِنَّمَا ٱلْخَمْرُ وَٱلْمَيْسِرُ وَٱلْأَنصَابُ وَٱلْأَزْلَٰمُ رِجْسٌ مِّنْ عَمَلِ ٱلشَّيْطَٰنِ فَٱجْتَنِبُوهُ لَعَلَّكُمْ تُفْلِحُونَ ۝ إِنَّمَا يُرِيدُ ٱلشَّيْطَٰنُ أَن يُوقِعَ بَيْنَكُمُ ٱلْعَدَٰوَةَ وَٱلْبَغْضَآءَ فِى ٱلْخَمْرِ وَٱلْمَيْسِرِ وَيَصُدَّكُمْ عَن ذِكْرِ ٱللَّهِ وَعَنِ ٱلصَّلَوٰةِ فَهَلْ أَنتُم مُّنتَهُونَ ۝ وَأَطِيعُوا۟ ٱللَّهَ وَأَطِيعُوا۟ ٱلرَّسُولَ وَٱحْذَرُوا۟ فَإِن تَوَلَّيْتُمْ فَٱعْلَمُوٓا۟ أَنَّمَا عَلَىٰ رَسُولِنَا ٱلْبَلَٰغُ ٱلْمُبِينُ ۝

O you who believe! Intoxicants and gambling, sacrificing to stones, and (divination by) arrows, are an abomination,- of Satan's handiwork: eschew such (abomination), that you may prosper. Satan's plan is (but) to excite enmity and hatred between you, with intoxicants and gambling, and hinder you from the remembrance of Allah, and from prayer: will you not then abstain? Obey Allah, and obey the Messenger. (5:90-92)

Last but the least, I pray to Allah to keep me Muslim, and whenever I die I pray to Allah to let me die as a Mu'min. I do plead my case to Allah to let me be summoned in the Day of Judgment with Prophet Muhammad, and all the other prophets, with the Shuhadaa' (The Martyrs) and the Saliheen (The good faithful believers). Allahumma Ameen

XII. GOING TO CANADA

Since I came to USA in 1962 till this year of 1999, I have been travelling quite often from place to place in the field of Islamic Da'wah for the love of Allah. In the 60's, we used to travel as a group by car, bus and train; we rarely traveled by plane because it was too expensive to do so. We tried to save money, and we did not have it either.

However, I graduated in the year 1966, and got a job. I realized that we should fly in order to save time and to be back to my job on time. Since then I have to follow this policy. I used to spend money from my pocket for Da'wah because I was earning from my job, Al-Hamdu Lillah. Later when a person has a family, he has to reduce his expenses and at the same time be resourceful to improve the quality of Da'wah activities. I tried to share the expenses with local communities as much as possible.

Canada is on the borderline with USA. Our Muslim Students' Association of USA and Canada demands from us to go back and forth. We had to visit Montreal, Kingston, Ottawa, Niagara Falls, Toronto, London, Windsor, Winnipeg, Edmonton, Calgary, Vancouver and other cities. Anytime we had to enter Canada, we had to present our passport for immigration and the custom declaration information. One has to wait in line for 20-30 minutes to finish the routine procedures. I find some of the questions that the immigration and the custom personnel asked to be silly and irrelevant. Some of the regular questions are as follows:

1. Are you coming by yourself? Yes!. (It is written on the paper that I am coming by myself, why do they want to ask such a silly question. Of course we can not teach them how to read the sheet of paper that one filled out).
2. For how long are you going to stay in Canada? For the weekend, sir.! (It is written for the weekend! I don't

know why he is asking such a silly question!!)
3. Is it for business or personal? It is personal! (It is already Written on the paper that I am coming for personal, why does he have to repeat something which is already there on the document? I don't know!..
4. Did you bring anything with you? No
5. Are you going to meet anyone here? No
6. Are you sure you are coming by yourself, and you are not going to meet anyone? Yes Sir!
7. In which place are you going to stay in the city? In a hotel, sir!
8. Which hotel? I don't know! Any hotel available.
9. Are you sure? Yes sir! (If we have to tell them that we are going to attend a seminar, a symposium, a conference, or to give a lecture, then a whole series of questions are to be asked.)
10. Where is the function going to be held? At the University, Sir!
11. Are you going to speak there? Yes, sir!
12. What topic you are going to talk about? Food, health and behavior, sir.
13. Are you going to be paid for the lecture? No, sir!
14. Are you sure you do this free of charge? Yes, sir!
15. How could you afford it? This is my humble contribution to the welfare of the society, sir.!

He stamps the documents, and sends me to another staff at the Airport. The other fellow staff repeats similar questions, and I answer him the same. Then he asks: Open your brief case? I open it. He tries to browse in the files of papers, letters, pens, pencils, etc so as to find something strange. But he does not find anything unique. He is not satisfied. He sends me to a third staff who is more cunning and stupid. He sees the documents again, and he repeats similar questions, I patiently try to answer him politely. He wants to examine more things. I try to open my suitcase to let him browse with my underwear and my pajamas. He gets scared. No! No! Close it. I close it, on the assumption that everything is fine. He takes it to the x-rays machine to find out if there is any material such as bombs or similar things. He comes back to me, and asks me to open the suitcase. I open it! He tries to search in every item he sees to see the unseen.

Sometimes he sees some of my personal books that I have published. He looks at them, and to his surprise he finds out that the author of those books is me, myself.. He looks at me with a surprise, and asks me: Is this your name? "Yes, sir!," I reply. He nods his head with double surprise!.. He asks:, "What do you do?" I say, as you can see sir, I am a retired professor, and I am an author of a series of books!

He looks at me with a triple surprise. He asks: where do you work? I used to teach in medical schools... I worked in mental hospital to see what's wrong with the brains of crazy people...(I want to say like yourself), but logic controls my emotions...Did you find out anything? Yes ! Sir! You are what you eat. Garbage in: Garbage out. Your personality and behavior are affected by the type of foods you eat, sir. The chemical compositions of the foods you eat, affect the chemistry of your blood, and in turn affect your brains, one way or the other.. He looks at me from behind his eye-glasses with surprise.

I continue talking to him, and he seems very anxious to listen to me. I say: sir. The foods could be micro or macro. The first could be vitamins, minerals, enzymes, co-enzymes, carbohydrates, proteins, lipids, and so on.

I continue saying to him: Sir, I also did my doctorate at the University of Illinois. It was about Atherosclerosis, and heart attack disease. Also, the influence of cholesterol on your aorta and the heart in general.

My role sir, is to educate people how to be healthy, how to live a happy life, how to reduce friction, and how to improve human relationship. I say: Ignorance about other people, other nationalities, other ethnic groups and others is the cause of many problems. People should travel to different parts of the world to see the beauty of life that God created for us to enjoy. However, there are many people who enjoy sticking their necks to their jobs. They isolate themselves too much, and therefore, they don't enjoy life. They don't understand the meanings of life. They don't understand other people, other cultures, ethnicity, colors, religions and so on. They don't even understand themselves and what they are doing.

The moment they dress shirts with a metal sign of immigration or customs, they think they are above people and humanity at large. They have the right to insult, demean, scare, and intimidate people. They forgot that they are employees to help the visitors, to guide them, and to welcome them with smiling faces. It seems they are not taught by their departments how to deal with visitors. It could be that the head Departments themselves lack the knowledge of courtesy and the knowledge of welcoming people.

What needs to be done, is to have a survey to be filled by the visitors stating their opinions about the different treatments they receive by the employees of the customs and immigration Departments. At that time people will wake up from being intimidated and assume their responsibilities. We live in a democratic society. The voice of the people is more important than the employees of the Government. Their voice is more important than the President of the country. After all, the President, the Senators, and the Congress people are to be elected by the people themselves. They are to serve their people, and not to harass or to scare their own citizens.

Those employees forgot that people are cursing them while they are alive. I am sure, people are also to curse them after they die. Such employees forgot that they themselves are going to go to the Day of Judgement. They are to be questioned at every check point by Angels from Hell. They will be scared to death. However, they do deserve the heavy penalty of the grave and the Day of Assembly as well as during the Day of Judgement.

If anyone assigns partners to Allah, he is as if he had fallen from heaven and been snatched up by birds, or the wind had swooped (like a bird on its prey) and thrown him into a far-distant place. (22:31)

XIII. TRIP TO PEORIA

On Friday, November 25, 1983, we made a visit to Peoria, Illinois. The whole family of six with nephew of the mother went in one car from the city of Lombard, Illinois. The trip was for the purpose of inaugurating the opening of the Masjid. The distance was about (150) one hundred fifty miles.

We arrived on time for Friday Prayer. I had to give the Khutbah and lead the prayer. The subject was on "Praise and Thanks to Allah (swt)". I tried to bring concept to Thanksgiving from the Islamic point of view.

In the evening, there was a speech and a dinner. The subject was on the "rewards in this World and in the Hereafter" for those who build a Masjid for the love of Allah. I had to inform them that any community can not establish itself without the establishment of Islamic institutions. Some of these institutions are: Mosques, centers, Islamic banks, Islamic hospitals, Islamic schools and universities, Islamic radio and TV stations, Islamic journals, magazines, and newspapers, Islamic slaughtering houses, Islamic industries and Islamic political systems.

The discussion was concentrated on Halal and Haram in Zabiha meat, while I was concentrating on establishing our identity and ourselves in this part of the world. I tried to talk about the American Islamic College as an example of an educational institute in America.

The dinner and the brotherly atmosphere were excellent. It should be mentioned here that we went seven of us early morning at 8:00 a.m. and returned home 11:30 p.m. of the same day. It is not easy to drive that distance back and forth; and at the same time to give the Friday Khutbah. Moreover, to give a lecture in the evening, and come back home is not easy.

Life is not easy. To get involved in the life of Da'wah is difficult. However, anything for the love of Allah should be easy. When the intention is for Allah, every thing becomes easy. One should recognize that Da'wah necessitates time, effort, energy, knowledge, wisdom, money and sacrifice. All of these are factors for Da'wah. Life is full of hardship, but the rewards are tremendous from Allah. Paradise is not free. Therefore, one has to work hard in order to obtain the Blessings and the Rewards from Allah. The Da'iyah should not expect any honorarium or any gift while he is serving his communities. He should not even expect any person to come to him and thank him for the good job he has done. His rewards are only from Allah (swt).

The reflections from Qur'an will definitely strengthen the Faith in the heart of a believer. One Ayah was brought to my attention from Surah Al-Nahl (The Bees). It goes as follows:

مَنْ عَمِلَ صَٰلِحًا مِّن ذَكَرٍ أَوْ أُنثَىٰ وَهُوَ مُؤْمِنٌ فَلَنُحْيِيَنَّهُۥ حَيَوٰةً طَيِّبَةً ۖ وَلَنَجْزِيَنَّهُمْ أَجْرَهُم بِأَحْسَنِ مَا كَانُوا۟ يَعْمَلُونَ ﴿٩٧﴾

Whoever works righteousness, man and woman, and has Faith, verily, to him will We give a life. That is good and pure, and We will bestow on such their reward according to the best of their actions. (16:97)

I pray to Allah (swt) to accept from us the work we are doing for His pleasure, and to forgive us for our shortcomings. Ameen.

XIV. WE NEED YOU ... BUT

As usual I am invited regularly to different places in North America. I have to fly from place to place in order to reach my destination to the community that has invited me. It takes me six to eight hours from the time I leave my home to my destination.

In November 1997, I was invited to a good number of places. In one day I had to go to three or four places. I was blessed by Allah to do such activities. Some of these places were by car fifty miles away from each other, while other places were by car and then by plane, Al-Hamdu Lillah.

In the third week of November of the same year, I was invited by Muslim Student Association (MSA) of San Diego, California; the MSA of Boston, Massachusetts ; the MSA at Mt. San Antonio College in California; the Islamic Center of South Bay, California; Operation Safe Community; the MSA of University of Southern California; the Islamic Information Service "Islam" TV ; the MSA of University of Illinois (Urbana); the Islamic Center of San Diego; the Islamic Education Center and the North American Islamic Conference in Cedar Rapids, Iowa. With all these challenges, I had to accept some of them and apologize to others whom I was unable to extend my help. Some groups however, were unhappy because I could not make it. I had to apologize to them as if I made a serious mistake for not being able to meet the demands of all. I recommended some other speakers from some areas, Al-Hamdu Lillah.

As far as the hosts of the North American Islamic Conference, (NAIC) are concerned, they insisted that I should participate in their Conference. They made sure that I should come because my presence is very important. They called me many times to make sure I will attend their conference even for just a day out of the scheduled three days. I received several faxes as well as the brochure about the conference, I felt morally obliged and I gave them the green light to be there. On the other hand I have to cancel other invitations because I cannot be in two places at one time.

Finally I received a fax about the conference program and about the importance of my presence for this particular conference. Their letter of November 8, 1997 reads as follows:

We are extremely pleased and honored that you accepted the invitation not only to the conference but to give the Friday, November 21st Khutbah. We know of your long relationship and love for the Muslims of Iowa; especially since your daughter and son-in-law spent time there.

We need your cooperation. We are hoping that your community or organization can assist us in raising the necessary funding to cover the direct cost for you to attend the conference. Your attendance will be a highlight of the conference and we hope your organization and community will find the means to get the support.

Dr. Sakr, we have found tremendous interest in the theme and endeavors of our conference as it is the first comprehensive understanding and attempt to research the History of Islam in North America from the first Muslim slaves from Africa through and to the immigration of Turko-Europeans, Middle Eastern Arabs, Indo-Pakistani to the most recent Southeast Asians. As one of the leading Islamic Scholars in North America, you will contribute tremendously to the conference and in turn we hope that you, too, will benefit. Please keep us advised as per your arrival schedule and the above.   *Yours in Islam.*

Most of the local people in that area are very successful business individuals. Even the host is very successful in his own business. They do know that I am a Roving Da'iyah. I left my teaching position for the sake of Da'wah. I left my business transactions for the love of Allah to spread His Message. I don't have even the benefits of an employee. In every trip I go to, I have to pay from my pocket in one way or the other. They are aware that I write and publish books. Those books are printed in the same city where the conference is to be held. I owe the local printer an average of forty thousand U.S. dollars due to lack of funds. They are aware that I distribute most of my books Free to so many people in North America and abroad. Moreover, the local community that I help here in California is the poorest one Al-Hamdu Lillah. We don't have a center of our own. We have been renting an office building with a warehouse for six years. It was difficult even to pay the monthly rent for that center.

With all these factors I ask myself how in the world the hosts of the conference want me to come on my own expense. I was shocked to read that in their letter that I should request the local people to give me money so as to participate in a conference which has nothing to do with the local community!...Yes I fly from place to place to raise money for the local communities themselves. I never went to any place to raise money even for the Foundation that is responsible for my books. I know how to beg for others but not for myself, or for our community center. These friends of the conference are courageous enough to request me to help them raising funds for my trip. It seems people want to hold conference to get recognition. I am already fed-up of attending conferences. They are tip-talks. People meet, talk and make good resolutions. But they don't know how to follow up to execute those decisions. For more than thirty five years we have been holding conferences and talking too much! We did not implement those resolutions as well as a the recommendations.

It seems people feel jealous of each other. Each person, group of individuals, or organization wants to call for a conference. Why? I don't know why. It seems they want to champion the Muslim Affairs. They want to be called the leaders of the Muslims of America. To be leaders, they should render services. They should initiate institutions for the Muslims. Unfortunately, we don't have a single hospital or a viable recognized Islamic University. We don't have an orphanage, senior citizen homes or shelter houses for the battered women or abused children... It seems we people would like to brag about being the leaders. We want people to attend the conferences, participate, give a lecture, and raise money for the so-called leaders.

Let everyone sacrifice their money, time, efforts, energy, wisdom and knowledge for the sake of those who want to champion false leadership. It is high time to stop such type of activities and start building institutions to take care of our needs. It is time that we should stop spending our money on fake conferences to produce fake leaders. It seems some of those champions may not be willing to practice the teachings of Islam. All what they are looking for is that people should give them pledge of allegiance to obey them.

These are some of my reflections while I was flying between California and Chicago. I was by myself next to the window. I was looking through the sky, mountains, snow, clouds, lakes, river and the plane was bumping because of air turbulence. I started **Reflecting as A Flying Falcon** about the invitations. I said to myself, why don't I jot down these reflections for the new generations to benefit from my experience. I did it with good intention. May Allah accept it. I did not mean to insult my good friends who invited me to the Conference. Allah is my witness. I ask Allah His forgiveness for our shortcomings. Ameen.

Then I had to remember the stories of all the prophets how they had sacrificed so many things with their local communities for the love of Allah (swt). All of them used to say:

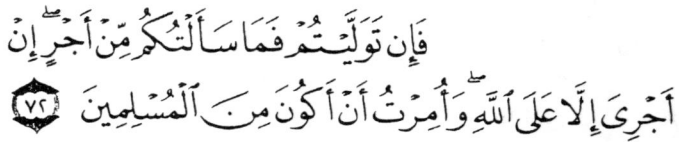

But if you turn back, (consider): No reward have I asked of you: my reward is only due from Allah, and I have been commanded to be of those who submit to Allah's Will (in Islam). (10:72)

It seems many Muslims who migrated from the Muslim World had the impression that Islamic Da'wah and services are to be done free. Every Da'iyah has to perform Da'wah from his personal expenses. He should continue these services day-after-day without complaining. He should never refrain or find excuses. The recipients are the beneficiaries, while the Da'iyah is the person who should sacrifice his time, knowledge, money, and even his own life while others are watching or benefiting. Muslims have to recognize that each and everyone has to share the happiness and the rewards by spending money, time or knowledge. Then and only then we can be successful in this world and in the hereafter.

I had to control myself, and submit humbly to Allah, praying to forgive me, and at the same time to help me continue my services to all. Ameen. I wish I have financial resources to help me rendering services free of charge. I want to be a Free-Lancer-Free. I try my best to help others as much as possible Free. However, as a human being with a family and relatives around me I feel obliged to take care of them. It is understood that family members come first. It became a habit that I help people to solve their family or business problems Free. I also give my books free to many people. If there is any reward it is only and only from Allah. I am grateful to Allah for giving me such type of opportunities to help others Free- Ameen.

Do they not look at the birds, held poised in the midst of (the air and) the sky? Nothing holds them up but (the power of) Allah. Verily in this are Signs for those who believe. (16:79)

XV. PARASITES

The journeys that the Falcon has to make are too many to count. He is being asked to go to different places for lectures to Muslims and non-Muslims. He has to fly from place to place in order to raise money for many local centers, communities, schools, and masajid. This poor fellow had learned from childhood not to say NO! Deep in his heart, he knows that he is doing these services for the love of Allah (swt).

In order to travel few thousand miles in one day and come back the second day, he has to wake up 4:00-5:00 A.M., pray Fajr, and drive his car and leave it at the airport. He has to accept all the challenges of jet lag, air turbulence, physical fatigue, no proper eating, eating at odd times and irregular sleeping. He has to continue rendering his services to all varieties of groups of people with a smiling face. Every time he goes to any particular function, he carries his books with him to give them as a gift to the local group. Sometimes he has to pay for his foods, liquids, parking at airport, pay for the shuttle bus, taxi, tips for several individuals, phone calls from his house to the local groups and vice-versa. Sometimes he has to pay for the hotel and he is forced to stay in.

Moreover, he has to raise money for the local group. The amount he raises is between $5,000-$500,000. Once he was able to raise $2,056,000. It is his hope and his prayer that Allah (swt) will accept his deeds and intentions, otherwise he will be a loser in the Day of Judgement. Local people feel happy with the series of lectures and the way he conducts the fund raising activities. However, he himself feels miserable after the function is over. He is tired, exhausted, his voice is lost, his leg muscles have spasms, and so on and so forth.

Local people feel happy: Everything was for them. No one is supposed to share money with them. In America, any fund-raiser charges 10% of what he raises. Our friends will never feel happy even to give any percentage. It is totally haram! A Da'iyah is supposed to make Da'wah free of charge. He should give his time, effort, knowledge and his personal money away Fee Sabeel Allah. He should leave his family for two days to two weeks. As if they say: do not worry! Allah (swt) will take care of them. The similitude of these people is like a person who says:

Ya Allah! You are for me!
My wife is for me!
My children are for me!
My relatives are for me!
The whole world is for me!
And I am for myself!

No one should share my happiness and my fortune with me! Such types of people are called parasites. These organisms in biology are to feed on others. They are to eat up the host. They are to destroy and to wipe out others to satisfy themselves. Such types of people in the society are very dangerous. They should be taught how to behave, and how to share the happiness and the fortune of this life with others. People are to sacrifice while they themselves are the recipients of fortune. Then later they brag about it on the assumption as if they did all these results.

Those people should recognize that in biology the parasites are to be destroyed. They should understand that there are other groups in biology who are wise enough. They also should recognize that happiness of life is a two-way street. Both groups are to benefit from each other. This type of a process is called symbiosis. Islam has taught humanity how to help one another: the rich is to help the poor through Zakat, Sadaqa, Qard-Hassan, grants, scholarships, Sadaqa-Jariya, etc. Islam has taught people how to be grateful and thankful to Allah by being thankful to those who help them and render services to them. Islamic teachings denounce those people who use others for themselves without sharing results.

This poor fellow the Flying Falcon (SAQR) starts asking himself so many questions as to why he is doing all these services while he himself is being denied the use or the benefits of the results. He cries not for himself and not about himself, but he cries for the situation of our people. He himself knows how to pacify himself. He tries to pacify his family when he comes back home with empty hands. The only thing he can do is to smile to them, to hug them, and to thank them for their patience during his absence. He cannot tell the local people about CARING and SHARING! He cannot tell them about the existence of parasites and they should not behave in that form! All what he can do is to pray to Allah (swt) to guide such people in the society to the Sirat Al-Mustaqeem.

The Flying Falcon recognizes that he has to continue to help others and to sacrifice. Life without sacrifice is meaningless. However, sacrifice with good intention for the love of Allah (swt) means complete happiness. For that reason, the Flying Bird (Assaqr Al-Taair) has written his thoughts while he was flying between Orlando, FL → Dallas, TX → Ontario, CA on his way home empty handed but full of Iman on December 26, 1997.

By reading Qur'an and studying the life history of the previous Prophets, one may recognize that all of them delivered the Message of Allah Free. For that reason they worked as business people first and some tried to continue to earn their living. In these days, a Da`iyah has to travel by plane and go from area to another one day-after-day. The question would be: How he is going to survive. He needs to live and raise his family with honor and respect. Otherwise he will be in trouble. We pray to Allah to guide all the Muslims to work together and help one another for the love of Allah. Ameen.

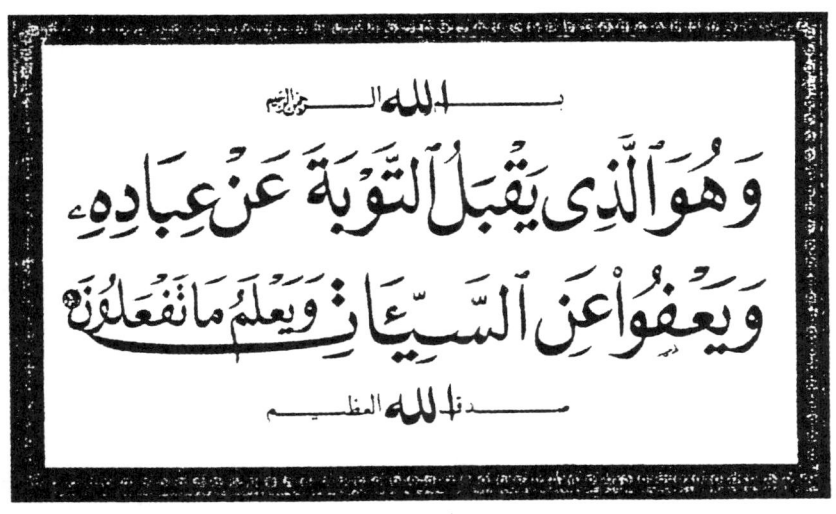

He is the One that accepts repentance from His Servants and forgives sins: and He knows all that you do. (42:25)

XVI. TELL US WHEN YOU ARE AROUND

I fly many times from place to place on a weekly basis and sometimes during the week. To satisfy more than one group, I have to fly in the same weekend to two or three different places: just jumping from place to place. Sometimes friends call me to invite me to their local community for an activity. Instead of inviting me and checking my schedule, they ask: when are you going to visit our neighborhood? I say I don't know. But we want to invite you to deliver Jumu'ah Khutbah, and in the evening to attend a function for our community. Please: Tell us when are you going to be in the region. I usually say in a friendly way: I don't know when I will be passing by your neighborhood.

They add, please brother Ahmad, let us know as soon as possible when you will be passing or visiting any local community in the vicinity. We want to invite you. We love you, we admire you, and our community would love to hear from you!. With an innocent voice, I usually say: Why don't we agree on a date from now and plan it for the future... Yes, brother Ahmad, but... I said, but what is the problem?! No brother Ahmad, there is no problem...But we prefer when a local community invites you, then you can drive to our community and help us. I say: Yes, brother I will be happy to do so, if and when a local community invites me. He feels happy; but brother Ahmad! Can you tell us now? I say: I am sorry! I wish I can tell you now, but I have no invitation in your region for the time being. However, I will let you know as soon as I get an invitation. Thank you brother Ahmad. This is our phone number and fax number. Please let us know. I usually say yes, Insha Allah and I do mean it.

Once I could not resist. I told the friend why don't your community and two other communities work out three (3) different programs one day after another, i.e., one day for each community. I will be happy to spend three days for all of you combined. I added: My services are free, and I will be happy to stay in a neighboring motel. I will be happy to take care of my accommodation. However, I mentioned to him, that the cost of the ticket could be shared by three communities. At that time, 1990, the cost of the ticket was less than $ 300.00. His polite answer was: No brother Ahmad... I don't think that our community can pay any penny. They want everything free. Therefore, do us a favor: Try to get an air ticket from the other community and let us know. However, we do need you to give Friday Khutbah, and a lecture in the evening. Then you are on your own for Saturday and Sunday. I thanked the brother for his invitation, and I told him that I will try to find the best way to come to him and his community. He felt happy, but he said to me: I like you very much; I am a good friend of you for a number of years; I like to hear you speaking to us; our community members do like you also; you know that; I thanked him tremendously for his good invitation. He wanted me to come form California to Chicago free of charge! For three days! On my own way! Ma-Sha-Allah!

Before I hang up the phone, he said: By the way! I said: yes, brother! Don't forget to get us your books for our community center. The library of the Masjid has no more of your books. I tried to find a polite answer to him. I told him: I will be happy to do so, but, by the way, if I remember well, I gave your community center all my books free! Yes!, he said, but it seems that the books have been taken away. I told him, whenever I plan to come, I will be more than happy to bring you another set of my books. He felt happy. Thank you, brother Ahmad. You are a good friend and generous. I look forward to meet you when you visit us. He thanked me and said to me Ma'assalama! Khuda Hafiz...

After closing the phone, I tried to reflect on this invitation: Everything should be given free: travel by plane, parking car at the airport, or taking a taxi, three days free, books free, giving a series of lectures free, hotel free, food free, and going from community to community free. It seems my best friends want from the speaker everything free, but they are not ready to assume the responsibility or even to share the expenses. They reminded me of Bani Israel, when they told Prophet Moosa: Go you and your God and fight for us. We are here sitting and waiting. If you succeed, we will come and take over the land! They thought that everyone is for them; even Allah is to serve them, while they are sitting at home!.

I wonder! Why these people are acting like that. They will not be successful unless and until they assume their responsibilities. They should understand that there is No Free Lunch in America, or in the whole world. Paradise is not Free. One has to work hard in order to earn Paradise and even to receive the Blessings of Allah (swt). Muslims in particular, should understand this concept before anyone else. It seems Muslims have to examine their faith. They should put themselves in the position of a Da`iyah. Would they like to be in such a humiliating position. The local communities want from a Da`iyah to come on his own expenses, or even other neighboring community should take care of the expenses, while they themselves are the recipient of the benefits Free-of-Charge. Muslims should study the teachings of Islam again and again through `Ulamaa', the scholars of Islam so that they will understand such teachings and act accordingly. By understanding the teachings of Islam is not enough. One has to practice such teachings in private and in public. One has to demonstrate in action that he means honesty and sincerity as well. We have to be selfless rather than being selfish.

I pray to Allah (swt) to guide us all, to help us work hard, and to assume the responsibilities of life. Ameen.

XVII. GORGEOUS BUT SCARY

Nothing in life compares to flying. One cannot enjoy the beauty of planet earth unless he goes up in the air and looks around, above and beneath. One should sit at a window seat, and start looking through space so as to enjoy the creation of Allah (swt) in this universe.

Since I came from the family of Sakr (Saqr), I had to convince myself that I belong to the family of Birds: Falcon, Hawk, Eagle, etc. This means that I had to fly regularly, and I had to fly high in order to survive.

Looking around, one may find that there are dozens of species of birds, some of which are as small as a butterfly, while others are as big as the family of falcons. All of them do fly in order to survive. They are considered a community of birds in a society with rules and regulations. Allah (swt) informed us about birds that they constitute a community similar to the human community. In Surah Al-An'am, (Cattle), Allah (swt) says the following:

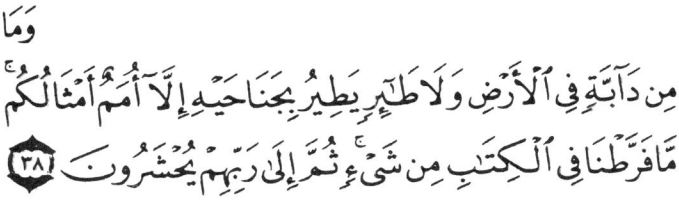

There is not an animal (that lives) on the earth, nor a being that flies on its wings, but (forms part of) communities like you. Nothing have We omitted from the Book, and they (all) shall be gathered to their Lord in the end. (6:38)

When I was a child I used to observe so many varieties of birds, as well as many varieties of planes. I tried to join the College of Engineering at the American University of Beirut in the 50's so as to learn how to design better airplanes, and fly fast as far as the horizon in a twinkle of an eye. Prophet Suleiman used to send people on a flying red carpet from place to place in a short period of time. His assistant was able to bring the palace of Queen Balqees from Yemen to Palestine before Suleiman was to twinkle his eyelids! All of these encouraged me to specialize as an aerospace engineer. I wish and I want, but I can't execute! However, Allah (swt) knows the best! I could not enter the Engineering College!...

Being involved in Da'wah, I had no choice but to travel locally, regionally, nationally, and internationally. My travelling was on foot, bicycle, motorcycle, car, bus, boat, train and by plane. Since I came to USA, I became more involved in Da'wah. I had also to travel and to fly. Flying by plane is so marvelous, so gorgeous, and so beautiful, but it is scary. Every time I had to fly I prepare myself to meet Allah (swt) as if that trip is the last one in my life. I start reading Qur'an and make special Du`a'.

There are so many things to narrate about the beauty of flying. Some of these reflections are the following observations:

1. Looking through the window of the plane, I start reflecting about the creation of the heavens and the earth. I contemplate. I had no choice but to be a humble human being. I remembered the Ayat in Surah Al-'Imran where Allah (swt) says the following:

Gorgeous But Scary

إِنَّ فِى خَلْقِ ٱلسَّمَٰوَٰتِ وَٱلْأَرْضِ وَٱخْتِلَٰفِ ٱلَّيْلِ وَٱلنَّهَارِ لَءَايَٰتٍ لِّأُو۟لِى ٱلْأَلْبَٰبِ ۝ ٱلَّذِينَ يَذْكُرُونَ ٱللَّهَ قِيَٰمًا وَقُعُودًا وَعَلَىٰ جُنُوبِهِمْ وَيَتَفَكَّرُونَ فِى خَلْقِ ٱلسَّمَٰوَٰتِ وَٱلْأَرْضِ رَبَّنَا مَا خَلَقْتَ هَٰذَا بَٰطِلًا سُبْحَٰنَكَ فَقِنَا عَذَابَ ٱلنَّارِ ۝

Behold! In creation of the heavens and the earth, and the alteration of Night and Day,-there are indeed Signs for men of understanding,- Men who remember Allah standing, sitting, and lying down on their sides, and contemplate the (wonders of creation in the heavens and the earth, (with the saying) Our Lord not for naught have You created (all) this! Glory to You! Give us Salvation from the chastisement of the fire. (3:190-191)

2. Looking and seeing the open atmospheres above while people are below is so gorgeous. I realize I am above all the agony of problems: fighting, cheating, lying, shooting, killing, backbiting, stealing, and so on. I am above all these vices physically, mentally, morally and spiritually.
3. Through the window looking down, I see the houses are so small, and the cars are smaller than toys. I am above driving and being scared from crazy drivers who are drunk and driving.
4. I am above pollution and smog. I can see the blue sky shining above my head. I can see the sun or moon and stars. I can reflect easily about their role and their benefits for us as human beings.
5. I see mountains, valleys, rivers, lakes, seas or even ocean passing under me in few minutes one after the other.

6. I see clouds above my head, facing me or even below me. The most gorgeous things in clouds are that none looks the same as others. Each cloud has different shape, color, size, and function. I can't help but to say: Glory be to Allah... Praise be to Allah... There is no god but Allah...And Allah is the Great.
7. Looking below I see villages, towns and cities. They are very crowded next to each other; while around them you see huge open areas. I say to myself, why they built those buildings next to one another so close that there is no privacy of life. There is no peace of mind and soul when they are too close to each other. More so! Why there are high and tall buildings to be above each other, when next to them there are the huge open areas that are free of congestion?
8. While flying at night and seeing below me, it gives me new dimension of reflections. You see the beauty of lights shining in the streets of the cities, but how often people abuse the darkness of the night by doing harm to others! It is really so beautiful to see this from the sky, but not to be yourself walking in any of those streets. You will be scared. I am reminded that we should read Surah Al-Falaq (The Dawn), so that Allah (swt) will protect us from all types of criminals at night.
9. Whenever I see a plane flying or whenever I am myself flying, I really appreciate how Allah (swt) taught human beings so many things that they did not know before. It reminds me of the Ayah in Surah Al-`Alaq (Iqra', Read, Proclaim) where Allah (swt) says:

Proclaim! (or Read!) In the name of your Lord the Cherisher, Who created- Created man, out of a leech-like clot: Proclaim! And your Lord is Most Bountiful,- He Who taught (The use of) the Pen,- taught man that which he knew not. (96:1-5)

People have reached a stage of knowledge so advance and superb; but they do not appreciate what Allah (swt) has bestowed upon them.

10. There are many more reflections that one wishes to share with the readers, but also I should share my worries when I fly, I am really scared!...I assume that the trip might be the very last one. I have the deep reflection that something wrong may take place to the plane, and it may crash!... That is the end of my life.

For that reason, before I leave home I make two Rakat Salat Widaa' (departure), and I read the Du`a' of travelling (please look for it in Addendum B). Anytime I try to enter the plane, a new reflection comes to me telling me, why are you going, get out, and cancel your trip. I get more scared!

While in the plane I see people happy relaxed while I am under tension!... They talk and laugh while I am silent and scared! Sometimes the plane passes through areas of turbulence, and it starts shaking! The pilot puts on light sign of "Fasten the seat belts". The plane passes the turbulence area for five (5) minutes to one hour or so. People are still talking, laughing and as if nothing happened.

If anyone wants to look at my face he will see it pale! I am totally scared! I am worried what to do. I say: It seems this is the end of my life! I start reading Ayatul Kursi seven times to pacify myself. I carry the Qur'an in my hands and squeeze it to my chest. If anything happens, I will meet Allah while the Qur'an is in my hands.

I find myself reading more Du`a' which are essential to be recited daily for many occasions. (please see Addendum C). When I land safely, I praise Allah (swt) and thank Him for taking me to the destination without any catastrophe. When I come back home safely I am really double grateful to Allah (swt) for all the favors He has done to me in the trip. I feel happy, at least, that I went to help the communities to raise money to build a Masjid or a school. I pray to Allah (swt) to accept me among others, and to give me credits and rewards for those trips. Ameen.

And the birds gathered (in assemblies): all with him did turn (to Allah). (38:19)

XVIII. AIR TICKETS ARE EXPENSIVE

Many times I am invited to travel to different communities in North America and overseas. I have the habit to accept many invitations without delay and without screening who is who. A good number of invitations in North America are mainly for fundraising. It is a matter of raising money and money only. I wish that they invite me to participate in giving lectures, to participate in panel discussions or otherwise. Sometimes I try to reflect and think that I should no more accept the invitations for fundraising. It sounds demeaning and also I have to act as a beggar on their behalves. Then I come to the conclusion that I should continue to accept any invitation as long as it is for a good cause. As such I continue to do whatever Allah (swt) wants me to do.

However, there are many who invite me in advance, and leave me without confirmation. Then they remember that they have to make arrangements for air tickets. They call me and say that the air ticket is a little expensive. But they continue to say that they found out that someone has a free ticket, but you have to be on stand-by. Otherwise, there may be another alternative whereby you have to take a particular airline that has to stop 2-3 times with change of airplane. This means that instead of coming with a non-stop which takes 3-4 hours, I have to spend 8-10 hour flight. I have to go from airport to airport, and to wait at every airport for 1-2 hours to make the connections. The other alternative is to come overnight, sleeping in the plane and spend the whole day (Saturday) till they start the function in the evening.

It should be stated here, that I always fly coach. I never feel happy to fly business or first class. I feel I would be extravagant in spending money for my luxury or prestige. I request the travel agent to find me the cheapest price . I do such type of reservation at least one month in advance in order to get the least expensive.

Many times one of the member of the host community calls to inform one that the air ticket is expensive. Therefore, they cancel my invitation. They will try to find another speaker somewhere in their locality so that they will not pay any penny to bring the speaker from out-of-town. I thank them very much and I tell them that they did the wise decision. They do not want to pay any dollar for any function, but they want to collect $100,000 without paying even the air ticket for their guest speaker.

I add my humble advice by telling them that the dinner to be served should be Free too from the restaurant. They say to me that: this is what they are trying to do. Sometimes I have the courage to tell them in a subtle way: If you wish I will be happy to come on my own. I will pay for the air ticket, and I will pay for the taxi to take me to the airport and back to my house. I will be happy to pay for my own accommodations in any hotel. Moreover, I will bring some of my books which consist of different varieties of subjects and I am going to donate them to their local community center. The host feels happy. He tells me to give him time to discuss this matter with his local community. That is the end of communication! Al-Hamdu Lillah.

Sometimes I try to joke with them by saying: You don't need to worry about that, I will come walking on foot to your community! I say this sentence in a very polite and firm way. The host gets shocked! Am I talking sense, joking, or mocking! I leave it up to him to think it over!

Finally! I try to reflect upon such groups of communities: They want to collect one hundred thousands to five hundred thousands. They don't want to spend any money at all. They want everyone to come forward with the money, but the leadership of such communities don't want to spend any pennies. They think that since the function is to build a Masjid or a school, everyone should contribute toward that goal. They should not spend any money at all. Some of the leadership themselves don't even contribute anything because they are the leaders!

Do these individuals think that paradise is Free?! Can anyone go to a Department store and pick up anything he desires and go out without paying at the cashier!? These individuals want the speaker to come on his own and help them to collect money without costing them a cent!

I reflect about such incidences, and I do cry! I say to myself shame upon such groups of individuals who have no respect for themselves. They should be ashamed of themselves. They want the speaker to leave his family, his job, and his other Islamic commitments. They want him as a slave free of charge! Even if a person has to have a slave, he has to respect him, feed him, provide him with clothes, and shelter him; they cannot have him free. I do reflect on these incidents, but I have no answer. Even when I go to a community I sit in the plane and reflect on such type of people on this planet earth.

I sit in the plane: I read Qur'an; I make Du`a'; I write some of these reflections while I am flying; and I ask myself again and again: why should I accept any invitation and then being mistreated, accused or blamed?! While I raise so many questions, I look through the window of the plane and I focus my vision toward the sky! I see mountains, lakes, rivers, and clouds. I see small houses and cars like toys under the plane. I ask myself again and again: Why should I continue to travel to such people?! The answer comes immediately: You are not doing any favor to anyone except to you, yourself. If I have been mistreated or insulted, I should feel happy, because the reward from Allah is according to the hardship that I pass through. While I was thinking about this subject, I remembered that all the prophets were mistreated, blamed, accused, or even assassinated by their local people. I remembered the following Ayah in Surah Al-Baqarah (The Cow) where Allah (swt) says the following:

$$\text{أَمْ حَسِبْتُمْ أَن تَدْخُلُوا۟ ٱلْجَنَّةَ وَلَمَّا يَأْتِكُم مَّثَلُ ٱلَّذِينَ خَلَوْا۟ مِن قَبْلِكُم ۖ مَّسَّتْهُمُ ٱلْبَأْسَاءُ وَٱلضَّرَّاءُ وَزُلْزِلُوا۟ حَتَّىٰ يَقُولَ ٱلرَّسُولُ وَٱلَّذِينَ ءَامَنُوا۟ مَعَهُۥ مَتَىٰ نَصْرُ ٱللَّهِ ۗ أَلَا إِنَّ نَصْرَ ٱللَّهِ قَرِيبٌ ﴿٢١٤﴾}$$

Or do you think that you shall enter the Garden (of Bliss) without such (trials) as came to those who passed away before you? They encountered suffering and adversity, and were so shaken in spirit that even the Messenger and those of faith who were with him cried: "When (will come) the help of Allah" Ah! Verily, the help of Allah is (always) near! (2:214)

It seems that these immigrant Muslims want to use, abuse and accuse the Muslim Da'iyah day-after-day. They should insult him, humiliate him and confuse him. He should never react negatively to anyone. He should render his services free, and at the same time, they should accuse him for all the good favor he does for them.

Finally I end up my reflections with thanks and appreciation to Allah (swt). I make Du`a' so that Allah may accept my humble efforts and my little contributions. ! Ameen.

XIX. I WISH I WAS NEVER CREATED

This question (I wish I were not created) is bothering many people in different parts of the world. Many times, I am asked by many friends: Why are we created, and why are we on this planet earth!? Anytime I travel anywhere in different places and in different countries, I am being asked these questions. To my surprise I used to ask myself why people ask the same questions irrespective of their color, nationality, ethnic background, language, position, gender, country of birth, creed or religion.

In one of my traveling, while I was in a plane, I thought let me write down some of my reflections. While I was trying to reflect on this subject, I also asked myself why Ya Allah: you created me. I wish I were not created... I wish I stayed soil so that people would step over me! Or even they use me to build their houses, shops, streets or even their own ovens. Some other ideas crossed my mind. I wish I were created as grass so that animals will eat me, and benefit from me. Otherwise, I wish I was created as a domesticated animal so that people will slaughter me, eat me and make use of me. Or I wish I were created as honey bees so that I will produce honey. People will benefit from me. I will be used as a healing medicine for them. All these ideas crossed my mind while flying in a plane. Many more ideas (wild and concrete) were passing through my mind: Either why and why!? Or I wish I was never created. It seems that I repeated subconsciously the people's questions. Such repetition is normal, because when a person hears similar questions over and over again, he himself will repeat these questions.

I took a few moments to reflect on these questions. I contemplated and meditated. I tried my best as a Muslim to ask myself First: Why many of us are asking these questions? I recognized that there are many reasons for such questions. People pass through tests and troubles in life. They got sick; they lose their jobs; they lose their houses. They lose their loved ones; they see people are involved in gangs, drugs, shooting and killing. They see homeless people, while next door to them they see the rich who don't care for them. They see hospitals full of sick people, and the senior citizens are sent to senior citizens homes without mercy, sympathy or even concerns by their own family members. When we see all these tragedies including refugees due to wars and conflict of interest, then we ask these questions. However, if we look at life from an Islamic point of view, we come to positive answers. We should be:

1. Grateful to Allah that He created us
2. That He made us human beings and entrusted us with the Message of Islam.
3. That He made us the supreme creatures
4. That He subjugated the animals, plants, angels, air, sun, moon, planets, mountains, rivers, seas, oceans, clouds, winds, etc. All are for our own benefits.
5. That He made us His vicegerents and His ambassadors.

I recognized that by creating me as a human being, I should appreciate God's creation of the whole universe. I can understand some of the wisdom of His creations in us and in other creatures. However, it is a responsibility to be assumed. If and when we fulfil such responsibility as being His vicegerents, His representatives, and His ambassadors, we would be rewarded tremendously on this planet as well as in the Day of Judgement. Many people who do not fulfill their obligations to the Creator, need to be reminded, to be informed, to be inspired, to be motivated, to be encouraged, and/or to be guided to God. If and when we do not want to follow the truth, we are to be charged, to be challenged, and to be tested with turmoil, sickness, loss of jobs, money, house, or otherwise. All of these tests are in our favor, and they are blessings from Allah to come close to Him. Life is short. We should plan for the big journey.

I wish that Allah (swt) did not create me, but He decided already and He already created me. I had no choice. Therefore, let me make of this golden opportunity while I am living. I recognized that I should be honest to myself and truthful. I should try to practice what is good for everyone and me. I should be good to all in spite of color, nationality, race, ethnic background, language, creed, or religion. I should help all while I am sacrificing my time, effort, energy, knowledge, wisdom, and money. I recognized that without this concept of sacrifice, I am not truthful to myself and to Allah (swt).

Finally, I said to myself: I am happy that Allah created me the way I am. While I am still flying like a falcon, I cried out of happiness! I looked through the window of the plane looking at the clouds above me, under me, and around me as well. I could not help but to cry! Ya Allah! Have mercy on me! If I have to die while I am in the plane, please Ya Allah! Le my death be when I am remembering You! When I am in a state of Wudoo', and when I am holding the Qur'an in my hands reading Your Message to all of us! I close my eyes looking for the Angel of Death! I know surely that he is going to come to me one day. Again I thank Allah for all what He has blessed me with. Al-Hamdu Lillah.

One more wish: Please Ya Allah! Whenever I am going to die, let my death be while I am fasting in the last ten days of Ramadan. Let it be during Lailatul Qadr, while I am in the Ka'bah and/or Masjid of Your Prophet Muhammad in Madinah. Let my death be when I am in a position of Sujood too. Ameen Ya Rabbal 'Aalameen.

XX. USE ME!

As an invited speaker in different parts of the world, I cannot say no to almost all of the hosts. I try my best to synchronize all these invitations so as to please Allah (swt) and to help the majority. My trips are to different parts of the world as well as in USA. As usual I am invited for many reasons: public speaker; dialogue with many Muslims; dialogue with non-Muslims; fund raiser; workshops; training programs; seminars; conferences; symposia; camping; giving Friday Khutab; leading different types of salat; officiating marriages; counseling; arbitration; burying the dead; radio talks and TV programs; giving a course on Islamic Shari'ah; and many more.

In many places I try to joke with the audience so that the speech or the session will not be monotonous. One of the famous statement I usually say without thinking too much is: USE ME! I usually say more than that: USE ME AND ABUSE ME, I DON'T MIND. You may use me as a janitor; custodian; a night guard; a catalyst; a coordinator; a cook; etc. I can do any of these services, I don't mind which type of a service you assign to me. I say more than that: USE ME... ABUSE ME... DON'T LOSE ME... DON'T REFUSE ME... RECYCLE ME. You may recycle me again and again as long as I am alive, Free- of- charge. If you can you may CLONE ME TOO...

I do know from the Hadith of Prophet Muhammad (pbuh), that when Allah(swt) likes one person, He uses him for the servitude of other people. Therefore, I want to encourage my friends to use my talent; my time; my little knowledge (if I have any!); my wisdom (if I have any!); and my muscles. This statement of USE ME became famous among my friends. They tell me that they do need my services even at the last minute. However, they try to be polite: we want to use you, but we are not going to abuse you! I tell them I don't mind how, where, and when they are to use me! I am grateful to all those who try to use my services, again and again.

Some of our friends are not well organized. They try to do things the last minute. I try to joke with them. I say to them that in the Middle East, there is a magazine called Aakhir Sa'ah (The Last Hour). However, our friends do things the last minute or even the last second. This is called in Arabic Aakhir Lahzah. They change their minds, their program as well as the speakers. In the last minute I am to be informed of such a change! They also give me topic to speak about in the last minute. Sometimes I have to tell them in a friendly and polite way: is it not true that all are highly educated, and well groomed in their professional backgrounds?! Don't you think that a speaker has to prepare his lecture well in advance, and that he should make a synopsis to be distributed to the audience?! Don't you realize that we are responsible for any function if we are not well organized?! Where is the Degree of Itqaan (well done)?!

Many times they try to give the most important sessions to many speakers. The very same speaker will be given more than one session. My speaking engagement is either a parallel session in a small room or to lead a parallel session. The general assembly session is given to all except to this humble writer. I don't know why! But I don't' mind at all. I don't go to a conference for the sake of talking and lecturing. I meet many friends and I share with them some of their problems. I try to find solutions to such problems. I do know that I am so insignificant in the eyes of some. I usually say it loudly:

1. I am the least knowledgeable and for that I try to read, study and understand.

2. I am the least significant and for that reason I don't mind to tell the hosts and the audience USE ME Fee Sabeel Allah!
3. If you wish to abuse me after using me, go ahead.... I don't mind. I am not here to please any person. I am here to please Allah and Allah alone.
4. I am only as important as a Catalyst. It is to be used to produce a product. Then it is to be recycled or to be dumped into the sink.

After using me in many functions, I am left behind to take care of myself. Either to find a place to stay overnight, or even make arrangements to go to the airport by Taxi or a shuttle. I feel I am so happy that I am Free from any bond or tie with any person, group, or society. My only hope and prayer that Allah is happy with me. I do remember that in the Day of Judgment I am going to be by myself in front of Allah. No one is going to help me. It is either that my intention is for the love of Allah or else I am a loser. I pray to Allah to keep my Iman high and strong.

I do know that flying is not easy at all! I still wonder why do I have to fly, to travel and to accept invitation after invitation?! I don't know either; but I do know that there is a higher Power above my head controlling me, inspiring me, guiding me, and showing me the way, Al-Hamdu Lillah... Please Ya Allah! Accept from me these trips, and please continue to USE ME for Your Love and Your Sake. Ameen Ya Rabbal 'Aalameen. Finally, I had to remember the following Ayah in the Qur'an in Surah Al-Anbiyaa' (The Prophets). Allah says:

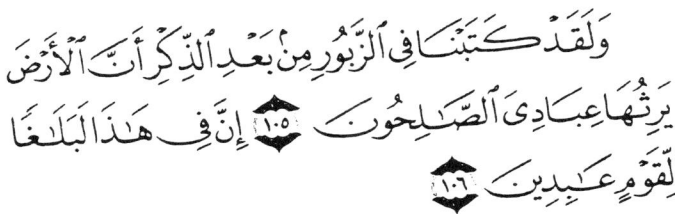

> *Before this We wrote in the Psalms, after the Message (given to Moses): "My servants the righteous, shall inherit the earth." Verily in this (Qur'an) is a Message for people Who would (truly) worship Allah. (21: 105-106)*

P.S. This is a Reflection written in plane while flying between Ontario (California), through Salt lake City (Utah) to Orlando (Florida) on December 24, 1997.

Seest you not that it is Allah Whose praises all beings in the heavens and on earth do celebrate, and the birds (of the air) with wings outspread? Each one knows its own (mode of) prayer and praise. And Allah knows well all that they do. (24:41)

XXI. HOMELESS IN PARADISE

I am invited by many Islamic Communities in North America and overseas. A good number of invitations are for Fund Raising. These functions are mainly to build mosques and schools. I have to travel by planes from the Pacific in California to the Atlantic in New York, Philadelphia, Baltimore and Florida. To fly such a long distance takes me an average of eight (8) hours. I have to fly back the second day. My flying time is early morning on Saturdays and my coming back is also early morning on Sunday. With an average of one day I have to travel back and forth from ocean to ocean when people are still sleeping

During the Fund Raising function, I try to inspire the audience through the quotations from Qur'an and the narration of a series of Ahadith. One Hadith is narrated by Uthman Ibn 'Affan ® and recorded in the books of Sahih Bukhari and Sahih Muslim that the Prophet (pbuh) is quoted to have said the following:

(٢) فضل بنائها :

١ — عن عثمان أن النبي صلى الله عليه وسلم قال : « مَن بنى لله مسجداً يبتغي به وجه الله بنى الله له بيتاً في الجنة » متفق عليه .

Whoever builds a house of worship (Masjid) for the Love of Allah, Allah (swt) will build him/her a house in Jannah (paradise).

To reflect on this Hadith, I request the audience if they hope to go to Paradise on the Day of Judgement. I also remind them by saying: "Anyone who wants to go to Paradise please raise your hands". Of course, everyone says yes, and all of them do raise their hands. Some raise both hands as a sign of great hope. They smile and one may see their faces glowing with good news.

I pause for a moment, and then I ask them: "Those who wish to go to Paradise: When you are to be there, try to look for your house. You look right and left, but unfortunately you cannot locate your house. Indeed, you will find out that none of the houses in paradise belong to you, or registered in your personal name. You look forward and backward, you go from place to place, but in vain. You stay there – homeless!"

You may go to Allah (swt) to complain and to find out that all the items you read in the Qur'an and the Hadith about the beauty of Paradise. The answer comes to you: "You are Homeless!" You will be shocked! "Why Ya Allah?!" And the answer comes to you: "Because you did not build a Masjid on this earth; you did not help others in building a Masjid; and you did not share with others in building a Masjid. Although you were asked to do so but you declined with false excuses. Therefore, you will stay in Paradise as Homeless…" You start to cry: "But Ya Allah! I was doing so many good things in life". "Yes! You did! And that is why you are in Paradise!"

A voice comes to you: 'You built a house for yourself on earth and you took care of it. It was so beautiful. After you died, you left it behind for someone else. You did not plan to build a permanent house for yourself in Paradise. You were busy for the temporary dwelling. You were not smart. You were dummy! You were ignorant! Yes, you were educated and you were rich! But none has saved you! So you better stay homeless in this Permanent Life.

You start crying. "Please, Ya Allah! Bring me back to the earth once again and I'll do my best to please You." The voice comes back to you: "No! It Is Too Late."

With this type of Reflection, I try to encourage everyone to donate money now for the purpose of building a mosque for the love of Allah. I tell them: 'Please don't be stingy! Be generous! The more you are generous, the more Allah will replenish you in this world and in the hereafter'.

I try to advise them not to listen to shaitan who is whispering to them. He scares you from being generous. Don't worry! Listen to Allah (swt) what He says in Surah Al-Baqarah (The Cow):

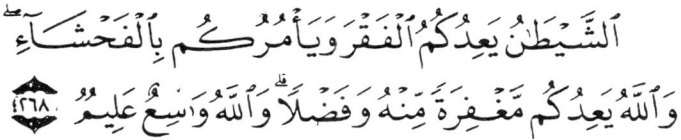

Satan threatens you with poverty and bids you to conduct unseemly. Allah promised you His forgiveness and bounties. And Allah cared for all and He knows all things. (2:268)

After we finish, I came back home Sunday at 5:00 AM from East Coast to West Coast of USA. The time in the West Coast is 2:00 AM when everyone is sleeping. Flying is not easy. Jet lag is not easy on my central nervous system. Eating time has to change too. While flying smoothly, you enjoy it, but when air turbulence takes place you want to cry. You realize that life is short. I start to read Ayatul Kursi from surah 'Al-Baqarah'. I start making certain Du`a' and ask forgiveness from Allah.. Questions cross my mind such as 'why I had to travel and to fly'. I should have stayed at home with my family. However, inspirations come to my heart informing me that I am doing all this for the love of Allah. Life is from Allah and death is from Allah too. One may die while in bed.

I look around and I see birds flying up and down as if they are happy. Then I say to myself: My last name is Sakr. And Sakr in Arabic means 'Falcon'. That bird has to fly to survive. You too have to fly to enjoy life and to see the beauty of the creations of Allah. You will never enjoy life without flying.

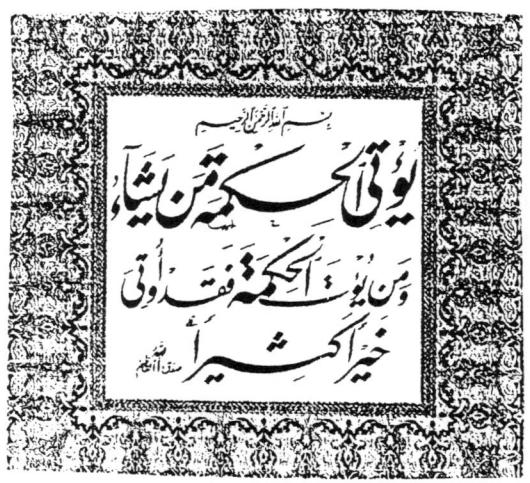

He granted wisdom to whom He pleased; and he to whom wisdom is granted received indeed a benefit overflowing. (2:269)

XXII. A CATALYST

Anytime I am invited to raise money for a local community. I am confronted with the idea that as if I am the one to raise the money from my personal pocket. Sometimes the local people may think that I already brought the money with me, or I am going to bring money from the oil producing countries. All of these ideas are false assumptions.

When I go to the podium to speak, I tell the audience that I am only a CATALYST. Of course some understand the meaning, but without knowing its application in that function. I try to explain its meaning and its implications so that they will work hard with me to raise the money from themselves. I start by saying that a catalyst is the least significant in any chemical reaction. However, the reaction does need two compounds to work with the catalyst to produce a product. These compounds are substrate (A) plus substrate (B) in order that the reaction can go through, and to get a product. The following formula is needed.

$$\text{Substrate (A)} + \text{Substrate (B)} + \text{Catalyst} \longrightarrow \text{Product (p)} + \text{Catalyst}$$

The catalyst is needed in very small quantities and it is insignificant. However, the reaction may not go through without him. This catalyst could be enzyme, coenzyme, mineral, vitamin, etc. Sometimes the effectiveness of the catalyst cannot be strong enough until we use heat, and/or adjusting the PH of the reaction. Then and only then, a product can be obtained plus the catalyst. As long as we get a product we may throw away the catalyst and dump it into the sink, or we may recycle him for future use.

To explain to the audience the implication of this concept. I say to them the following: Substrate (A) is you yourself; while substrate (B) is your hands to be put into your pockets to pick-up your money and to donate it for the love of Allah (swt). Without these two there is no hope to get a product. However, as a catalyst, I will do my best to inspire you and to motivate you. I will use certain Ayat from Qur'an, and certain Ahadith from the Prophet. Such type of inspiration and motivation should excite and encourage all of you to come forward and to bring your money out of your pockets.

After getting the product you may throw me away, or dump me into the sink. I don't mind, because I came to you to perform the role of a Catalyst. I am to leave you alone with your project. I am not going to interfere with your work. It is your project and you are responsible for it in front of Allah (swt). You are going to be asked in the Day of judgement as to what did you do with the Project.

After we finish collecting money for them, I leave them alone and I say to them Bye...Bye! I go back home by flying like a Falcon high in the sky at an average of 33,000 feet where all other birds and small planes are way below us.

I really appreciate how Allah (swt) made people to learn flying up in the air. I realize as if I am outside this planet earth. Everything is below me. If I have to thank anyone, I have to thank Allah (swt) alone Who made people to invite me for such activities.

I am happy that I acted as a Catalyst. I am not going to be involved with them everyday. My responsibility was over Al-Hamdu Lillah.

XXIII. A MOSQUE OR A CASTLE ?!

The new Islamic Center of Toledo was inaugurated on Saturday, October 22, 1983. Delegates and representatives from different parts of the world attended the occasion. Non-Muslims attended the function too. Official people from Ohio including the governor, the mayors, the senator, police officers and mass media were there.

While establishing a new mosque in America is not a new thing, it is a replica of previous efforts. This particular community is a unique one. They had a center built in the city and it was the third center in the history of mosques in America. The community increased in number and the mosque could not accommodate them. Instead of expanding it (which they could do because of extra property of theirs), they built a huge center on the farm 15 miles south of the city.

The mosque is built on a farm in the city of Perrysburg, Ohio. One may be able to see the mosque while driving on the highway. It is a huge one with a dome and two minarets.

The mosque has all types of glass designs similar to those of the churches except that they have verses from the Qur'an, the Most Beautiful Names of Allah (swt) and the picture of the Ka'bah. All impregnated into the glass windows throughout the Masjid.

Few reflections passed my mind. Some of which are stated here:

1. The name of Toledo in Arabic is Tulaitalah, a city in Spain where Muslims were ruling, and their civilization was flourishing.
2. Early Muslim settlers of Toledo were mainly from Lebanon. They came after being deprived of religious and academic

teachings. They had hard time to establish themselves in Toledo.
3. Their children and grandchildren are highly educated and well to do financially.
4. There are only three families living in the town of the Mosque including the Imam himself.
5. The mosque looks like a castle in its design and in its facilities. This is the first phase too. It is very beautiful and magnificent.
6. The mosque is open daily for administrative work of the Imam, while the community is at work.
7. The Masjid is to be used officially on Fridays and Sundays, each of which is for few hours.
8. The Masjid cost the community few million dollars as an investment for teaching Islam to the community.
9. Muslims of Toledo can not move to live next to the Masjid because of the necessity to be next to their daily work.
10. Muslims of Spain have already built the best masajid in the world, but they did not use them effectively. They were busy in the worldly affairs of the modern society.
11. They lost Spain and we had nothing to inherit from them. Ten million Muslims were killed, butchered, slaughtered through the Inquisition of the Francos.

What made me think of all these ideas is that during the inauguration ceremony, people were clapping and whistling in the mosques. Non-Muslim ladies were passing inside the Masjid with all types of cosmetics, with American dresses and uncovering their heads. Some Muslims were kissing American ladies who were visiting the Masjid as signs of appreciation.

What type of Islam that we are looking for to establish in America!? Is it Americanized Islam!? Is this the type of Islam that America wants us to adopt, to establish and to maintain!?

If Muslims want to build mosques, they should build them very close to their houses. Otherwise, they should move immediately and build their houses around the Masjid. Our Prophet migrated from Makkah to Madina. The first thing he did was to establish the House of Allah. He established his own house next to the Masjid: wall-to-wall. He advised the Muslims to live around the Masjid. In this fashion, they established their own community, and they were able to protect themselves.

I had to reflect by remembering the following Ayah in Surah Al-Tawbah (Repentance):

$$\text{إِنَّمَا يَعْمُرُ مَسَاجِدَ ٱللَّهِ مَنْ ءَامَنَ بِٱللَّهِ وَٱلْيَوْمِ ٱلْءَاخِرِ وَأَقَامَ ٱلصَّلَوٰةَ وَءَاتَى ٱلزَّكَوٰةَ وَلَمْ يَخْشَ إِلَّا ٱللَّهَ فَعَسَىٰ أُو۟لَٰٓئِكَ أَن يَكُونُوا۟ مِنَ ٱلْمُهْتَدِينَ ۝}$$

The mosques of Allah shall be visited and maintained by such as believe in Allah and the Last Day, establish regular prayers, and pay Zakat, and fear none (at all) except Allah it is they who are expected to be on true guidance. (9:18)

One has to recognize that 'Imarah Al-Masjid is not only building it, but by praying in it five times daily, and the Jumu'ah Congregation salat as well.

By the way! This is not the only Masjid built far from the community. Many more Masajid are built in the 90's in similar way. We hope and pray that things will be better in the future. Ameen.

P.S.   I do appreciate what this community has done and has achieved. I respect them since I got to know them in 1963. I visited them so many times, and I do admire their sacrifice. May Allah reward them.

And He sent against them Flights of Birds, striking them with stones of baked clay. (105:3-4)

XXIV. WANTED AS HONORED GUEST

The Muslim community in Milwood, Alberta are living in the south suburb of Edmonton. They invited me for a fund-raising dinner during the month of November, 1983. They held the dinner at the Islamic Center of Edmonton. The dinner was a success and the local Muslims were able to raise $70,000, Alhamdu Lillah for building a Masjid.

In the month of May, 1984, they called again and insisted that I should come again to be their honored guest. I was reluctant but due to their insistence, I accepted the invitation for Saturday, May 12, 1984.

The Muslim community of Calgary, knew of my coming. They insisted that I should visit them, as they are in the process of raising fund for the Muslim cemetery. They needed me to be their honored guest on Sunday noon, May 13, 1984. Reluctantly, I had no choice but to accept the invitation and delay my visit till Monday, May 14, 1984. I requested both groups to get in touch with one another so that they make one ticket. Hence money can be saved.

Few days later the Muslims of Fort McMurry, Alberta, called and requested me to visit them on Monday, May 14, 1984. I could not accept or refuse, but I requested them to get in touch with the other two groups and make one ticket for the three communities. This means that I have to stay till Tuesday, May 15, 1984.

Confirmation of the program was made and the ticket was sent with discrepancy. On the letterhead of the travel agent in Edmonton, it is recorded that I should come back to Chicago on Tuesday, the 15th of May, while on the ticket of Northwest Airlines, it is recorded that I should come back on Monday, the 14th of May.

I called the airline in Chicago and confirmed that my coming back is to be on the 14th but not on the 15th. I called Calgary and Edmonton and I found out that there is a confusion. The two intimate friends of Edmonton (Hatem Malhem) and of Calgary (Mohammad Aziz) tried to help as much as possible. They called me more than half a dozen times to straighten out the mess.

The ticket made by the Muslims of Milwood was a restricted one. I am supposed to be on May 13-14 in Calgary, I am supposed to leave on May 14 from Edmonton which is 179 miles away. My departure is to be early morning too. My questions were not solved: How can I be in Calgary on May 14, while I am supposed to leave that day early morning from Edmonton? How can I visit the third community in Fort McMurry on May 14, when I am supposed to leave Edmonton early on May 14. Finally, they informed me that I should come with the ticket, and when I'll be in Canada, they will make the rest of the arrangement.

After arriving at Edmonton Airport, I found about twelve Muslim brothers welcoming me. After greetings, hugging and shaking hands, I realized that they were disputing to which house I am supposed to visit and stay with. My understanding that I should go to Brother Malhem's house. The dispute turned to be a hot discussion and few of them started insulting one another. I tried my best to pacify some, but I could not. I informed them that I will be happy to go back to Chicago. Finally, they agreed that we go to Brother Melhem.

There, we had a heavy dinner at 10:30 p.m. which is 11:30 p.m. Chicago's time. We stayed there till 1:00 a.m. reviewing few items in the teachings of Islam, how we should control our emotions whenever we are faced with a situation. People started talking where I am going to stay. I invited them all to go with me to the Masjid and be guests to Allah (swt). It turned out that the Masjid is too far in the North side of Edmonton. Finally, we agreed that I can stay at Brother Melhem. However, we have to go for Fajr Salat to Brother M. Saeed's house at 5:00 a.m.

Brother M. Aziz, his son Basil and myself stayed in one room, Sister Mona and Nahla stayed in one room, the children stayed in a third room and Brother Melhem stayed in the living room.

At 4:30 a.m., I woke up and went with a brother to Saeed's house for Salatul Fajr. We were there about 14 persons. After Fajr, we had discussions on different topics including American Islamic College and the procedures to be used for the fund-Raising Dinner to maximize collection.

We spent most of the day with Brother Melhem at his house. In the afternoon, we visited the office of the popular conference and they confirmed that they will give American Islamic College three (3) partial scholarships for their students. In the evening we went to the Masjid for dinner and we started collecting money. Between 8:30 to 9:30 p.m., we were able with the help of Allah (swt), to collect (cash, pledges, checks) about $40,000. Brother Hisham Badran was able to inspire them through his songs.

After Maghrib Salat, they could not resume the meeting for speeches. Hence, we attended a special meeting with Mr. Faiz Al-Sabbah and the Executive Committee of the Masjid. Mr Sabbah is a blind person and lost his hands. He is from Lebanon working at UAE. He and his wife are on tour to Canada, USA, South America for Fund-raising for the handicapped and the blind. It was an emotional meeting. It was agreed to raise funds for them by approaching Muslims and non-Muslims as well.

The second night we stayed at Melhem's house being split with Brother Ali Amqi taking family of Aziz. On Sunday we were to go to Calgary. The people there were having fund-raising dinner for their cemetery. I found out, that the Calgary community did not share in the ticket cost. They did not send anyone to pick me and to take me to Calgary. I realized yesterday, Saturday that Mr. Abbas, a member of the Executive Committee, passed by Edmonton to pick me up, but he had to attend a wedding at Lac Bich. He informed me that he will see me at Calgary instead of taking me.

I made arrangement of my own with the Brothers of Edmonton. These brothers were kind enough to bring two cars for 14 people including children.

We packed ourselves in two cars. I remember the pleasant personalities of Melhem, Talal Ajaj, Mohammad Rahimi, Jamil El Zarif, Najib Quadri, Abdel Aziz Saj, all came from Edmonton to Calagary to take me and to share the responsibility.

At Calagary, we had lunch at Aziz house. In the evening, we went to the Masjid. Dr. Qureishi and Iman Al-Mahruqi welcomed us in the basement. After dinner and speech, collection of cash and pledges were done. After Maghrib Salt, continuation of speech was conducted till 11:00 p.m.

We left to Aziz's house and had refreshment. Some of the brothers from Edmonton left after Maghrib Salat. Three of whom may become students at American Islamic college. We slept at 1:00 a.m. including Hisham, Talal, Hatem, Abdel Aziz and myself.

At 4:00 a.m., four of us (Hatem, Talal, Aziz and myself) woke up, performed our Fajr Salat and left silently by car without bothering anyone. We arrived at Edmonton airport at 8:00 a.m.

I thanked the three brothers with deep thanks and appreciation for their kindness, generosity, hospitality, help, sacrifice, companionship and all the favors.

It should be stated here, that Brother Hatem Melhem is living without the two kidneys of his. He had to do dialysis Monday, Wednesday, and Friday. He had to go as soon as he arrives home to hospital to start his dialysis. I felt very much sorry, that a man who is sick with kidney problems had to take the responsibility of hospitality, accommodation, transportation, travelling and has to live a rough life. I pray to Allah to recover him and find him a solution to his health, Ameen.

I had to lose the visit to Fort McMurry because of lack of coordination, lack of communication and lack of proper airline ticket reservation.

P.S. WHAT TYPE OF AN HONORED GUEST!

They desperately needed him to raise funds for the Center and cemetery but:

1. They needed him for every hour of his time without notifying him about his program.
2. They are ready to argue among themselves at the airport to get hold of the guest in the house of their choice without informing him in advance.
3. The community of Calgary was in need of him, but no arrangements were made to pick him up from Edmonton. They did not worry about his return to Edmonton at 5:00 a.m. They did not either ask the chief guest about his stay overnight in Calgary. Finally, they did not share with the cost of the supersaver airline ticket that the community of Edmonton bought.

4. To keep the chief guest till after midnight is satisfactory, but to plan a program for him during the day does not seem to be necessary.
5. They needed his time, energy, efforts, knowledge and finally they needed him personally and physically but they are not.....!

Finally, I had to reflect about prophet Ibrahim toward his guests. In Surah Az-Zariyat (The Winds that Scatter), Allah (swt) says the following:

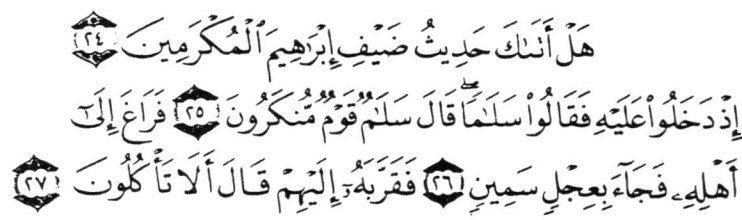

Has the story reached you, of the honored guests of Abraham? Behold, they entered his presence, and said: "Peace!" He said, "Peace!" (and thought, "these seem unknown people.)" Then he turned quickly to his household brought out a fatted calf, and place it before them he said, " Will you not eat?" (51:24-27)

Finally, I learned a lesson from this incident. During my childhood and youth life, my beloved Muslim teachers and scholars taught me to accept any tests and trials. All of these tests are for our benefits, credits and rewards from Allah (swt). One has to accept all types of exams. After all, this life on this planet earth is a life of tests. The more the trials are the more the rewards are from Allah. I don't mind to be an honored or a non-honored guest.

I want to please Allah and Allah alone. I am not interested to be treated with kindness or otherwise. My interest is the pleasure of Allah. All what I pray that Allah will accept my activities and my services. Ameen.

WHAT A FORTUNATE CHIEF GUEST SPEAKER IS HE?

There is not an animal (that lives) on the earth, nor a bird that flies on its wings, but (forms part of) communities like you. (6:38)

XXV. POST MORTEM

I was invited by the local MSA Chapter at Temple University in Philadelphia to speak on Islamic Fundamentalism on Wednesday, November 16, 1983. I was supposed to be the only speaker. The agreement was that I will present a historical survey of Fundamentalism in Christianity, Judaism, Communism, Buddhism and Islam.

To my surprise, I had to be informed that a Christian theologian will speak on Christian Fundamentalism and I had to speak of fundamentalism from an Islamic perspective.

To my surprise I did not receive the poster informing me of a change of the title. I was not informed at all of the type of audience, the expected discussion, the background of the internal disputes going on even among the Muslims themselves.

To my surprise, I had to find later that some Muslims had deep rooted understanding of orientalist approach towards Islam. Others have understood Islam as a history of Muslims, a history of intellectual forum of philosophers, a history of Islam as being practiced by local traditions, and a history of different movements. Anytime, I had to speak of Islam, the intellectual Muslims could not differentiate between Islam and Muslims. It was totally in their minds, that the two are one. This is not true, although it is a wish and a hope and it should be both in one.

I realized that a good number of the audience are graduate students in Islamic Studies and religion. Those students came from different parts of the Muslim world.

The audience was mixed of both Muslims and non-Muslims. The majority of those who raised questions were trying to demonstrate their intellectual understanding to the others. Most of them got involved in semantic dialogue: arguing, disputing, rejecting and introducing their personal feelings and understanding, as if these are Islam. Anything else is not true and could not be true. Of course, the whole session was a frustrating one to the speaker and to the silent majority.

To my surprise, I realized that some members of the audience had to leave the session as a protest, because they could not tolerate what was said. To my happiness and surprise, I had to go at night to the Masjid to get together. In that session, the brothers requested a post mortem session.

In that session it was agreed to have an evaluation of what went wrong in the meeting, so as to be corrected for the future. It is a healthy attitude to have such a session, but it would be far better to have a prerequisite session before the lecture was delivered. I had to request them the following:

1. There should be good communication between the host and the guest speaker.
2. The speaker should be informed in advanced exactly about the whole situation. Any changes to take place are to be communicated directly to him.
3. He should be informed about the type of audience, their local problems and disputes.
4. He should be given ideas as an outline to his subject to be covered by him.
5. The host has to act as a HOST not only to the speaker, but to every non-Muslim attending the session.
6. Muslims in the audience should seek the opportunity of such as session to make Da'wah to Muslims and non-Muslims rather than expressing their frustrations.

7. Muslims are to recognize that they are to compliment their ideas and not to dispute in public.
8. Muslims are to recognize that the speaker can't cover the topic in a short period of time and that they are to request him to elaborate on certain areas of his speech.
9. Muslims are to polarize the teachings of Islam and not their local traditions, customs and habits.
10. Muslims are to communicate with logic, with understanding and with courtesy in order to present the true image of Islam.
11. Muslims coming from different parts of the world are to assimilate themselves into the melting pot of Islam.
12. Muslims have to recognize that their loyalty is to Allah (swt) and His teachings. They have no loyalty to the teachings of their professors, and they are not to defend such teachings.
13. Muslim intellectuals are to get out of their hierarchy of brain exertion into reality of life. They should get rid of the sementie of the Mu'tazila and orientalists. They should not dilute the subject by arguing some philosophical ideas that they have learned in classes from the orientalists.

After thinking about what I mentioned above, I tried to reflect:

1. Why should I go and talk to those who claim themselves superiors than the guest speaker.
2. If those people in the audience believe that they are more knowledgeable than the guest speakers, then they should never ever invite any speaker like me in the future. They themselves are qualified for the function. They could have done it themselves without troubling the speaker to travel from Chicago to Philadelphia.
3. I have a second thought: Should I accept any invitation in the future to any university students and/or faculty members? Or should I apologize to them in advance?

4. Should I concentrate my time, efforts, energy, and humble knowledge for reading, doing research, and trying to finish my writings of my books? Or I should continue helping others.
5. What do I get from these invitations except headache, jet lag, lack of sleep and money spending?
6. I had to convince myself that I am ignorant and the least knowledgeable, the most arrogant, and a lousy speaker.

Then I recognized that our Muslim friends will not believe me with these excuses. Therefore, I said to myself: I will continue to make Jihad against myself for the love of Allah by serving the communities at large. If I want to earn blessings and rewards from Allah (swt), I should continue rendering my services, even if people did not like me or like my lectures. However, I learned from experience to improve my presentations.

My experience in Da'wah is that it is very difficult to talk to Muslims whether they are intellectuals or others. It is easy to talk to non-Muslims than Muslims. Our Muslim friends try to argue too much about so many trivial items, while non-Muslims try to listen to understand the basic principles of Islam. One has to have Patience, Endurance and Steadfastness. These factors are considered to be the Golden Rules of Success in this world. Along with good intention, the success will be in the hereafter too. Insha-Allah.

Finally, we prayed to Allah (swt) to give us rewards and blessings for our efforts as long as our intentions are right. Ameen.

XXVI. EMPTY BUILDINGS

I have to travel hundreds and thousands of miles to help local Muslims – helping-themselves. In order to fly those thousands of miles. I have to leave my house at 5:00 a.m. to go to the Airport, and jump from Airport to another in order to reach my destination on time. This means that I have to wake up at 4:00 a.m. to make my Fajr Salat. Hence I cannot sleep properly except for few hours. I don't mind to do so, as long as it is for the love of Allah, and for the sake of helping Muslims in different parts of North America.

Since I came to America in 1962, and to this day, Muslims have been preoccupied with establishing Masajids. Recently they started establishing schools. They have a long way to build their infra-structural institutions so as to establish themselves as a community.

Many times I am asked to raise money from within the local community through a Fund Raising Dinner. I don't mind to sound as a beggar; but such type of activity is not for me, but for the local host community. As such I don't feel bad to raise money for them. Raising money is the most demeaning activity for any person, but it could be the most rewarding in the Book of Allah (swt). One has to stand at the podium and start inspiring the audience to donate . It takes minimum two (2) hours to fulfill the job.

Some Muslim communities have no properties at all, and they want to start from the scratch. Others have already property, but they want to expand. Some other communities have the most sophisticated properties such as a Masjid, classes, lecture hall, library, gymnasium, etc. The cost that the local communities had to pay between 1.5 millions to 9 millions. The buildings are gorgeous, beautiful and worth admiring the decorations that the architect had designed.

Many of these communities cannot afford to employ an Imam, a director, a secretary, a custodian.., etc. They rely heavily on volunteers to run the affairs of the center and the community at large. Some of them put a recorded message. You leave a message, but no one will answer. You try to go during the week, you find the place is locked and you cannot enter the buildings. If the Masjid is open, you will find it empty. No Imam, no director, no secretary, no security and no custodian. You get shocked and you feel lonely in the house of Allah. You start asking yourself:

1. Why the local community had to build such fancy buildings?
2. Where is the Muslim community? Are they living around the Masjid, or they live 10-20 miles away from the Masjid?
3. It seems the Masjid has been built in the suburb or on a farm away from the city. You ask yourself as to why they did such a thing.

The buildings are empty, the Masjid is occupied on Friday for Salatul Jumu'ah. The school building is occupied on Sunday for the children. On both days the buildings are being used for 2-4 hours a week. You try to analyze the situations and ask the question: Is it worth investment such amount of money being put in stones, walls, and fancy buildings for the sake of keeping them closed and for the sake of DUST, GHOSTS, OR ANGELS ???

Muslims of America in the late 90's are well to do financially, but they are not ready to employ well qualified personnel to run the services professionally. Even if they employ certain individuals they will not give them reasonable salary. Moreover, they will not give them benefits like other employees outside the Muslim community. Such benefits would be: social security, disability, medical insurance, life insurance, unemployment compensation, retirement, etc.

Therefore, the Masajid, and the community centers became vacant and empty except from dust. I hope and pray that angles are there to bless the places and to protect them. The number of Muslims in America has increased tremendously and especially in the 90's where very many refugees are being brought in to this country by United States Christian Churches (USCC) as well as by the Jewish Foundation. These refugees are mainly from Bosnia, Somalia, Kurdistan, Afghanistan, Iraq, Iran, Kosova, Albania, etc. Most of them do need counseling, and they do need a variety of help. They need Islamic teachings of Qur'an, the language of the Qur'an and they need orientation, workshops and advice as to how they can live in North America. They need a scholar, an 'Alim, an Imam, a family counselor, and jobs. Who is going to do all these services when the buildings are empty?

The number of the children born and raised in America is tremendous. They are youth by now. They need guidance, otherwise they will be lost in the society.

Other centers have Imams, Directors, Custodians, and Secretaries, but they don't care to render social services because it is time consuming. They have the best facilities, but they don't want to spend time to help others. They are <u>Not</u> Da'iyah. They fit as employees sipping coffee and tea. They spend time in chatting here and there, without knowing how to use their precious time for the love of Allah, and for the sake of humanity at large.

We ended up having fancy buildings without services. We leave them empty till the Day of Judgement. My personal reflections would be: why should I go to such communities to help them build centers to stay empty? My answer would be, I am not doing these services for me, or for the present families. I am doing it for the future generations who are more committed towards their religion. While reflecting on this topic, an Ayah crossed my mind. It is in Surah Al-Tawbah (Repentance). It goes as follows:

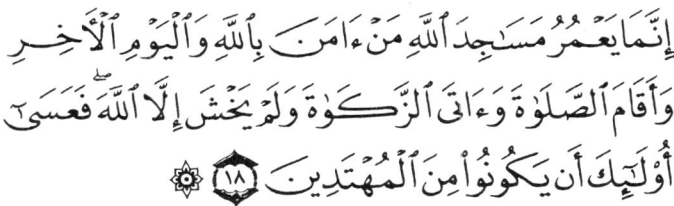

The Mosques of Allah shall be visited and maintained by such as believe in Allah and the Last Day, establish regular prayers, and pay zakat, and fear none (at all) except Allah. It is they who are expected to be on true guidance. (9:18)

Muslims have to recognize that our beloved Prophet (pbuh) built a humble Masjid. He lived wall-to-wall to the Masjid. He asked the Muslims to live around the Masjid. They all were to pray with the Prophet five times a day. He used to advise them, and answer their questions. Therefore the Masjid of the Prophet became a hub of every service that the community needs. The early Muslims succeeded in building an Ummah of Muslims who care for one another. Indeed they formed an Ummah of Islam, and a Muslim State under the leadership of our beloved Prophet (pbuh)

Finally, I raise my hands and pray to Allah to accept my efforts, time, energy, knowledge, and the passing times that I am using in these activities. Please Ya Allah! Forgive me for my shortcomings; and please, Ya Allah! Guide us all to the Sirat Al-Mustaqeem. Ameen.

XXVII. A WALL IN THE MASJID

This subject has bothered many Muslims in different parts of the world, and especially in America. Muslims Sisters are not to come to the Masjid. If they want to come, they are prohibited or discouraged. If they insist, they should be in different building or a room hidden somewhere in the building. If members of the same family come to the Masjid, they don't know how to meet one another at the time of departure.

As a frequent traveler, and a flyer, I started writing this article, and then finalized it while I was coming from Orlando, Florida to Los Angeles, California, on Sunday April 4, 1999. The idea of isolating sisters in the Masjid and keeping them separated from the general body of the Ummah of Islam, has nothing to do with Islam. It is a Bid'ah that Muslims have invented to prove that they are better Muslims than the companions of Prophet Muhammad (pbuh). Allah never asked Muslims to isolate males from females in Masjid, except in the performance of Salat (Prayer). Men are to pray together shoulder-to-shoulder. The same applies to women.

The Prophet was the role model, and it was he himself who organized us properly. We are being instructed that men should be in the front, followed by children (boys), followed by children (girls) followed by women. The best rows for men are the first ones, while the best rows for women are the last. Children are used as a buffer zone.

The Qur'an talks about separation but not isolation. In Surah Al-Hijr, chapter 15 verse 24, Allah (swt) inform us that He Knows who sits in the front rows, and those who wish to stay in the back rows. He knows the intentions of each one. It seems there were few individuals at the time of the Prophet who wanted to stay at the back so that they may look at women.

A Wall In The Masjid

It was stated that Aisha, ® the wife of the prophet (pbuh) used to say that men were praying in front of women without any wall. Women were only one row away from men. Most men used to have short Thawb (clothing), thus when they pray in front of women, their legs are exposed. Therefore the women used to keep their sajda longer till all men stood up so that no one will be distracted with the appearance of men's legs in front of them.

These days, Muslims don't encourage women to come to the Masjid. They consider it to be Haram, Bid'ah or Makrooh. However, Muslim Women are allowed to drive cars, go to the banks, grocery stores, department stores, and attend universities. They are even allowed to be employed by non-Muslim institutions. They mingle and work side by side with non-Muslim men. However, these Muslim men object to their women coming to the Masjid. They themselves are working with women in their jobs. It seems it is Halal for Muslim men and women to work with non-Muslims, to talk to each other, and to socialize together. On the other side, it seems it is Haram for Muslim Sisters to enter their own Masjid, to learn more about Islam, to be inspired, and to be motivated. They want the Sisters to remain ignorant in matters of their own religion. One should ask: Is there any place outside the Masjid where Muslim Sisters can learn their religion. One has to remember! We live in a non-Muslim Society. There is nothing good about Islam in the American Society. It is on the contrary! Everything is against Islam, Muslims, families and morality.

Muslims have to encourage our Sisters to come to the Masjid. They should be advised to dress with modesty. At the same time men should dress with modesty. By coming to the Masjid, Muslims will get to know each other; they will feel the sense of belonging to the Ummah of Islam. They try to help each other, while they are learning the teachings of Islam.

A Wall In The Masjid

One has to add one more thing. When we go to Makkah to perform Umrah anytime throughout the year, we don't see a wall separating women from men. They make Tawaf around Ka'bah together. Al-Masjid Al-Haram is a sacred place. It is not the exception, but a good example for Muslims to learn how to live peacefully together, and how to work together without being harsh against each other. Men should control their ego as well as their own lusts when they see the other gender. They should encourage Muslims Sisters to come to the Masjid in order to be respected more and more. Muslim men should protect Muslim Sisters wherever they are in the society. Muslim Sisters will feel proud if and when they are in safe places. The best place is the Masjid.

Moreover, we should recognize that mothers are the ones who really take care of their children better than the fathers. They are the ones who rear them, raise them properly, train them, mold them and shape them rightly. If mothers are going to stay ignorant about Islam, then they cannot perform their duty properly toward their children. These children will be away of Islam. They will miss the opportunity of learning Islam as a way of life, and they will be lost in the society.

Therefore, we should try our best to help our families to live in peace and harmony. The best place to get to know one another is the Masjid while the worst place is the market. Hence we should encourage all Muslims to come to the Masjid for all their needs Insha-Allah

I hope and pray that Muslims will assume their responsibility properly, and act accordingly. Ameen

XXVIII. TRYING TO TAKE-OVER

We learned from our religious teachers that we should take the initiative and do something good to the Society at-large irrespective of color, nationality, ethnic background, language, position, social status, gender or creed. They taught us to do good for the love of Allah (swt) and for the benefit of all without bragging or showing-off our accomplishments. They reminded us to build institutions for the future generations. They instructed us to train individuals to help them to assume the responsibilities for these institutions. They made sure that we are not for titles or positions, otherwise we will lose our credits in the Book of Allah (swt).

I for one, tried my best to apply what I learned from those noble teachers. It was not easy at the beginning, but later I realized that my aims and objectives in life are to work hard to please Allah (swt) alone. I am convinced that life on earth is not the true life. The real life is the one in the hereafter. The turmoil in this life are but tests, and preparation for the next life. Therefore, I am convinced to work hard, and to do pioneering projects, activities, services, and etc. I do not mind if people appreciate my help for them or not. I realized that many people do not appreciate what you do for them in time of their needs. It is on the contrary: The more you help them free, the more they may criticize you, blame you, denounce you, and suspect your intentions. As a human being it is not easy to accept this type of relationship among people, but later I had to absorb this fact with a grain of salt (as it is said!).

By going back to the Qur'an, one finds out that human beings are in general ungrateful to Allah. He gave them all the blessings free of charge, but very few who are thankful to Him. Allah tells us in Surah Al-Adiyat (or Those that run) the following:

Trying To Take-Over

$$\text{إِنَّ ٱلْإِنسَٰنَ لِرَبِّهِۦ لَكَنُودٌ ۝ وَإِنَّهُۥ عَلَىٰ ذَٰلِكَ لَشَهِيدٌ ۝}$$

Truly Man is, to his Lord, ungrateful; and to that (fact) he bears witness (by his deeds). (100:6-7)

Finally, I had to realize that there will be more difficult situations ahead of me than the previous ones. Many people may criticize, suspect, blame and sit and watch. I learned that I should take the initiative and assume a larger responsibility to start a project single-handedly for the community. I worked hard: day-and-night, for a number of weeks, months and years. When the project becomes successful as an entity, then I start to recruit individuals and assign them certain responsibilities within the project. Unfortunately, some of them feel jealous of me personally and my success. Some of these friends were out of jobs and I already gave them a good job, with a good title and a good salary. They tried to stab me from the back: Spreading rumors, accusing me by fabricating lies, and even trying to get me out of the project completely. **Some of them were planning to get a gun to shoot me and kill me!!...yes, this is all true.**

Some other friends have to circulate a letter to all the Islamic Centers in North America accusing me by fabricating lies against Me! By the way! I gave them the mailing list of those centers to send them their local magazine. Instead of that, they circulated a letter defaming me and my services that I rendered beyond and above any imagination.

After some thirty years of experience in assuming pioneering projects in the U.S., I had learned some lessons in life:

1. I will (Insha-Allah) continue to initiate pioneering services to the whole Ummah of Islam, but those services are within my capacity.
2. I will continue to initiate institutions, but not by myself. For those who are interested in having any institution, I will work with them. I will help them, advise them, and show them the way.
3. Anytime the project is ready, I will turn over the whole project back to the group.
4. I had to learn that anything that comes easy, will somehow go away easy from our hands. Therefore, I should teach others: planning, strategies, alternative routes, financing, management, supervisions, delegation of responsibilities, training individuals to run and manage the project, continuity of the project for 100 years or more, and so on.
5. Many Muslims are inclined toward Free services. They want your time free; your knowledge free; your efforts and sacrifices free; they feel happy that you spend money from your own pocket for their own benefits. They may not compensate you at all; and even if you want to ask for your right they turn you down. They got what they wanted from you.
6. I had to accept the fact that even when I render my services free, some will come and suspect me!? How in the world do you render your time, effort, energy and knowledge free? My answer is that I am doing it for the love of Allah (swt). They look at me with suspicious eyes!.. They do not believe that somebody do help others Free: Family counseling; business counseling ; officiating marriages; burying the dead; giving Shari'ah courses; giving lectures at different places and different universities; giving your own books free; giving Friday Khutab at different places and leading Salatul Jumu`ah; and many more services!! They forget that all the

prophets of Allah (swt) used to do favors to their local communities free too. Whenever people used to suspect the prophets, those prophets used to say according to Surah Ash-Shu'araa' (The Poets) the following:

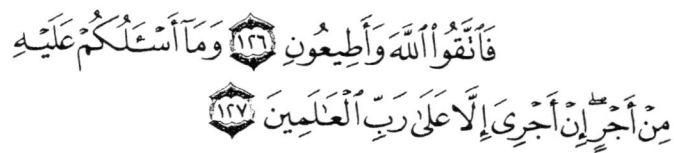

So fear Allah and obey me. No rewards do I ask of you for it: my reward is only from the Lord of the Worlds. (26: 126-127)

7. I had to learn the hard way, that anytime I go to a group to help them, I should expect someone to come to me to blame me for something he thought it was wrong. There are others who insist that what they tell me is 100% right!. I have no right to discuss the matter with them. I have to thank them and to promise that I will follow their instructions to the letter!...
8. I had to accept the fact that after I develop a project and after being successful, a group of so called friends try their best to take over the project after playing the dirty game! They claim that the project is theirs, and as if I stole it from them!.. Those people never even rendered any effort for the project. They were sitting and watching the success of the project . I wish they came to me asking me to turn it over to them peacefully!..

I asked myself what is the difference between these so called good friends, and the reign of colonialism, imperialism, and exploitation!.. the others were European non-Muslims!.. But ---

these are so-called Muslims! Masha-Allah! It seems they have learned from the enemies of Islam how to hurt Muslims. They are acting on behalf of the enemies of Islam to hurt Muslims. They cannot even talk or challenge non-Muslims, they obey them and follow their footsteps.

Final Remarks

The more I read Qur'an, the more I learned about the prophets, their struggles and how their people treated them with hostilities. With that knowledge I feel more relaxed, happy and contented. I say to myself that those people are looking for titles, positions, money, recognition and reputation in this world. They are looking to grab anything and everything for themselves irrespective whether the method is Halal or Haram. Even if the whole world is given to them, they will not be satisfied. Death is the only criterion that scares them, but unfortunately, they do not learn a lesson.

Let them try to take over anything and everything from me. Let them try to take over the whole world. However, they should recognize that the whole world and what it contains do not equate to a wing of a small mosquito. They should also recognize that nothing goes with them to save them from the Day of Judgment. Unfortunately they are my friends that I helped in many aspects of life. They are educated in fields of science and technology; but they are not educated in Islamic Shari'ah. They are ignorant, but arrogant, vicious, selfish and proud of nothing!.. It seems they have been possessed by the devil. They already surrendered to him instead of submitting to Allah.

I pray for them as much as I pray for everyone to be guided by Allah including myself, too.

O Allah! Forgive us for our mistakes and for our short comings!

O Allah ! Guide us to the straight path of Your Prophets and Messengers.

O Allah! Help us to live honest and sincere Muslims.

O Allah! When we are to die, help us to die as Mu'mins.

O Allah! Help us to be summoned in the Day of Judgment with all the Prophets and Messengers, as well as with the righteous believers, and the martyrs.

O Allah! From us is the Du`a'; and from You is the acceptance.

Allahumma Ameen

If Allah helps you, none can overcome you: (3:160)

XXIX. SLEEPING IN THE SAME BED

I was invited by my good friends in Singapore on September 1996 for a series of lectures to be delivered in Sarawak (Malaysia), and in Singapore. My good friend in California Dr. Kameluddin Chang, asked his son Ali in Singapore to take care of me. The local friends in Singapore put me as usual in Golden Landmark Hotel. However, Mr. Ali Chang put me in a suite of two rooms in the same hotel, and took care of lodging and other expenses.

Flying 20 hours from the U.S. to Singapore through Tokyo, and going to Sarawak continuously and coming to Singapore to do similar activities without rest is very difficult, but I had to accept it because the functions are for the love of Allah. In the hotel, I need my privacy to read Qur'an, to pray and to do my own writings accordingly. The suite in the hotel is composed of two rooms, but it has only one bed. One guest from Sarawak came with us to Singapore. The local host did not pay for my room in the hotel. It was Mr. Ali Chang who did that as a matter of respect to his father Dr. Y. Chang.

The local host in Singapore requested me in front of their own guest who came from Sarawak if he can stay with me in the same suite. I said Yes! But it has only one bed. He said you can share it together! I was shocked and I was mentally disturbed. I thought I could arrange the couch in the other room to be a bed for him, but it was not meant for that purpose.

Muslims are well aware about the moral life in Islam. Even children at the age of ten have to sleep separately as the Prophet of Islam have instructed the Muslims. Moreover, the Qur'an made sure that children have no right to enter the bedroom of their parents without permission. Morality and family life are very important. While sleeping, no one knows where he put his hands as the Prophet mentioned. Therefore, separation in sleeping is a must.

Sleeping In The Same Bed

It was only a couch. I was more disturbed. The host did not pay for my room, and he did not want to pay for his other guest too. I was planning to give them my suite and rent another room on my own. Any move I take in that direction is going to disturb the host and his guest. I said to myself: La Hawla Wa La Quwata Illa Billah.

I welcomed the guest of my host. The only arrangement I was able to do is to divide the bed with pillows in between both of us. I could not sleep all night long! I do know that the host and the guest are very good and practicing Muslims. I do know also it was not a matter of lack of money. It was lack of thinking right. Anyone may misunderstand the mismanagement and the lack of courtesy in such a decision. Luckily the bed was wide enough (king size). There was enough space for each; and luckily the pillows were used as a partition in between both of us.

I thought of the alternatives: I should have given him the bed while I can use the couch for myself; but I thought he may feel uneasy. Also I thought that I would give him the room with the bed, and I will sleep on the floor in the other room. To me it would have been much easier to do so, because I enjoy sleeping on the floor. I do this type of habits many times to reduce the pressure on my back. I do know that during Hajj, Muslims are to stay in tents on floor or on couches. However, for the sake of the guest, I had to absorb it and to accept such a challenge.

I was deeply affected by such an incidence. I did not want to mention it or to write about it. Those friends are extremely good. They never meant anything wrong. It was a bad decision. I did not want even to write it here in this book, but for the sake of those who are involved in Da'wah, they should prepare themselves for the worst. Finally, I said to myself I had to fly thousands of miles to make Da'wah from country to country. Why should I have to fly and to receive such treatment! Then I came back to my conscience! It is a matter of delivering the Message of Allah to all people of the world. Then I ask myself: I am already doing such type of Da'wah with the local communities in U.S.A.. Why should I go all over the world with all the headaches, with jet lag, being away from my family, with change of weather, with different types of foods that may not be accustomed to!!? Why!? I realized the following: Most of the time during Salat Al-Witr I make a series of Du`a'. One of them is: Please Ya Allah! Use me wherever You want, whenever You want, and to whomever You want. When I remember such a Du`a' I keep silent and I have no choice but to accept the challenge.

In writing this article I want to make sure that all those who are Da'iyah have to expect all varieties of unexpected experiences. They should prepare themselves for any and every type of test. I, for one, am working in the field of Da'wah since I was 17 years old. I never expected or anticipated such type of test. Therefore, I am mentioning this incident so as to prepare the other friends in the field of Da'wah to have immunity against this type of test. Da'wah necessitates patience (Sabr), wisdom (Hikmah), faith (Iman), good intention (Niyah Sadiqa) and hard work (Juhd). Allah (swt) will give success to them in this world and in the hereafter.

It seems a Falcon is a Falcon. He has no true life without flying. I accept the challenge and I pray to Allah (swt) to keep me happy, healthy and strong. Above all, I request Allah (swt) to continue to use me in the right direction. Ameen.

XXX. I DON'T WANT TO DIE

I was in Edmonton, Alberta, Canada during November 4-6, 1983, for a fund-raising dinner for a new Masjid. After making Isha prayer, I met a young Muslim from Saidon, Lebanon. He tried to express himself by stating his wish. The first thing he said to me: I don't want to die! I was shocked to hear such a statement. However, I realized immediately what he meant. He was frustrated what was happening in the Muslim world and especially in Lebanon. He started pouring his ideas one after the other without allowing me to share with him his ideas except by nodding my head and saying to him yes, yes. Some of his expressions and his comments were the following:

1. I don't want to die like others. It is very shameful.
2. I don't want the worms to eat my flesh and my body when I am in the grave.
3. I want to stay alive till the Day of Judgement.
4. I want to make Jihad for the love of Allah and be killed.
5. I want to be killed in the battlefield for Allah so that I will be a martyr (Shaheed).
6. Allah (swt) informed us in the Qur'an that whoever is killed in the way of Allah (swt), he is a martyr and he is alive.
7. I hate my job, I hate this type of life, and I hate to wait to see the Muslims losing their countries. I hate to see the enemies killing Muslims and I am sitting here to enjoy life.
8. Please Brother Ahmad, where is the Islamic State in the Arab world so that we can make Jihad in the way of Allah (swt).
9. I am preparing my grocery store to be given to my younger brother to take care of it, and to take care of my family after I leave.
10. What is the use of this world! All of us are to die. Our eternal life is not here in this world, but in the hereafter. So I am anxious to liberate my land, the land of Islam, and the land of

Allah (swt). I want to liberate it from the Israelis and all other enemies of Allah (swt).

O Allah! make me among the martyrs. O Allah! make me a Shaheed. O Allah! make me to die in your way so as to Live an eternal life.

P.S.:

1. -This story was written at Minneapolis Airport while coming to Chicago and waiting for the flight schedule.
2. -As the reader is aware by now, that I fly regularly. It is not my decision that I should fly, but it was a necessity to help the communities as much as possible.
3. -By the way! I do not plan these trips. It is Allah alone Who makes these trips available for me. I have no choice but to accept them as long as they are for the love and the pleasure of Allah.
4. -It should be stated here that travelling and flying is no more fun. They became a mode of life for those who are involved in the field of Da'wah. One has to accept whatever goes on during these trips. It is Allah and Allah alone Who gives credits as long as the intention is for the love of Allah.
5. -This incident reminded me of the Ayah in the Qur'an in Surah Al-Baqarah (The Cow) whereby Allah (swt) says the following:

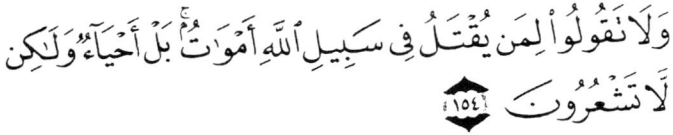

And say not of those who are slain in the way of Allah: "They are dead," nay, they are living, though you perceive (it) not.   (2:154)

Finally, let us pray to Allah to accept our deeds, our intention, and our Iman. We try our best to please Allah alone. We are sure He will not let us down. Ameen.

Praise Be to Allah, Lord of the worlds.

XXXI. GREEN AND DRY LEAVES

On Sunday, November 13,1983 I could not go anywhere and so I stayed at home. Our house was in Lombard, Illinois. It is in the west suburb of Chicago. I took care of writing few articles and then I tried to rake the garden around the house. It took me two hours to finish the job. While raking the dry leaves, reflections passed over my mind. Among others, the following are some reflections regarding "Green and Dry Leaves".

1. During Spring and Summer seasons, trees were full of green leaves, flowers and fruits.
2. People were happy to see them, to benefit from them and to sit by them. They were admiring the varieties of the flowers and the green scenery of the trees and shrubs.
3. People rush to pick up fruits or flowers and enjoy having them during these two seasons.
4. During Autumn, leaves fall down after they become yellow, red, brown or gray. They wither down from the trees and people start to step down over them. Very few really care for them at all.
5. One person or two may come close to them to rake them and put them in a trash bag to be disposed. Very few people may be looking at them and contemplating the relation between the life of the leaves and the life of the people.
6. When a person is active, young and useful, many people ran after him to use him and to make use of his services. When he is incapacitated, many disregard him completely. Very few care for him. No one may call him or visit him. Very few may ask where is he…or where about he is.
7. When a person is actively giving his time, energy, effort, knowledge and money for Allah (swt) to inspire, motivate, and mobilize his fellowmen, a good number of people surround themselves around him. They do so to get recognition through

him. As soon as the opportunity prevails, they start attacking him, assaulting him and take over his place. They look for recognition to themselves.
8. Such type of people start fabricating lies to please their ego and to impress on others. They fear no one, even Allah (swt). Their lusts and desires are for themselves. Their ambition is to Be recognized as the previous person had been recognized. However, such type of people who have no fear of Allah (swt), and fabricate lies to satisfy their ego, such type of people do exist in the society everywhere.
9. Finally, one should recognize the story and life of green and dry leaves on trees. If you wish to listen to my advice prepare yourself for a number of cycles of this type of malaise in the society. Remember that the trees don't mind to repeat their cycles even if people don't care much. Trees always give fresh leaves, flowers and fruits. They don't mind to lose them for others. They adapt themselves to different seasons. They continue to grow taller and taller, while they produce more and more. People have to climb on ladder to reach the fruits. The tree became taller than people, and the latter had to look up to the flowers, leaves and fruits. People are the beneficiaries while the trees are the ones that sacrifice for us as human beings. Do people appreciate?! I don't know. I hope so!...

Finally, I wish to remind my readers to go and visit farm lands or go to mountains and live in camping areas. In so doing, they will live amongst trees, shrubs, flowers, leaves, birds, insects, animals, and etc. They will have many reflections better than this reflection. May Allah bless us all Ameen.

XXXII. A CHILD IN THE HOSPITAL

Our only daughter Sarah was admitted on Wednesday, October 27, 1983 to Elmhurst Memorial Hospital for the removal of her tonsils. She was scared but one of her girl friend had to do the same few months before. Hence, she was somehow relaxed. I had to take off from my work so as to share the load of the family. My wife had to take care of the children when I had to take care of Sarah.

At the hospital, I was there Thursday at 7:00 a.m. to give my daughter some company, to encourage her and to give her moral support. I asked her to read Ayatul Kursi, Surah Iklass, Surah Al-Falaq and Surah Al-Nass. Sarah was relaxed when she was going to the operating room at 8:00 a.m.

My wife came after 9:00 a.m. after she dropped the children at school and especially Basil the baby of the family. She was very much scared and worried. She was shaky and shivering. She could not control her emotions. She said: "Now Sarah is still under operation …. She is now in the recovery room….How come the doctor never called…. I am worried …. Maybe the girl did not make it …. The physician did not come yet to the waiting room to inform us. May be there is a problem. Ahmad! Please help me! I cannot wait.

I had to pacify my wife saying to her: Why don't you make a Du'ã'. Why don't you read Ayatul Kursi ….read Surah Iklass, Surah Al-Falaq and Surah Al-Nass. The wife read all of these and still her anxiety was never over.

I had to remind her, how difficult it was for me during her first delivery with Sarah herself who is now at the hospital. I was by myself with no friends around midnight at the hospital in Macomb. The two physicians had to perform C-section. I was alone by myself. My wife had to go to the operating room. Here I am

A Child In The Hospital

standing by myself, trembling, shaking, pondering what is going on. I had no one to talk to ... No one to comfort me .... No one is to remind me of anything. I had to submit myself totally to Allah (swt).... Let Him do what He pleases. I am to accept from Him all circumstances.

The mother is still worried .... The receptionist announced: The family of Sarah kindly come to the reception area. The mother jumped hurriedly while she was shaky toward the reception area. Before picking up the telephone she thought that the daughter died! How come! The doctor never came down to meet us and to give us the good news! How come! The Doctor had talked on the phone! She picked the phone while her face was pale! Dr. Farnotto! Yes ... Can ...Can you ... Tell me ... How is Sarah? Sarah is fine, the doctor said: Yes ... Yes ... continue ... she is doing fine... How about her tonsils? They were very large: they affected her ears. They were very bad to keep them. Did you have to withdraw liquid from her ear, Doctor? No, because they were o.k. Can I see her tonsils, Doctor? Yes, they are in the pathology Department. You can see them tomorrow after the Pathologist find out the result.

All these talks were going on between the physician and my wife, while the poor father standing trying to understand what was happening. The only thing that he could do was to look at the face and eyes of the mother and read her face reactions. Poor father, he had to control his emotion, to pacify himself and to be patient till he got the news later from the mother.

While we were waiting till Sarah comes out of the recovery room, Shahida, a friend of the family and a clinic dietitian came to visit Sarah. Shahida took us to her office and showed us the hospital and its facilities. The mother was anxious to see the tonsils, we went to the basement. While we are entering the pathology department, here we see the Pathologist showing us two large balls in a bottle. The mother could not control herself started asking many questions. Finally she said can I take these tonsils with me? He said yes after we find out. She was relaxed because she wants to preserve them. She wants them as souvenir.

We rushed up to see Sarah if she has come from the recovery room. When we reached her room, the nurse said that we should wait few moments because Sarah is being admitted. The mother was shocked! What! Admitted again to the operating room?! No! but to her room. We entered the room and there was Sarah on her bed... We remembered the Du`a' of the Prophet when he said:

٣- «اللَّهُمَّ رَبَّ النَّاسِ أَذْهِبِ الْبَأْسَ وَاشْفِ أَنْتَ الشَّافِي لَا شِفَاءَ إِلَّا شِفَاؤُكَ شِفَاءً لَا يُغَادِرُ سَقَمًا». (٢)

It was narrated by Aisha ® that the Prophet (pbuh) said:

Ya Allah! You are the Lord of Mankind. Remove the sickness, and give healing. You are the Healer. There is no healing without You. Let the healing stay till sickness is over. (Agreed upon)

P.S.

All of us as human beings are liable to get sick. Whenever we get sick we should be patient. We should make sadaqa (charity), read Surah Yaseen in the Qur'an, and make Du`a' Shifaa' (Healing). Allah is the Only Healer. We pray to Allah (swt) to keep us happy, healthy, and to have strong Iman. Ameen.

XXXIII. SHOVELING SNOW

One Sunday I had to convince myself not to attend the activity of the Muslim community in our neighborhood in Villa Park, IL. My wife had to go to teach the children of the Muslim community. So she went with our children and left me alone at home in Lombard, IL, writing my articles and speeches. I got tired and so I went out door to shovel the snow.

During shoveling, some ideas crossed my mind. I admired the white color of the snow. It represents purity of everything around me. I was amazed how the colorless water becomes whitish when the temperature drops down to make the colorless water white snow.

While shoveling the snow, I was interested to see how snow flakes are formed; by removing the snow from one area to the other, one can see easily waves of flakes cracking over one another. I asked myself why in the world I had to remove the beautiful whitish snow from the driveway? It looks beautiful; it covers the concrete dry color, giving a whitish pure color? Why in the world, the whitish color is not needed in this area? How could it be that the snow is flaking after cracking smoothly and keeping silent? How could it be true that they are not complaining? Who knows! May be they are crying and shouting, but their cries are falling on deaf ears like mine. I wish I can talk to them, or listen to them.

With all these thoughts, I had to whisper to the snow layers: I have to remove you from the driveway, while I like to see your beautiful color around me. Remember, I want you to stay next door to the driveway. I like you to be a member of my family, but instead of staying on the driveway area, I want you kindly to stay around it.

On the other hand, I remembered my case with my own Muslim community. With all of fraternal bonds for more than a decade, I can't understand, why in the world we had strain relationship with some members of the Board. I asked myself, am I not needed any more on the Board or in the community itself? Am I to be shoveled away as the snow layers on the driveway? How come that I have to be shoveled away with disgrace and mistrust? Why in the world backbiting was going on among some of the Board members? What crime I have done against anyone of them, all of them or against the community itself.

Then, I said to myself: I am shoveling away the white snow with sympathy and concern. I am shoveling them with compassion and mercy. How come I have been shoveled away with disdain and hate. I asked myself again and again: What type of hearts do my friends have? Don't they have white hearts as white as the snow? Or do they have dark hearts as dark as charcoal? Don't they remember that all of us are human beings and each one of us has his own feelings? While today they played it rudely against me and Brother Zayd, tomorrow they will play it against someone else. Don't they recognize that next time, someone else is going to attack them vehemently and without mercy. Wait and see what the future is planning for them! O Allah (swt) forgive my friends for their wrong doings.

I served the community for more than ten years. We established that community from my house in Lombard, IL. We used our basement for Friday Salat. My wife used to make refreshments and sweets for those who attend the Salat. We then rented the Lombard Park District to continue serving the community, such as the Friday Salat, the Sunday school, evening classes, and etc. Moreover, Allah helped us through our humble efforts to get financial grants from Saudi Arabia to build a Masjid.

With more services rendered to the community free of charge, I was to be rewarded. Their reward was to excommunicate me from the Board of Trustees, and from rendering services, and especially that of Friday Khutbah.

Then I remembered that my wife and myself were running full time summer school for their children free of charge for a number of years. We conducted few summer camps for their children. All these services were conducted free of charge. We never asked for any compensation or rewards. We prayed to Allah to reward us.

As a human being you feel sorry!. But our condolence is our Prophet Muhammad and his companions (Sahaba). They did every good to their people, but they were mistreated, persecuted and tortured. I also remembered that a candle usually burns itself to give light to others. Therefore, there is no harm if I am burned, tortured, persecuted or excommunicated. If this generation of immigrant Muslims don't appreciate our favors to them, their own children may do so.

Another Reflection crossed my mind. I remembered that our beloved prophet was persecuted so many times from his own community members. He had trouble in Makkah, in Taif, in Madinah, and around. Every time he used to pray to Allah (swt) to guide them. Never he cursed them. He never requested Allah to send them any earthquake or otherwise. He used to say: Allahumma forgive my people, because they don't know the meaning of Real Life. He used also to say: Please Ya Allah don't curse them. Their children may become Muslims.

Therefore, I had to learn a lesson: I should continue rendering our services to all whether they appreciate or not. O Allah! Please accept our deeds and actions. Please Ya Allah! Guide us to the Sirat Al-Mustaqeem. Ameen.

XXXIV. 'ILM AND 'ULAMA'

The title of a Khutbah given at Downtown Islamic Center of Chicago, on Friday, May 20, 1983 was about 'ILM (knowledge) and 'ULAMA' (The knowledgeable People). 'ILM is very important in Islam. The best word to define 'ILM could be knowledge, and it may include science, technology, education, languages, business, religion, politics and so on. Islam emphasized 'ILM more than 700 times in 87 different forms. In fact, the very first few Ayahs revealed to Prophet Muhammad (pbuh) were about 'ILM. When Muhammad (pbuh) received the Message and became Prophet, Allah (swt) asked Muhammad (pbuh) through angel Jibril to read. In this regard, Allah (swt) says in Surah Al-'Alaq (The Clot) the following:

Read: In the name of your Lord Who created. Created man from a clot. Read: And your Lord is the Most Bounteous, Who taught by the pen, taught man that which he knew not. (96:1-5)

'ILM is a must on every Muslim, and the appropriate 'ILM is to be selected rather than a general one. Allah (swt) does honor the 'ULAMA' (The knowledgeable People), and they themselves are the ones who really appreciate Allah (swt) and His creations. They are the inheritors of the Prophets, and as such they are to deliver the Message of Allah (swt) properly to mankind. The 'ULAMA' are more honored by Allah (swt) than the worshippers. They cannot be compared with the ignorant people. In this regard, Allah (swt) says in Surah Al-Zumar (The Troops):

$$\text{قُلْ هَلْ يَسْتَوِي ٱلَّذِينَ يَعْلَمُونَ وَٱلَّذِينَ لَا يَعْلَمُونَ إِنَّمَا يَتَذَكَّرُ أُولُوا ٱلْأَلْبَابِ ﴿٩﴾}$$

"...Say (unto them, O Muhammad): Are those who know equal with those who know not? But only men of understanding will pay heed." (39:9)

Allah informs us that it is only the knowledgeable people who do appreciate Allah's creations, and they are the ones who respect Him. In this regard, Allah says in Surah Al-Fatir (The Creator):

$$\text{وَمِنَ ٱلنَّاسِ وَٱلدَّوَابِّ وَٱلْأَنْعَامِ مُخْتَلِفٌ أَلْوَانُهُ كَذَٰلِكَ إِنَّمَا يَخْشَى ٱللَّهَ مِنْ عِبَادِهِ ٱلْعُلَمَاءُ إِنَّ ٱللَّهَ عَزِيزٌ غَفُورٌ ﴿٢٨﴾}$$

And so amongst men and beasts and cattle, are they various colours. Those truly fear Allah, among His Servants who have knowledge: For Allah is Exalted in Might Oft-Forgiving. (35:28)

The 'ULAMA' are supposed to inform, educate and train their people how to be closer to Allah (swt) through 'ILM. The 'ULAMA' are not to run after the political leaders, but the latter group are to come to the 'ULAMA' to get the proper education and information. The first school of education in history was that of Masjid of Prophet Muhammad (pbuh) in Medina, followed by Mosque of Zaitoona in Tunisia, Masjid Qarawiyeen of Fez in Morocco and Masjid of Azhar in Cairo. Muslims are to build educational institutions in every corner of the world. They are to give scholarships to students, graduates and professors. They are to open Research Centers, Information Centers and Training Centers as well. While millions of people go to schools, institutes, colleges and universities to seek education and knowledge, let me remind you of the following important points:

1. Getting knowledge is more important than seeking a certificate or a degree.
2. Knowledge and education are more important than fame and reputation due to certificates and/or degrees.
3. The degree of knowledge is not only through formal education, but also through tutoring and experience that one gets in the field.
4. Visiting different parts of the world is a type of education. Allah says in this regard in Surah Al-`Ankaboot (The Spider):

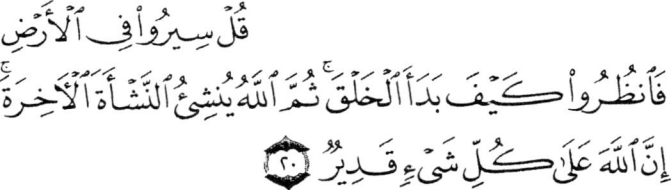

Say: (O Muhammad): Travel in the land and see how He originated creation… (29:20)

5. The place of Masjid is the best place for education.

The knowledge of this world should be inspired by the knowledge of Religion. Otherwise the scientific knowledge and technology while it is a blessing from Allah (swt), it will be a curse on the person himself as well as on the society as well.

XXXV. A VISIT TO THE VATICAN

As usual I am a frequent flier. The trips that I go to are not by my choice, but I am always being invited, and I cannot say no or I am sorry. I was invited by a good friend of mine Dr. Muhammad Ahmad El Sharief, the Secretary General of the Islamic Call Society in Tripoli, Libya, to attend a Conference in the Vatican. I could not believe myself that I will visit the Vatican and to meet the Bishops, Cardinals and the Pope. I was asked to prepare a paper about the Concept of Da'wah in Islam. Dr. El Sharief happened to be a good friend of mine in the late sixties when both of us were in Chicago area. He was the President of the MSA in Chicago, and I was the President of the MSA of USA and Canada. We were working together to help the students and the community at the same time. We stayed good friends, and we hope to stay like that till the Day of Judgement.

By the way! I requested Dr. El Sharief to invite a good friend of mine. He is Mr. Rafael Narbaez. He used to be a Minister for Jehovah Witness, and accepted Islam. They agreed to my request. The Conference was on April 27-30, 1997. We met the first night in a hotel as guests with some host members who happened to be priests, fathers, sisters, bishops, and one cardinal. We had dinner, and introduced ourselves to one another. The Conference was held the second day of our arrival in one building of the Vatican. It is a conference room. To my surprise, the hosts refused to allow us to record the dialogue on audio cassettes, or on video. They preferred to keep everything private!.

I was requested to start the meeting with a recitation from Qur'an. I read the last three Ayat of Surah Al-Baqarah, and gave their meaning in English.

The first day there were two papers to be presented about the Concept of Da'wah in Islam, and the Concept of Mission in

Christianity. I presented my paper that took about thirty (30) minutes and the rest of the session was spent discussing the topic. By the way I made enough copies of my paper, and I distributed it to the participants. One may read my paper somewhere else in a book called Da'wah Through Dialogue, by the same author.

The second day the session was about the achievements of the Muslims and Christians for the last one hundred years in Da'wah and in Mission. The session of the third day, was about the plans and strategies for both Muslims and Christians for the coming one hundred years to come.

The fourth day we had to go and attend a congregation to be held under the leadership of the Pope at St. Peter's Square! We also visited the Church of Basilica, and the museum of the Vatican. During that day we were taken to visit an Islamic College run and conducted by the Vatican. We were informed that the Vatican has three (3) Islamic Colleges. They bring young men and women from Muslim World. Some of them are Christians while others are Muslims. The Vatican offers degree in Islamic Studies. To our surprise, they teach Qur'an, Hadith, Sirah, history, Arabic, Friday khutab, and etc.

We were told that there is a huge Islamic Center in Rome. We went few of us to visit the Masjid. It was Wednesday, and it was closed. We were told it is open as a museum on Thursday and Saturday in the morning only. As far as the Masjid is concerned, it is opened only on Friday for Salatul Jumu'ah. We tried our best to enter but we were denied. It was a real shock to us.

Some of the highlights of this visit are the following:

A Visit To The Vatican

1. We got to know that the Vatican does not believe in the Bible as the word of God, but it is a book that has been rewritten for the last one thousand six hundred years ago (1600 years), over and over again. They considered it to be a book of collections of customs, habits, and wisdom of previous people. Therefore, it is a book of history rather than a Divine, Revealed Book.
2. The only ones who are considered Christians are those who follow the Pope, the cardinals, and the Vatican. The rest of the Christians are not Christians. They are off-shoots of Christianity. The Vatican has nothing to do with them. Protestants and all other denominations are outside the main stream of Christianity.
3. They believe that no one will go to paradise unless he believes in Jesus as his personal savior, and that Jesus is not only the only son of god, but God himself.
4. We found out that the Vatican has a special department for Dialogue with Muslims. They hold seminars and workshops with Muslim officials from different parts of the Muslim world.
5. It seems there are few thousand statues and idols. Wherever one goes he sees nothing but statues. They reminded me of Prophet Ibrahim when he was young. He destroyed all the idols except the biggest one.
6. By visiting the museum., one sees nothing but statues of every variety one can think of. It gives you sign of depression, and a sign of paganism. Islam came to liberate and free people from this type of life to a better life. I wonder how the people there were proud of each and every statue. May Allah guide them to the Siratul Mustaqeem.

My visit to the Vatican was an eye-opener. One can write a book of what has been seen there, or has heard. This is only a reflection from the Flying Falcon about such a trip. It is the hope that more Reflections will be written and shared with others.

XXXVI. MUSLIMS AND CATHOLICS DIALOGUE

I. Introduction

The Dialogue between Muslims and Catholics is a noble effort. May God bless all those who took the time, the efforts, the knowledge and the wisdom to call for such an occasion. We pray to God to bless all those who accepted such invitation. It is really a challenge to all of us. We are grateful to Dr. John Borelli and his group from the Secretariat for Ecumenical and Inter-Religious Affairs. They called a preliminary meeting on May 10, 1999 at the Islamic Society of Orange County, in Garden Grove, California, under the direction of Dr. Muzammil Siddiqui. We are also grateful to Dr. Borelli for his memo of May 27, 1999 reminding us to meet today, February 1, and tomorrow, February 2, of the year 2000, at the Center for Spiritual Development in the city of Orange, California. This meeting is being sponsored by the Islamic Society of Orange County and the Catholic Diocese of the city of Orange.

It should be stated here that this meeting is not the first of its nature, and it will not be the last of its kind. Many more Dialogues were conducted between the Vatican in Rome with a good number of Muslim Governments, and some International Muslim Organizations. I, once, was invited to participate with the Bishops and Cardinals in the Vatican in 1997. I was asked to present a paper about Da'wah in Islam. I enjoyed it very much, and I learned so many things. I do encourage the Muslims and the Catholics of America to continue such Dialogues. In so doing, it brings better understanding between both groups, and at the same time, we will be able to solve many problems in America, and the world.

II. Challenges

Now that you and I have accepted the invitation, we are faced with many challenges:

1. Some of us are Muslims while others are Catholics, but all of us are God-fearing, and God-faithful.
2. We have differences in approaching God, but we have more commonalties among ourselves.
3. We have different methods of solving the problems in the society, but we face the same problems in the whole society.
4. If we sit and watch the society, more and more problems will be coming out; they will definitely hit us, and hit our faith and our religious teachings.
5. Many families are broken: There are more single parents than before. Children don't know their fathers, and sometimes they don't even know their own mothers.
6. The Society is hit with Divorce. Husbands and wives cannot tolerate each other anymore. Instead of seeking counseling and arbitration, they break their relationships and their commitments. Their children are suffering as well as the society at large.
7. The moral life is lost in many areas of the society. Every year one finds out that more and more there is the existence of night clubs, topless shows, x-rated films and movies, xxx-movies, drinking, mixed dancing, use of drugs, and so on.
8. The moral life in family relationship is changing from two genders joining one another to establish a noble family, we see that the society is accepting families of the same gender. The sad part about this problem is that some politicians are supporting them and defending them. They are unfortunately asking the society to accept this type of a life style. Moreover, some so-called scientists are putting the blame on God by

saying that such a life style is due to a gene on the chromosome. They lied to themselves and to the society. It is due to the type of foods that they eat which are polluted with steroid hormones such as Diethylstilbestrol and Estrogen.
9. We are faced with other problems. Our youth are following different gangs. They shoot and kill without respect to life. Some of them killed even their own loving parents! They spoil the beauty of the society by using graffiti in many streets and on many buildings; they destroy the beauty of the traffic signs and signals.
10. We are faced with a challenge of those who are homeless, as well as those who lost their jobs. They ended up by losing their houses, and finally losing their families.
11. We are faced with Economic problems. This country is built economically on Capitalism. The Banking System is considered to be like Economic Slavery. The rich becomes richer, while the poor becomes poorer. They have no mercy on their customers. Those clients work days- and nights to make the Bankers richer-and richer, but when any customer is in trouble financially, they exploit his situation.
12. We are faced with the Economic Exploitation of the IRS, and the taxation system laid upon the citizens. It ranges from Federal Tax, to State Tax, County Tax, Sales Tax, Property Tax, etc. The other taxes may be called benefits taxes such as: social security, unemployment, disability, health insurance, car insurance, life insurance, retirement benefits and so on. It ends up that a person has to work as a slave almost all his life, and he will get nothing or the least. It becomes a life of economic exploitation.
13. We are faced with another challenge. Religion has been isolated from the society. The politicians informed the people to keep their religions inside their places of worship. When

they come out they should follow the society as being dictated by the politicians. They ended up in having a secular society without respect to the Role of Religion in keeping the society at high standards. We ended up in having two gods: One inside the places of worship, and the other god is the Congress in the hands of either Democrats or Republicans or both.

14. The other big challenge that we are also facing is the ethnic cleansing and religious cleansing. People talk about Human Rights and Civil Rights. People talk about Freedom of Speech and Freedom of Religion. But we find out that even some so-called Religious People teach hate, and pass stereotype remarks against other religions, or religious people. This type of religious hate has created animosity among the God-Fearing, and Faithful- people. If the Religious people are to hate one another, whom in the society is going to respect each other!?

III. Living Together

The theme of this section poses a series of questions: How can we live together peacefully and happily? Who are we that have to live together? When, where, and how to live together? All these questions and many more have been raised.

People are already living together. If they are not living next to each other, they are working together in one place irrespective of color, nationality or creed. People go to the same stores to buy their necessities of life. People have to eat, drink, work and sleep. People have similar biological make-up. All have eyes, ears, a nose, a mouth, hands, legs, a heart, lungs, a stomach, a liver, a spleen, etc. Above all they have brains in their skulls.

People may see things differently because they may have been taught and raised differently. The basic measures and standards with which people evaluate and assess things are different, and, as such, their approaches to life are different.

In order to live peacefully among other people, one has to realize that it is the concept of IGNORANCE about others that makes people denounce one another. To be stubborn, arrogant, haughty, vicious, or close-minded does not help solve any problems. Remaining ignorant and unwilling to learn about others will definitely augment the problem. It is only through proper education, information and communication that people may come to understand each other. Then and only then will they appreciate one another.

As far as Muslims are concerned, they were instructed to live in peace and harmony with the Creator, themselves, their families, their relatives, their neighbors, their society, the environment and with the universe. Muslims are also instructed to believe in all the prophets and messengers of Allah to mankind. They are to honor, respect, and speak about them with good will. The Qur'an mentions twenty-five prophets. Of these, five are considered to be Mighty Prophets. These are Noah, Abraham, Moses, Jesus and Muhammad. This illustrates that the prophets of Judaism and Christianity are also the prophets of Islam. In the Qur'an one can read in Surah Al-Baqarah (The Cow) the following:

قُولُوٓا۟ ءَامَنَّا بِٱللَّهِ وَمَآ أُنزِلَ إِلَيْنَا وَمَآ أُنزِلَ إِلَىٰٓ إِبْرَٰهِۦمَ وَإِسْمَٰعِيلَ وَإِسْحَٰقَ وَيَعْقُوبَ وَٱلْأَسْبَاطِ وَمَآ أُوتِىَ مُوسَىٰ وَعِيسَىٰ وَمَآ أُوتِىَ ٱلنَّبِيُّونَ مِن رَّبِّهِمْ لَا نُفَرِّقُ بَيْنَ أَحَدٍ مِّنْهُمْ وَنَحْنُ لَهُۥ مُسْلِمُونَ ﴿١٣٦﴾

> *Say: We believe in God, and in what has been revealed to us, and what was revealed to Abraham, Ismail, Isaac, Jacob, and the Tribes; and in (the Books) given to Moses, Jesus and the Prophets, from their Lord: We make no distinction between one and another among them, and to God do we bow our will (in Islam).*
> *(Qur'an 2:136)*

Muslims are instructed in the Qur'an to invite People of the Book under common terms with the Islamic philosophy: To worship the Creator alone without associating partners or progeny to Him. The Qur'an states in Surah Al-Imran (The Family of Al-Imran) the following:

قُلْ يَٰٓأَهْلَ ٱلْكِتَٰبِ تَعَالَوْاْ إِلَىٰ كَلِمَةٍ سَوَآءٍۢ بَيْنَنَا وَبَيْنَكُمْ أَلَّا نَعْبُدَ إِلَّا ٱللَّهَ وَلَا نُشْرِكَ بِهِۦ شَيْـًٔا وَلَا يَتَّخِذَ بَعْضُنَا بَعْضًا أَرْبَابًا مِّن دُونِ ٱللَّهِ فَإِن تَوَلَّوْاْ فَقُولُواْ ٱشْهَدُواْ بِأَنَّا مُسْلِمُونَ ﴿٦٤﴾

> *Say: O people of the Scripture! Come to an agreement between us and you: that we shall worship none but Allah, and that we shall ascribe no partner to Him, and that none of us shall take others for lords beside Allah. And if they turn away, then say: Bear witness that we are they who have surrendered (to Him).*
> *(Qur'an 3:64)*

To live together, one has to realize that others might be as good as you are if not even better. One cannot know what is in the hearts of other people, and one does not know the intention of others. It is Allah alone, the Creator Who knows everything.

Muslims are told in the Qur'an that among the People of the Book there are those who are staunch believers and good practicing servants of God. In Surah Al-Imran (The Family of Imran) Allah says:

﴿ لَيْسُوا۟ سَوَآءً مِّنْ أَهْلِ ٱلْكِتَٰبِ أُمَّةٌ قَآئِمَةٌ يَتْلُونَ ءَايَٰتِ ٱللَّهِ ءَانَآءَ ٱلَّيْلِ وَهُمْ يَسْجُدُونَ ۝ يُؤْمِنُونَ بِٱللَّهِ وَٱلْيَوْمِ ٱلْءَاخِرِ وَيَأْمُرُونَ بِٱلْمَعْرُوفِ وَيَنْهَوْنَ عَنِ ٱلْمُنكَرِ وَيُسَٰرِعُونَ فِى ٱلْخَيْرَٰتِ وَأُو۟لَٰٓئِكَ مِنَ ٱلصَّٰلِحِينَ ۝ وَمَا يَفْعَلُوا۟ مِنْ خَيْرٍ فَلَن يُكْفَرُوهُ وَٱللَّهُ عَلِيمٌۢ بِٱلْمُتَّقِينَ ۝

They are not all alike. Of the People of the Scripture there is a staunch community who recite the revelations of Allah in the night season, falling prostrate (before Him). They believe in Allah and the Last Day, and enjoin right conduct and forbid indecency, and vie one with another in good works. They are of the righteous. And whatever good they do, they will not be denied the need thereof. Allah is Aware of those who ward off (evil). (Qur'an 3:113-115)

Therefore, Muslims should be the most tolerant people in the world toward the non-Muslims. And indeed, they have proven this to be throughout history. They have coexisted with Christians, Jews, Hindus, Persians, Sikhs and Buddhists, regardless of whether the Muslims were in the majority or minority. They have lived together throughout most of their history on good terms with these people.

What is needed now from all the God-fearing, loving, and faithful people is to realize that they should open a new page and chapter in life. They should try to open the door for dialogues and trialogues among the God-conscious. They should rediscover their roots and their faith not as someone wants it, but as it should be. With this approach the faithful can be able to live together unanimity and wholesomeness.

IV. Final Remarks

In presenting this paper, the author wants to make sure that each group knows their faith, their history, their culture, and their own civilization. Each group should be aware of their assets as well as their liabilities. Finally, each group should study the faith, culture and history of other people of the world. In so doing, people can understand their position in today's society.

In order to live peacefully, and work together with integrity and honesty, one has to recognize the following:

1. People should think of their duties and responsibilities before they ask for their rights and for their privileges.
2. One has to remember that he is not the only person that God has created, and that the brain in his skull is not the only one in the world. That his wisdom is not the only idea found in the world. Also, his method is not the only way to lead people to the right resolution of life.
3. The God-fearing people should recognize that their method to reach and/or to approach God, is not the only way. It is not the method that counts, but the good intention, the good will and the good methodology as well.

4. God has created people with a rainbow of colors, a rainbow of races, a rainbow of nationalities, a rainbow of languages, and a rainbow of creeds. They were put all together on this planet to compose a coalition, to work together, to help one another, and to respect one another.
5. People have to understand that they can differ from one another, yet they have to work together despite their differences.
6. People should recognize that the future will not be better unless they can benefit from one another's background, faith, culture and civilization.
7. Those who claim to be God-fearing have to realize that none of them has been given the authority to judge people. There will be a Day of Judgment and it is God Almighty Who is the sole authority in judging people.
8. People should be equal in the eyes of the law. No one is better than the other. No one should be considered superior; and no one group is better than the other due to their biological composition.
9. People have to understand that they should render their services to others without exploitation, coercion or conversion.
10. Leadership is not bestowed on anyone, and it will never be offered freely to anyone. It has to be earned with blood and sweat.
11. Whoever wants his rights has to understand that rights are not acquired freely. Someone else has worked hard to earn them. Hence, everyone should realize that rights must be earned through hardship.
12. Might should not be considered to be right, rather right is might. Those nations that think they are mighty because of military power should be condemned if they use their power to subjugate other nations.

13. People have to be freed from colonialism, imperialism, capitalism and communism. All of these systems are meant to exploit others and keep them under governmental control.
14. Charity starts at home. America is exporting freedom to other nations, while millions of Americans have been exploited by the economic system of the banking systems. The rich ones become richer and the poor become poorer. There are few hundred thousand Americans who are homeless and they live on the streets even in the cold weather. Many millions of Americans have lost their jobs and houses, becoming beggars or drug pushers. If the American Government does not change its economic policies and take care of its own citizens, American Capitalism will be dismantled in the same fashion as that of the Russian Communism or the Soviet Union.

Therefore, those who claim to be God-fearing, and faithful believers are to come out of their hiding places, and face the reality of life with all its problems. We should all work together and be in the front line to solve the problems of others. We should encourage the other groups of believers to come forward and join our hands in solving the problems of the society. We should continue these meetings, and we should deliver certain responsibilities to some of us so as to achieve our aims and objectives.

Again I wish to thank all of you for attending and participating in this Dialogue. I wish to thank the organizers and the hosts for rendering their facilities and their services to us. God bless you and reward you all. Ameen.

XXXVII. VISITS TO TRINIDAD

As a flying falcon, Allah (swt) has blessed me so many times to travel to different parts of the world. Most of my travels are flying of course. It is not easy to do so, because one gets tired, exhausted, jet-lag, a change in climate and time, etc. The night becomes day, while the day becomes night, and so on. One has to accept these challenges, adapt and adjust to such changes, as long as he is doing these activities for the love of Allah (swt).

Trinidad and Tobago constitute one country in the Caribbean sea. They are close to Venezuela. The climate is hot and humid. Most of the people are the by-products of India, Africa and Latin America. It was a British colony, therefore, one can see the traces of England in that part of the world.

I was invited four times to that part of the world: in the sixties, in the seventies, in the eighties, and the most recent one is in July 14-20, 1999. Each invitation was from different groups: The Anjuman, The Muslim World League, the Islamic Call Society, and the Jama'at Al-Muslimeen. Each time I go there, I was to participate in a seminar, a conference, and a series of lectures in schools, university, mosques, camping, etc.

Between the sixties and the nineties, the Muslim population increased from six percent (6 %) to fifteen percent (15%). Most of this was due to the Africans who were able to find a better life in Islam than the western lifestyle. Most of these who came from the old India became highly educated; and they were able to enter into the political arena to a certain extent. Some of them became members in the parliament, others became ministers, speakers of the house, judges and president of the Country.

Most of the Arab descendants stayed as business people trying to make money. They isolated themselves from the rest of the other Muslims. I don't know why!! The rest of the Muslims have built enough Masajid, Islamic schools for boys, and other schools for girls. By the way: There are a good number of Christian Arabs who are very successful in business too.

Every time I go to Trinidad, I have new experience. The following is a partial list of experience:

1. The country has a democratic system, and as such the political system follows the western countries with different political parties.
2. The economic system is a capitalistic one, and as such the banks control the money. The rich people become richer, and the poor ones become poorer. While touring the country, one can see a poor neighborhood next to a rich area. One can see a slum area similar to Harlem in New York City, and high rise buildings next door to it similar to Hollywood and Wilshire areas in Los Angeles, California.
3. Poverty is a by-product of Capitalism; and Capitalism these days is similar to human slavery. It is considered as economic slavery.
4. The country is overexposed to the immoral life of the west and especially to Hollywood. It is easy to find in many places: Drugs, alcohol, dancing, night clubs, pornography including the TV programs as well.
5. The climate is hot and humid most of the time. I for one, cannot tolerate such a weather. As such I don't think I can live in that part of the world. The country has beautiful scenes. It is good to visit the country and enjoy the creation of Allah (swt) in that part of the world.

6. Being hot and humid, many people walk in the street with the least clothing on their bodies. You feel sorry for them. Either they don't recognize the concept of modesty and decency, or they don't mind to do what they do.
7. The Christians and Hindus are very active in their missionary works, much more than the Muslims. Every place you go, you will be able to see churches, and temples. You will see schools built by missionaries. The Christians try to invite the poor Muslims to visit the churches to help them in one way or the other.
8. There are off-shoots of the main stream of Islam; such as the Ahmadiya (Qadiani) movement, the Bahais, Nation of Islam, and the Shi'ah as well. All of these groups are very active indeed with the African people.
9. Muslims were able to organize themselves. They established the Islamic Secretariat for all the Caribbean Islamic centers. This is a good venture. We pray for their success.
10. A good number of the Muslims were able to establish financial institutions away from Riba, such as Islamic Banking systems, Takaful institutions, etc.
11. Some of them became very successful business people. One family developed a supermarket devoid of alcohol, pork, cigarette, or even lottery. Masha Allah!

By the way! In my last trip I was asked to present a paper on the subject of : **Islam and other Faiths: call to them with wisdom and understanding**. I made a synopsis for that talk, and distributed it to the delegates. It is as follows:

Islam and other Faiths
A Call with Wisdom and Understanding

I. Introduction

Islam is the most recent religion revealed by Allah to all humanity. Prophet Muhammad was sent to the Christians, Jews, Pagans, Atheists, Agnostic, Confused and those who went astray. He did not come to abolish, but to purify, admonish, approve, correct and to complete the previous messages that were revealed to all the previous prophets who came before him. Among those prophets were Jesus, Moses, Abraham, David, Jacob, Isaac, Ishmael, Noah, and many more.

Islam is not a religion as the latter being defined in the Western societies. Islam is a complete and a total way of life. It includes spirituality, as much as it gives guidance to live in a system of a government. It includes economics, social, cultural, education, politics, banking system along with methods how to deal with non-Muslims individually and with government as well.

I. Da'wah

A Muslim Da'iyah is to invite people to Allah. He is to do good for them without obliging them. Finally, he should identify himself as a Muslim without any prefix or suffix. This concept of Da'wah is depicted from the Ayah in Surah Fussilat. It reads as follows:

> *Who is better in speech than one who calls (people) to Allah, works righteousness, and says, "I am of those who bow in Islam." (Qur'an 41:33)*

At the same time, Da'wah necessitates wisdom and goodly approach. Each and every person is not the same. In this respect, Allah (swt) demanded us to call people with good manners. In Surah Al-Nahl (The Bees) Allah says the following:

$$\text{ادْعُ إِلَىٰ سَبِيلِ رَبِّكَ بِالْحِكْمَةِ وَالْمَوْعِظَةِ الْحَسَنَةِ وَجَادِلْهُم بِالَّتِي هِيَ أَحْسَنُ ۚ إِنَّ رَبَّكَ هُوَ أَعْلَمُ بِمَن ضَلَّ عَن سَبِيلِهِ ۖ وَهُوَ أَعْلَمُ بِالْمُهْتَدِينَ ۝١٢٥}$$

> *Invite all to the Way of your Lord with wisdom and beautiful preaching; and argue with them in ways that are best and most gracious: for your Lord knows best, who have strayed from His Path, and who received Guidance. (Qur'an 16:125)*

Muslims are not to convert people to Islam as there is no compulsion in religion. Allah says in Surah Al-Baqarah (The Cow) the following:

$$\text{لَا إِكْرَاهَ فِي الدِّينِ ۖ قَد تَّبَيَّنَ الرُّشْدُ مِنَ الْغَيِّ ۚ فَمَن يَكْفُرْ بِالطَّاغُوتِ وَيُؤْمِن بِاللَّهِ فَقَدِ اسْتَمْسَكَ بِالْعُرْوَةِ الْوُثْقَىٰ لَا انفِصَامَ لَهَا ۗ وَاللَّهُ سَمِيعٌ عَلِيمٌ ۝٢٥٦}$$

> *Let there be no compulsion in religion: Truth stands out clear from Error: whoever rejects Evil and believes*

in God, had grasped the most trustworthy hand-hold, that never breaks, and God hears and knows all things. (Qur'an 2:256)

II. People of other Faiths

As far as the People of the Book are concerned, Allah has advised the Muslims to call upon them for the universal concept of Tawheed, the living of a moral life, and that all should cooperate on the common and mutual terms. Allah says in this regard in Surah Al-`Imran the following:

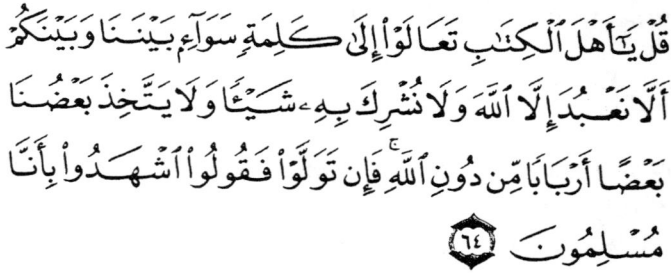

Say: "O People of the Book! Come to common terms as between us and you: that we worship none but God; that we associate no partners with Him; that we erect not, from among ourselves, lords and patrons other than God." If then they turn back, say you: "Bear witness that we (at least) are Muslims (bowing) to God's Will." (Qur'an 3:64)

It is to be recalled here that Allah has reminded us to use the best approach when we are talking with People of other Faiths. In this regard Allah says in Surah Al-'Ankaboot (The Spider) the following:

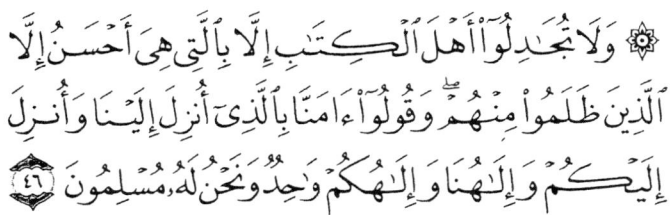

And dispute you not with the people of the Book, except with means better (than mere disputation), unless it be with those of them who inflict wrong (and injury): but say, "We believe in the Revelation which has come down to us and in that which came down to you; our God and your God is One; and it is to Him we bow (in Islam)." (Qur'an 29:46)

III. Final Remarks

People may see things differently because they may have been taught and raised differently. The basic measures and standards with which people evaluate and assess things are different, and as such, their approaches to life are different. In order to live peacefully among other people, one has to realize that is the concept of IGNORANCE about others that makes people denounce one another. To be stubborn, arrogant, haughty, vicious, or close-minded does not help solve any problems. Remaining ignorant and unwilling to learn about others will definitely augment the problem. It is only through proper education, information and communication that people may come to understand each other. Then and only then will they appreciate one another.

Therefore, Muslims should be most tolerant people in the world toward the non-Muslims. And indeed they have proven this to be throughout history. They have coexisted with

Christians, Jews, Hindus, Persians, Sikh, and Buddhist, regardless of whether the Muslims were in majority or minority. They have lived throughout most of their history on good terms with these people. What is needed now from all the God-fearing, loving, and faithful people is to realize that they should open a new page and chapter in life. They should try to open the door to dialogues and trialogues among those who are God-conscious. They should rediscover their roots and their faith not as someone wants it, but as it should be. With this approach the faithful can be able to live together in unanimity and wholesomeness.

The trip for the conference took one whole week so as to present a paper for only (30) minutes! I asked myself and the audience whether it was worthy or not!? To be considered worthy, a friend of mine took me to a waleemah whereby I gave a talk to the people who were attending it. Also, we went to a Muslim camp and spoke to the youth about the benefits of camping. I also had the golden opportunity to visit my old friend Dr. Wahid Ali, the former president of the Senate, and Acting President of the country. I visited some of the business people. Then I felt very happy that my time was useful.

I pray to Allah to accept from all of us our deeds, and forgive us for our shortcomings. Ameen.

Allah is the Greatest

XXXVIII. UNEXPECTED EXPERIENCES

In the following section there are some incidents that took place. They were unpredictable, and sometimes shocking. These experiences are written here so that other speakers will take it easy on them. Life is full of stories, incidents, experiences and surprises. One should listen to stories of others, and benefit from them. The list of incidents are very few and they took place at different places, and at different times. These stories are quotations and they are excerpts as they happened.

A. No One Was At Airport

I arrived at La Guardia Airport. No one was waiting for me. I did not know who is going to pick me up. I stayed for one hour at the Airport trying to find my way. I did not have the phone number of the host. I called my wife at home to look for it and to call me back at the Airport. After getting the number, I tried to call one member of the host. He was not home. His wife took the message and my phone number at the airport. She tried to reach her husband but in vain. Finally, she requested someone to come to the Airport to pick me up, and take me to the function. It took another hour waiting at the Airport. What a guest speaker! Free of charge.

I had to come all the way from the West Coast to the East Coast. It seems that this is the way I had to be treated. I did not mind it at all, as long as I was doing this for the love of Allah. Our beloved Prophet had to go all the way to the City of Al-Taif to deliver the Message of Allah. He was not welcomed at all. Instead, the gang threw stones at him till his feet were bleeding. Therefore, Da'wah necessitates patience, sacrifice, and wisdom. Please Ya Allah! Accept from us our deeds and activities. Ameen

B. Good Friends

In one community in Dearborn, Michigan, a good number of my friends had to take me to stay overnight in their houses. I ended up having my suitcase in one house, my brief case in another, my overcoat in a third house, and I, myself had to stay in a fourth house without having my personal items. I had to sleep with my suit without changing my clothes. The second day, I had to leave to the Airport, and I had to relocate my personal belongings. I had either to miss my plane or some of my belongings. I chose the latter and I requested them to ship them back to my house in Chicago.

I had to learn a lesson: To keep everything in one car wherever I move from center to center. I had to learn another lesson. I had a good number of friends who want to please me. All want me to be in their local houses. Therefore, I decided that I prefer to live in a motel or hotel. I am ready to pay money for my stay overnight. I don't mind to do so, in order to have peace of mind during my trips.

C. Stay With Us In Ramadan

One time I was out of job and I was in desperate need of financial help to survive. I was invited to a local Muslim Center. I left Chicago and went to Ohio in the late eighties (1987). I gave Friday Khutbah; and immediately after that I had to give two consecutive lectures to a group of non-Muslim university students who visited the Masjid. Later in the evening, I gave a lecture at the Masjid to all the Muslims. The whole day was very busy and Al-Hamdu Lillah the program was a success. The local people knew that I was out of job. They offered me to come and stay the whole month of Ramadan in the Masjid. They informed me that I will sleep in the Masjid and I will lead the daily Salat, and give

Qur'an Tafseer. Since I was free and out of job, they requested me to leave my family in their home town without any financial help. They will let me live inside the Masjid free. During Iftar I will eat with them. This should be enough for me!! The local people were honest and sincere in their generous offer... what else you need?! A place to stay on the floor, and Iftar to eat with us. In return you lead us, guide us, educate us, inspire us, and help us to make Da'wah to Muslims and non-Muslims. They did not think of my family's needs at all. My daily expenses and other items of life existence! What type of a generous offer?!!! Yes! Indeed it was a good offer. Their intention was good. They were students. They do need a scholar to help them, to guide them, and to inspire them. They meant good. I did not suspect them at all. I hoped I had income somehow, and somewhere. I would have devoted the month of Ramadan with I'tikaf for the whole month of Ramadan. I cried! O Ya Allah! Please help me, guide me, and use me in the right way for Your love. Ameen

D. We Need That Money

Once I was invited to give a lecture at the University of Wisconsin, Milwaukee. I drove from Chicago with a good number of friends. After I gave the lecture, the local Muslims students were kind to make arrangement with their University to give an honorarium to the guest speaker. However, I was asked in front of others: We need the money. The University will give you an honorarium. Please sign these papers and write your social security number so that we collect the money for us.

At the same time I was without job, and I did need money too. In a friendly way I had to say I don't need money. I signed the check for them. They collected the money and I had to report it as an income for me to the IRS without having proof of donating it to any. They themselves never sent a receipt or even acknowledgement. However, they were kind enough to embarrass me in front of others without courtesy. They could either send me a receipt for my donation to them, or they could have split the money between both of us. They were selfish, but innocent. They had to learn more and more how to share the happiness and the miseries with others. I did not mind what happened. I knew that Allah (swt) was testing me to let me know whether I am doing Da'wah for the love of Allah, or for the love of money, position, recognition, etc. I had to reflect for sometime: All the prophets did not ask for honorarium. In Surah Ash-Shu'araa' (The Poets), one may find out that a good number of Prophets did not ask any honorarium. The honorarium is coming to them from the Creator of the Whole Universe. The Qur'an states the following:

"I am to you a messenger worthy of all trust." So fear Allah, and obey me. No reward do I ask of you for it: my reward is only from the Lord of the Worlds. (Qur'an 26:143-145)

If I do not read Qur'an daily, I would have reacted bluntly against those students. But with the Blessings of Allah, I felt happy in a way: The money was not meant for me in this world, but it is (Insha-Allah) for me in the Day of Judgement. I had to learn a lesson, that I have to travel on my own, take friends with me while I am driving, and I have to give the series of lectures. All of these services and many more are Free of Charge. I do pray to

Allah (swt) to accept what we do, to reward us for such activities, and to forgive our shortcomings. Ameen

E. Homeless

In many places I found out that the local community did not make arrangements for my stay. They were perplexed about what to do with me. I realized that each one was finding excuses in not taking care of me. I volunteered myself to stay in a hotel/motel; and I will take a taxi to the Airport. They ran away from me, and I was left homeless! Such incident took place after exhausting myself and after raising a large amount of money for their local project without asking any honorarium. What type of a guest speaker for a good host community!... To raise money for them, and they did not care to host me or even to allow me to take care of myself. Ma-Sha-Allah.

As I frequent traveler, I had to learn a series of lessons. One of them is to expect the worst while doing the favor for others. The only source of satisfaction is the expectation of rewards from Allah (swt). Otherwise, why one has to help those who are egoistic, selfish, stingy, and don't know the idea of symbiosis. They act as parasites. One cannot help, but to feel sorry for such groups of people on this planet earth. It seems they forgot the idea of hospitality for their guest. The guest was invited to help them raise money. He had to come from a long distance by flying from his place to them. He had to leave his family also. He did his homework properly. They benefited from him. A lesson has to be learned! One has to expect the worst while he is doing favors to others. One has to remember something important in life. For pilgrims, they have to experience during their ritual rites, to live in tents as Refugees in Mina and Arafa. They have to spend one night in Muzdalifa as homeless!.. Therefore, the more a person goes through hardship, the more reward he will get.

I had to be grateful to Allah (swt) for allowing me to render my services to different groups of Muslims in North America. Please Ya Allah! Accept from me whatever I am doing, and forgive me for my shortcomings. Ameen.

F. We Expect You To Donate

I was invited to a good number of Islamic Centers to raise money for their local communities. Al-Hamdulillah we were able to raise enough money for them. Once I was out of job. Someone from the organizers looked at me and at the audience, and then he asked me publicly, "we want to hear from the speaker himself how much he is going to contribute himself to us!" They forgot that a speaker had to leave his family and his local town, his leisure and his work. He is raising money for them instead of paying him an honorarium. They were demanding him to pay money for them above what he had incurred expenses during his trip. What type of a Deal is this?!!.. Is he an Amir, or a person who has oil fields or a king with the luxury of the world?!

They forgot that any money collected by intimidation is Haram. Any money earned by asking each person in name is also Haram. But to ask the guest speaker himself publicly to donate is difficult to believe. They do not know seriously that he is to be given an honorarium or a gift for his services rendered to them. He is a Roving Da'iyah. He does not earn money from a professional job in a University or an industry. They forgot that the Da'iyah himself is not an angel or a prophet. He is a human being as any other person. He has his family, he has his needs, and he has his obligations to survive in the society with honor and dignity. It seems our good friends did not know, or they did not want to know all of these facts. They are too selfish! I do pray to Allah to forgive me by expressing my feelings for such incidents. Never I meant wrong! All what I want that the educated Muslims of America should assume their responsibility and act professionally. Ameen.

G. The Guest is Responsible

Two speakers were invited in the nineties (1992) to a local community. We were sitting with the Board members few hours before the main function, discussing the strategy for a better fund raising. We asked the Board to lay down the strategy and we then requested that someone who is generous should be the first to pledge. We found out that the President and the Chairman of the Mosque project were both medical doctors. We requested them to start the pledge with their community. They refused. They were hoping that we the guest speakers are to raise the money from somewhere other than themselves. I had to ask politely, if you are not interested to pay, to pledge or to encourage people to donate, then how in the world you want us to raise you money!! Their answers was: this is why we brought you here to raise for us money. I said: but from where do you want us to raise for you money? Do you expect that we are millionaires, and we came to donate our money? Don't you know that we are small and insignificant employees, and we came to help you collect the money from your community? The president's response was, this is now your problem! This is your homework! We invited you here so that you do something about it. We leave it up to you. As long as we brought here, it becomes your responsibility to raise the money for us. Of course! I did it Free without honorarium. What type of a deal!…

When I was coming back in the plane, I had to reflect about such type of members of the Board of that Community Center. They are medical doctors!! They are the leaders of their local community!!. They do not know that they are living in America!! There is no Free lunch... There is no Free services... Jannah (paradise) is not Free... The speakers had to leave their family, their local community and travel by plane to help other communities on a regular basis Free. Why those speakers had to continue such type of services, to such type of so-called local leaders! Do those local executives think that they are the dictators, while the rest of the world are slaves in their hands! Do they think that the speakers who had Ph.D degrees are servants for them Free!? Such types of individuals are nothing but parasites!!

To be a leader, a person has to serve the community. Leadership is not to be given free. It has to be earned with blood and sweat. Such type of individuals are going to face the worst position in the Day of Judgement. All what I had to do is to pray to Allah to forgive those people, and to show them the right way so that they will be forgiven by Allah.

I for one, will continue my work Insha Allah for any noble work, as long as it is for the love of Allah. But at the same time, I should learn a lesson, by not going again to the same community to spoil the so-called leaders, unless they change their attitude, manners, behaviors, and understand their responsibilities.

XXXIX. UGLY... UGLY... UGLY

Allah has blessed me to travel from place to place quite often. Throughout my traveling I had to go from airport to another. While going and coming back I see a large number of people traveling too. I got surprised! Every airline and every airport is full with people. I ask myself how can they afford the money to pay for all their traveling. I myself cannot do it, unless the host group takes care of it. This article was written when I was in Washington D.C., on August 31 – September1,1999. I was invited for deposition to defend the inmates so that they will receive Halal foods.

I see people with strange appearances. They look strange and scary. The style of their hair is unique and ugly. Some use metal rings on their nose, eyelids, ears and tongues. Others use tattoos on their body: ugly and scary. Ladies use too much cosmetics on their faces to the extent you doubt the appearance of their faces as human beings. The type of dress that men wear is ugly. Their dignity as people has been lost. One would ask the question: Are they animals in the shape of human beings? Are they human beings trying to look naked like animals, or are they satans in the shape of distorted human beings? It seems those people lost their honor and respect. They forget that they are human beings. They forget that Allah has made them the supreme creatures, and all other creatures are to serve them.

Moreover, the dress of women is so ugly and very obnoxious to the eyes. It seems that such women don't look at the mirror to see themselves how ugly and intimidating. They don't feel ashamed of themselves. They lost their respect by wearing miniskirts or short pants, and showing their legs and thighs. They wear very tight blouses that intimidate the other gender. They show their arms, neck, chest, breasts, etc. They wear high heels with tight clothing. They don't see themselves while walking: Their chests and butts are shaking one way or the other as if they are dancing! Many times when I see these things, I request Allah (swt) to protect me and to save me. I say to myself: I wish I had the power to stop all those people from doing satanic behavior and appearance. I do remember that Satan is behind all those people. He falsely promises them Paradise while he himself is going to Hell. He inspires them to do the wrong activity so that they will fall into his trap. The Qur'an informed us in Surah An-Nisaa' (The Women) how Satan instructs people to change their appearance. The following Ayat have been revealed:

لَعَنَهُ ٱللَّهُ وَقَالَ لَأَتَّخِذَنَّ مِنْ عِبَادِكَ نَصِيبًا مَفْرُوضًا ۝ وَلَأُضِلَّنَّهُمْ وَلَأُمَنِّيَنَّهُمْ وَلَآمُرَنَّهُمْ فَلَيُبَتِّكُنَّ ءَاذَانَ ٱلْأَنْعَٰمِ وَلَآمُرَنَّهُمْ فَلَيُغَيِّرُنَّ خَلْقَ ٱللَّهِ وَمَن يَتَّخِذِ ٱلشَّيْطَٰنَ وَلِيًّا مِّن دُونِ ٱللَّهِ فَقَدْ خَسِرَ خُسْرَانًا مُّبِينًا ۝ يَعِدُهُمْ وَيُمَنِّيهِمْ وَمَا يَعِدُهُمُ ٱلشَّيْطَٰنُ إِلَّا غُرُورًا ۝ أُوْلَٰٓئِكَ مَأْوَىٰهُمْ جَهَنَّمُ وَلَا يَجِدُونَ عَنْهَا مَحِيصًا ۝

Allah did curse him, but he said: "I will take of Your servants a portion marked off. "I will mislead them, and I will create in them false desires; I will order them to slit the ears of cattle, and to deface the (fair) nature created by Allah," Whoever, forsaking Allah, takes Satan for a friend, has of a surety suffered a loss that is manifest. Satan makes them promises, and creates in them false hopes, but Satan's promises are nothing but deception. They (his dupes) will have their dwelling in Hell, and from it they will find no way of escape. (Qur'an 4:118-121)

One may see more ugly things in society. Men and women hugging, kissing, flirting, and goofing around without feeling ashamed of themselves, and of what they are doing. They don't recognize how ugly they look, and how ugly they behave!!!

Some men dress like women, while women dress like men. They look strange and ugly. You drive around, and you will be able to see some advertisements on the stores with ugly pictures of naked women. You open newspapers and you will be able to see advertisements of different department stores. Most of what one sees are the women with their underwear clothing fitted on them. They look very ugly and disturbing.

If you are invited to a wedding party, you think you are going to a respected Muslim family. During the reception, you realize that some do drink alcohol, dance, and sing non-Muslim songs. You get astonished, and you are shocked of what you see and what you hear. Their behavior is very strange. Their dress is ugly. Their faces look ugly and their function is ugly. One cannot tolerate what he sees. Either he has to stop them, or to leave. Most of the time I had to leave those functions, because I cannot tolerate being in their place.

Once I requested the orchestra people to stop for an emergency announcement. The whole function stopped, and those who were dancing stopped for the announcement. I took the microphone, and I gave the Azan. Then I invited them to relax and come with me to pray Salat of Maghrib. They were mad at me, of course, they hated me, but they could not do anything bad to me except frowning faces.

Ugly...Ugly...Ugly

Their faces are ugly; their dresses are ugly...Their appearance are ugly...Their activities are ugly...Their services are ugly...Their lifestyle is ugly...Their eating habits are ugly...Their speeches are ugly...Their whole life is ugly! I asked myself: if everything became ugly, why are they still living?! Allah (swt) is the Most Merciful. He is still giving them the chance to repent and come back to a normal life of modesty, and decency. They are to follow a life with morality and respect as human beings, not as animals. Muslims have to recognize that Shaitan is their first enemy. He tries his best to destroy them. However, Allah (swt) has already warned us not to follow him. In one Ayah in Surah Al-Noor (The Light) Allah (swt) says the following:

﴿ يَٰٓأَيُّهَا ٱلَّذِينَ ءَامَنُوا۟ لَا تَتَّبِعُوا۟ خُطُوَٰتِ ٱلشَّيْطَٰنِ وَمَن يَتَّبِعْ خُطُوَٰتِ ٱلشَّيْطَٰنِ فَإِنَّهُۥ يَأْمُرُ بِٱلْفَحْشَآءِ وَٱلْمُنكَرِ وَلَوْلَا فَضْلُ ٱللَّهِ عَلَيْكُمْ وَرَحْمَتُهُۥ مَا زَكَىٰ مِنكُم مِّنْ أَحَدٍ أَبَدًا وَلَٰكِنَّ ٱللَّهَ يُزَكِّى مَن يَشَآءُ وَٱللَّهُ سَمِيعٌ عَلِيمٌ ﴿٢١﴾

O you who believe! follow not Satan's footsteps: If any will follow the footsteps of Satan, he will (but) command what is indecent and wrong: And were it not for the grace and mercy of Allah on you, not one of you would ever have been pure: but Allah does purify whom

He pleases: And Allah is One Who hears and knows (all things) (24:21)

Sometimes Allah (swt) sends them earthquakes, hurricanes, tornadoes, firebrush, floods, and other so-called natural catastrophes to bring them back to normal life. It seems people don't learn, and don't correlate these uncontrollable incidents with their social behaviors. They need someone to remind them so that they will get out of the ugly life, to the beautiful life. This latter life, is a life of decency, modesty, morality, a life of respect with dignity as human beings. It should not be a life of satans or a life of animals. We pray to Allah (swt) to shower His blessings on us, and to guide all of us to the right path. Ameen.

الله اكبر
ALLAHU AKBAR

الله اكبر
ALLAHU AKBAR

XL. SHAME... SHAME... SHAME

In a previous article, the title was "Ugly...Ugly...Ugly." At that time I was reflecting about those women who put on ugly clothing, and behave ugly. At that time I did not blame them much, but it seems Satan had already possessed them tremendously. Any person who is not in touch with Allah, and does not follow the teachings of Allah, then Satan has to posses them. They will make them behave like Satan's or even worse. They dress like Satan and they lose human feelings and behaviors. They will not even recognize the big mistakes that they are committing.

While flying from city to city, I still see the ugly people behaving and acting as animals in the shape of human beings. I had no choice but to request Allah to help me to advise some of them anytime I had the chance to. One time while flying, a reflection crossed my mind. I said to myself, it is not enough to say: Ugly ... Ugly...Ugly, I should say: Shame...Shame...Shame. Then I asked myself shame on whom? The answer came to me as follows:

1. Shame on those women who do what they are doing ugly at any time.
2. Shame on those women who try to dress like men or even behave immorally and in public.
3. Shame on those women who are Lesbians. They think that they are better citizens. They forgot that they are worse than animals. Allah (swt) says in Surah Al-Furqan (the Criterion) the following:

> *Or think that most of them listen or understand? They are Only like cattle; -- Nay, they are farther astray from the way. (25:44)*

4. Shame on those men who allow their wives and daughters to look ugly. The blame is not only on women but much more on the men.
5. Shame on those men who encourage women to look ugly.
6. Shame on those men who abuse women by using them for commercial purposes with ugly appearance.
7. Shame on those men who enjoy dancing with women in public without feeling ashamed of themselves.
8. Shame on those men who claim themselves to be Gay! They reduced themselves to a lower level than animals. At least animals behave morally between genders.
9. Shame on those men who refused to study the history of other nations. The people in Palestine during the days of Prophets Ibrahim and Loot were destroyed because they practiced Homosexuality. They were advised by prophet Loot, but refused to listen to him. Finally, Allah sent them an earthquake, and showered them with brimstones from Hell. Then Allah showered them with hot salty water to get rid of them. One can go to Palestine and visit the Dead Sea there. Moreover, one has to read from the Qur'an about those immoral people who were practicing homosexuality. In Surah Hood, Allah says the following:

وَلَمَّا جَاءَتْ رُسُلُنَا لُوطًا سِيءَ بِهِمْ وَضَاقَ بِهِمْ ذَرْعًا وَقَالَ هَذَا يَوْمٌ عَصِيبٌ ۝ وَجَاءَهُ قَوْمُهُ يُهْرَعُونَ إِلَيْهِ وَمِن قَبْلُ كَانُوا يَعْمَلُونَ السَّيِّئَاتِ قَالَ يَا قَوْمِ هَؤُلَاءِ بَنَاتِي هُنَّ أَطْهَرُ لَكُمْ فَاتَّقُوا اللَّهَ وَلَا تُخْزُونِ فِي ضَيْفِي أَلَيْسَ مِنكُمْ رَجُلٌ رَشِيدٌ ۝ قَالُوا لَقَدْ عَلِمْتَ مَا لَنَا فِي بَنَاتِكَ مِنْ حَقٍّ وَإِنَّكَ لَتَعْلَمُ مَا نُرِيدُ

قَالَ لَوْ أَنَّ لِى بِكُمْ قُوَّةً أَوْ ءَاوِىٓ إِلَىٰ رُكْنٍ شَدِيدٍ ۝ قَالُوا۟ يَٰلُوطُ إِنَّا رُسُلُ رَبِّكَ لَن يَصِلُوٓا۟ إِلَيْكَ ۖ فَأَسْرِ بِأَهْلِكَ بِقِطْعٍ مِّنَ ٱلَّيْلِ وَلَا يَلْتَفِتْ مِنكُمْ أَحَدٌ إِلَّا ٱمْرَأَتَكَ ۖ إِنَّهُۥ مُصِيبُهَا مَآ أَصَابَهُمْ ۚ إِنَّ مَوْعِدَهُمُ ٱلصُّبْحُ ۚ أَلَيْسَ ٱلصُّبْحُ بِقَرِيبٍ ۝ فَلَمَّا جَآءَ أَمْرُنَا جَعَلْنَا عَٰلِيَهَا سَافِلَهَا وَأَمْطَرْنَا عَلَيْهَا حِجَارَةً مِّن سِجِّيلٍ مَّنضُودٍ ۝ مُّسَوَّمَةً عِندَ رَبِّكَ ۖ وَمَا هِىَ مِنَ ٱلظَّٰلِمِينَ بِبَعِيدٍ ۝

Then after him we sent Messengers to their people, They brought them When fear had passed from the mind of Abraham and the glad things tidings had reached him, he began to plead with us for Lut's people. For Abraham was, without doubt, forbearing, compassionate, and given to penitence. O Abraham! Seek not this. The decree of the Lord has gone forth: for them there comes a Chastisement that cannot be turned back! When our messengers came to Lut, he was grieved on their account and felt himself powerless to protect them. He said: "This is a distressful day." And his people came rushing towards him, and they had been long in the habit of practising Abominations. He said: "O my people! Here are my daughters: they are purer for you if you marry! Now fear Allah, and cover me not with disgrace about my guests! Is there not among you a single right-minded man?" They said: "Well do they know we have no need of the daughters: indeed they know quite well what we want!" He said: *"Would that I had power to suppress you or that I could betake myself to some powerful support." The messengers said: "O Lout! We are Messengers from the Lord! By no means shall they reach you! Now travel with your family while yet a part of the night remains, and let not any of you look back: but the wife will remain behind: To her will happen what happens to the people. Morning is their time appointed: Is not the morning yet?" When our decree issued, we turned the cities upside down, and rained down on them brimstones hard has baked clay, Spread, Layer on Layer, -- Marked from the Lord, nor are they ever far from those who do wrong! (11:77-83)*

10. Shame one million times on those men who call themselves The Muslim Gay Club. Such dirty people did not want only to proclaim themselves to be dirty, but they want to insult the best religion of Allah. Those people are trying to abuse the name of Allah Who created them with mercy. They do not only insult the name of Allah, but they do insult Allah Himself Who is giving them life with all its needs free of charge. While flying from New York City to California, I asked myself as to what I should do. I remembered that I should write about it and talk against that type of life. Then I prayed to Allah (swt) to protect me in case He has to get rid of them. I remembered the following Ayah in Surah Al-Mu'minoon (The Believers) whereby Allah (swt) says the following:

Say: "O my Lord! If you will show me in this lifetime which are Warned against, Then, O my Lord! Put me not amongst the people Who do wrong!" And we are certainly able to show thee in fulfillment that against which they are warned. (23: 93-95)

Finally I remembered to read the following Du`a' from Surah Al-Imran:

ٱلَّذِينَ يَذْكُرُونَ ٱللَّهَ قِيَٰمًا وَقُعُودًا وَعَلَىٰ جُنُوبِهِمْ وَيَتَفَكَّرُونَ فِى خَلْقِ ٱلسَّمَٰوَٰتِ وَٱلْأَرْضِ رَبَّنَا مَا خَلَقْتَ هَٰذَا بَٰطِلًا سُبْحَٰنَكَ فَقِنَا عَذَابَ ٱلنَّارِ ۝ رَبَّنَآ إِنَّكَ مَن تُدْخِلِ ٱلنَّارَ فَقَدْ أَخْزَيْتَهُۥ وَمَا لِلظَّٰلِمِينَ مِنْ أَنصَارٍ ۝ رَّبَّنَآ إِنَّنَا سَمِعْنَا مُنَادِيًا يُنَادِى لِلْإِيمَٰنِ أَنْ ءَامِنُوا۟ بِرَبِّكُمْ فَـَٔامَنَّا ۚ رَبَّنَا فَٱغْفِرْ لَنَا ذُنُوبَنَا وَكَفِّرْ عَنَّا سَيِّـَٔاتِنَا وَتَوَفَّنَا مَعَ ٱلْأَبْرَارِ ۝ رَبَّنَا وَءَاتِنَا مَا وَعَدتَّنَا عَلَىٰ رُسُلِكَ وَلَا تُخْزِنَا يَوْمَ ٱلْقِيَٰمَةِ ۗ إِنَّكَ لَا تُخْلِفُ ٱلْمِيعَادَ ۝

Men who remember Allah standing, sitting, and lying down on their sides, and contemplate the (wonders of) creation in the heavens and the earth, (with the saying) "Our Lord not for naught have You created (all) this! Glory to You! Give us salvation from the

Chastisement of the Fire. Our Lord! Any whom You do admit to the Fire, truly You covered with shame, and never will wrong-doers find any helpers! Our Lord! We have heard the call of one calling (us) to Faith, 'Believe you in the Lord, and we have believed. Our Lord! Forgive us our sins, blot out from us our iniquities, and take to Yourself our souls in the company of the righteous. Our Lord! Grant us what You did promise unto us through Your Messengers, and save us from shame on the Day of Judgement: For You never break Your promise. (3:191-194)

Please ya Allah! You are Ar-Rahman and Ar-Raheem. You are Al-Ghafoor and Al-Wadoodd. Please take care of us and save us from the satanic people. Ameen.

"And our Lord says.: Call on me: I will answer your prayer...."
(40:60)

"Supplication is the brain of worship."

XLI. DIRTY... DIRTY... DIRTY

As a flying Falcon I see so many things: some are good, others are bad and still others are in between. In a previous article I wrote: Ugly...Ugly...Ugly. At that time I was very disturbed to see women dress in an ugly fashion. I put the blame on them and on others. Later I wrote another article under the title of Shame... Shame... Shame. At that time, I put the blame on men who allow such women to dress ugly or even force them to do so.

Today is May 27, 2001. I was coming back from Oakland Airport to Ontario Airport in California. We tried to raise money for the Tracy Islamic Center. While I was at the Airport in Oakland, a new Reflection came to my mind. It is Dirty...Filthy...and Bad Smell. However, I put this article under the title of Dirty...Dirty...Dirty. I hope I can reflect properly on this subject.

Yes indeed! Anywhere I go I see very ugly women with their shameful clothing. It is not enough that they dress bad, but a good number nowadays dress with dirty clothing. This applies mainly with men. They wear dirty jeans...Some go to public places and sit next to you in the plane with dirty jeans. They smell like tobacco, smokes, others and others without the need for mentioning the rest of the other dirty names.

Others could be Muslims as well. They come for Jumu'ah Salat with Dirty clothing. Blue Jeans that smell like car machines, with dirty grease too. They forget that Allah (swt) instructed Muslims to come to the Masajid with the best clothing. In Surah Al-A'raaf (The Heights), Allah (swt) Says the following:

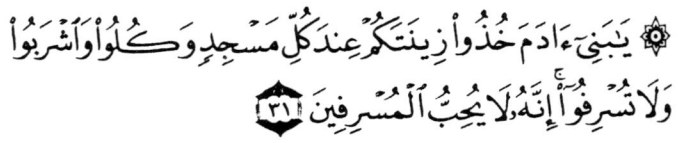

> *O Children of Adam! Wear your beautiful apparel at every time and place of prayer: eat and drink but waste not by excess for Allah loves not the wasters. (7:31)*

Our beloved Prophet used a special gown for Jumu'ah and for the Eids. He instructed Muslims to have a shower on Fridays, have the best clothing, abstain from eating garlic, and encouraged them to use 'Itr (oil perfume).

One reflection is the following: Dirty bodies, dirty brains and dirty hearts. Some Muslim youth come to the Masjid with Dirty blue short jeans, with dirty hair and ugly appearance on their faces, ears, noses, lips and so on. Some of them sit in an ugly position and talk to each other while the Khatib is giving his Friday Khutbah. Some chew gum all the time during prayer and Khutbah, and some come with their cellular to talk while the Imam is leading Salat. It seems that Shaitan has possessed such people and force them to change their appearance, and to dress dirty and fashionable clothing. While closing my nose from the dirty smell in the airport, and in the plane, I remembered one Ayah in the Qur'an in Surah Al-Nisaa' (The Women). It goes as follows:

لَعَنَهُ ٱللَّهُ وَقَالَ لَأَتَّخِذَنَّ مِنْ عِبَادِكَ نَصِيبًا مَّفْرُوضًا ۝ وَلَأُضِلَّنَّهُمْ وَلَأُمَنِّيَنَّهُمْ وَلَآمُرَنَّهُمْ فَلَيُبَتِّكُنَّ ءَاذَانَ ٱلْأَنْعَٰمِ وَلَآمُرَنَّهُمْ فَلَيُغَيِّرُنَّ خَلْقَ ٱللَّهِ ۚ وَمَن يَتَّخِذِ ٱلشَّيْطَٰنَ وَلِيًّا مِّن دُونِ ٱللَّهِ فَقَدْ خَسِرَ خُسْرَانًا مُّبِينًا ۝ يَعِدُهُمْ وَيُمَنِّيهِمْ ۖ وَمَا يَعِدُهُمُ ٱلشَّيْطَٰنُ إِلَّا غُرُورًا ۝

> *Allah did curse him, but he said: "I will take of Your servants a portion marked off: "I will mislead them, and I will create in them false desires; I will order them to slit the ears of cattle, and to deface the fair nature created by Allah," Whoever takes Satan for a friend, has of a surety suffered a loss that is manifest. Satan makes them promises, and creates in them false hopes, but Satan's promises are nothing but deception. (4:118-120)*

Finally, I prayed to Allah (swt) to guide those people, and bring them back to the level of human beings. Indeed, their behaviors, attitudes, manners, clothings, and smell are worse than animals. I remembered another Ayah whereby Allah (swt) says in Surah Al-Furqaan (The Criterion) the following:

> *Or do you think that most of them listen or understand? They are only like cattle; nay they are farther astray from the way (25:44)*

Therefore, one has to pray daily and request Allah to protect him from both human Satan as well as Jinn Satan. Ameen.

XLII. DEPOSITION

Since I came to USA in 1962, I was involved in Da'wah. I had to travel from place to place with different means of transportation. The more I give my time through Da'wah, the more I was needed. Some of those activities were: Lectures, Friday Khutbah, Dialogue with non-Muslims, Family Counseling, Fund Raising, Visiting Inmates, Deposition for one way or the other, officiating Marriages, Burying the Dead, etc.

As a frequent flier, and as a Falcon I had no choice but to accept those invitations. Among the most unique invitations are those for Depositions. Most of those situations are not to defend myself, but to defend others, or to solve complicated problems that need solutions. Some depositions were for the inmates against the local governments. Other depositions were meant to elaborate about Family Laws concerning marriage, divorce, alimony, custody of the children, dowry, and inheritance. Some other depositions were about business people, and what Islam says about Islamic arbitration, and Islamic solution to such problems.

Some of those depositions were done by lawyers who represent government, industry, or independent legal firms. Certain individual lawyers are very rude and tough as if I am a criminal in front of them. They try to intimidate me in one way or the other. They also try to corner me and at some point they try to offend me. I tried to control myself otherwise I will lose the case. Several times the lawyers were shocked when they find out that I am doing such services free of charge! To be more specific I was asked by a law firm in Washington D.C., to come all the way from California for a Deposition that might take about 3-4 hours. I had to leave my home Monday August 30, 1999, at 5.00 a.m. to take a plane from Ontario Airport, in California, to go through Chicago airport, and then to Washington Airport. It took me the whole day because I had to lose three (3) hours in time difference between the west coast and the East coast.

That particular trip was to defend the inmates so that they will receive Halal Foods. I had to spend Monday to Wednesday for the sake of three (3) hours deposition. The lawyer defending the inmates was a very nice Caucasian lady. The lawyer who was representing the local government was straight forward person. He never tried to intimidate me. However, the lawyer of the catering company was rude and tough. He tried to corner me in many ways. He was shocked when he knew that I am doing this type of services Free. He could not imagine that a person like me is spending three (3) days free. He asked me as to why I am doing it Free. My answer was that I was looking to get credits from God. I am not looking for money. I am ready to go from place to place for the sake of helping people free of charge. I am ready to help people irrespective of color, ethnic background, race or religion. People are people, and they were created by the same God. If I want to please God, I should go out of my way to help people for the love of God (Allah), otherwise I will not be rewarded.

The other astonishing question was raised to me. Why you are helping someone that you don't know. They did not call you and ask you to help them. Moreover, a law firm called you without knowing you, and you don't know them as well. You come as a volunteer. You are even paying your travel expenses with the hope you will be paid in the near future. You don't want honorarium or per deem !! What is going on! Are you a millionaire or out of your mind?!!1 I replied politely: Money comes, and money goes away. If I don't earn credits in the Book of Allah, I would be the loser in the Day of Judgement. Money will never help me in the Hereafter, it might be a curse! God will ask me for every penny how I earned it, and how I spent it!! Therefore, it is better not to have too much money in as much as I should look how to earn credits and blessings from Allah the Creator.

Our beloved Prophet told us:

All people of the world are the Creation of Allah. The most beloved ones to Allah are those who are of beneficial to them.

Therefore, we should help people without exploitation or even without proslitization or coercion.

P.S.

1. This article was written when I was in Washington, D.C. August 31, 1999. While sitting in Marriott Hotel, I felt the impact to write such an article, immediately after I finished the Deposition.
2. By the way! There were too many points that were raised during the deposition. However, for the sake of brevity, I brought only the aforementioned points.
3. Attached is a copy of my deposition submitted through the local law firm, for the sake of the readers to benefit from.

IN THE UNITED STATES DISTRICT COURT
FOR THE DISTRICT OF COLUMBIA

| ABDUS SHAHID M.S. ALI, SEIFFULLAH ABDUL-LATIF ALI, a/k/a ALBERT GRIMES, Plaintiffs, v. DISTRICT OF COLUMBIA, et al, Defendents. |)))))))))) | Civil Actions Nos. 97-0456 and 97-0489 (HHK) |

Statement of Ahmad H. Sakr

1. My name is Ahmad H. Sakr. I have been retained by the law firm of Arnold & Porter to consult on issues relating to the requirements of a Muslim diet in the above-captioned cases.

2. I am a practicing Muslim. I was tutored in Islamic religious law for 12 years and have taught courses about Islam and Islamic Jurisprudence. I have held positions of leadership in Islamic Centers and other Islamic organizations. Currently, I am the Religious Director of the Islamic Education Center and President of the Foundation for Islamic Knowledge. I also hold a Ph.D. in Food Sciences from the University of Illinois and have taught course on food chemistry and nutrition in several universities. I have published numerous books and articles on subjects relating to Islamic law and the Muslim diet. A current Curriculum Vita is attached.

3. The concepts of *halal* and *haram* in Islam are very important in the life of every practicing Muslim. *Halal* is an Arabic word that means allowed or lawful. *Haram* is an Arabic word which, in general, means prohibited or unlawful.

4. The sole legislator of *halal* and *haram* is Allah (or, "God"). According to Islamic jurisprudence, human beings cannot change the unlawful (*haram*) to lawful (*halal*). By the same token, it is unlawful under Islamic jurisprudence for a human being to make the lawful unlawful. To follow the dictates of one who presumes to approve the unlawful or to prohibit the lawful is to attribute a partner, or an equal, to Allah:

> *Those who give partners (To Allah) will say: "If Allah had wished, We should not have given partners to Him nor should we have had any taboos." So did their ancestors argue falsely, until they tasted of Our wrath. Say: "Have ye any (certain) knowledge? If so, produce it before Us. Ye follow Nothing but conjecture; Ye do nothing but lie." Say; "With Allah is the argument that reaches home; if it had been His Will, He could indeed have guided you all." Say: "Bring forward your witnesses to prove that Allah did forbid so and so." If they bring such witnesses, Be not thou amongst them; Nor follow thou the vain desires of such as treat Our Signs as falsehoods, and such as belief not in the Hereafter, for they hold others as equal with their Guardian-Lord.*

(Surah Al-An`am [or, "The Cattle"] 6:148-50, **Holy Qur'an** [Abdullah Yusef Ali, trans.]) (emphasis supplied). This passage clearly expresses Allah's strong disapproval of one who presumes to forbid what Allah has permitted to the Muslims. In this passage, Allah commands the faithful to not follow those who contradict the dictates of Allah, for they have presumed themselves to be partners, or equal to Allah. It is a very serious sin to attribute partners to Allah; showing regard to one who presumes to be Allah's partner is deeply offensive in Islam.

5. Most diets and foods are considered *halal* unless they are specifically otherwise identified in the Holy Qur'an or the Hadith, which is a compilation of the sayings of the Prophet Muhammad. In Islam, the following foods *haram:* pork and its by-products, carrion, animals

slaughtered in a name other than Allah, blood, alcohol and other intoxicating drugs. Meat that comes from animals slaughtered according to Islamic law is called *zabiha*. This term connotes that the meat is *halal*. Because blood is *haram* animals must be slaughtered in a manner that facilitates the draining of the blood from the body if the meat is to be *zabiha*. In addition, in order to be *halal*, the name of Allah must be invoked at the time of slaughtering;

O ye who believe! Eat of the good things that We have provided for you and be grateful to Allah, If it is Him ye worship. He hath only forbidden you dead meat, and blood, and the flesh of swine, and that on which any other name hath been invoked besides that of Allah.

(Surah Al-Baqarah [or, "The Cow"] 2:172-73, **Holy Qur'an.**

6. All varieties of fish and seafood is *halal* according to most schools of Muslim thought and on this point the **Holy Qur'an** is clear:

Lawful to you is the pursuit Of water-game and its use For food-for the benefit Of yourselves and those who Travel;

(Surah Al-Ma'idah [or "The Table Spread"] 5:96, **Holy Qur'an**).

7. Muslims are not vegetarians by dictate of their religious laws. Islamic law commands Muslims to include in their diet fruits, vegetables, legumes, meat of herbivorous

animals and fish. Allah created all of these for all human beings' consumption. Allah specifically encouraged and approved the eating of properly slaughtered meat:

So eat of (meats) on which Allah's name hath been pronounced, if ye have faith in His Signs. Why should ye not eat of (meats) on which Allah's Name hath been pronounced, when He hath explained to you in detail what is forbidden to you-except under compulsion of necessity?..

Surah Al-An'am [or "The Cattle"] 6:118-119, **Holy Qur'an**]) (emphasis added).

8. The **Holy Qur'an** does not directly address the practice of vegetarianism because it is a recent development, yet Islam disapproves of asceticism. Restating the prohibition on transforming the lawful into the unlawful and thereby usurping divine authority, Allah cautioned ancient ascetics:

O ye who believe! make not unlawful the good things which Allah hath made lawful for you, but commit no excess; for Allah Loveth not those given to excess. Eat of things which Allah hath provided for you, lawful and good; but fear Allah, in whom ye believe.

(Surah Al-Ma'idah [or 'The Table Spread"] 5:87-88, **Holy Qur'an**]) (emphasis added).

9. Muslims are required to abide by what Allah instructed them to do; otherwise they are to be blamed in this world and the Hereafter for deviating from the commands of

Islamic law. To force Muslims to accept diets that do not conform to what Allah has prescribed is not acceptable under Islamic jurisprudence. Muslims are required to follow the teachings of Allah. They are instructed not to imitate or follow people of other cultures or religions in their customs, life style, habits, eating or drinking, such as Hindus, who are vegetarian by virtue of Hindu religious law.

10. To force a Muslim to accept a meatless diet as a religious diet is obnoxious to the Muslim faithful and contrary to the dictates of Islamic law. It has the effect of forcing a Muslim to imitate another's religious dictates (e.g., that of the Hindu), which is forbidden. It has the effect of forcing a Muslim to be excessive in his practices; Allah has cautioned against excesses in all things and specifically discouraged asceticism. It has the effect of placing a human authority on the same level as the divine authority, Allah, or making a partner to Allah, which is explicitly forbidden. A Muslim is bound by faith and by command from Allah through the scripture to resist allegiance to such authority that usurps the authority of Allah.

11. The foregoing statement reflects my expert opinion based on the materials and information I have received to date, which include the complaint filed in this action and portions of the discovery responses from the defendant Aramark. I understand that discovery is ongoing and that I may be asked to consider additional information, in which case I may wish to supplement or revise my opinions expressed herein.

June 26, 1999   Ahmad H. Sakr, Ph.D.

After I came back, I had to ask myself several questions, as well as I had few reflections: (1) Am I doing these services free for the love of Allah and for the sake of humanity at large or not. (2) Am I supposed to spend time, efforts, energy, and money for these activities to get rewards from Allah alone or not (3) Would I continue to render similar services free of charge or not. The answers came to my mind: Yes Ya Allah! Please Ya Allah! Help me, guide me, and give me moral support so that I will continue to do these services for Your Love and Your Pleasure. Ameen

I pray to Allah (swt) to accept from me and to forgive me for my shortcomings. Ameen

Pilgrimage thereto is a duty men owe to Allah, those who can afford the journey (3:97)

XLIII. I DON'T KNOW

- You Don't Need To Know!
- Why Should You Know?!
- You Will Know Later!
- You Are Invited For A Celebration! Really! Yes! Of Course---
- What Type of A Celebration?!
- The Centennial?!. Ma-Sha-Allah!
- Which Centennial?! Don't You Know?
- I felt embarrassed to ask anymore questions.
- I thanked the host for their kindness in inviting me.
- I could not stop asking. I said: Any special programs? Yes! Of course---
- Can you send me the program so that I will be able to orient myself. Yes! Indeed -

When you come here, you will have it—But I requested the host to fax it to me, he said: No problem—But I never received it. I was confused whether I should travel from California to Washington, D.C. without knowing what is going to happen1.. or what am I supposed to do!—The host tried to get my airline ticket, but it was not convenient—I will lose the Friday Salat. The travel agent did not communicate with me till five days before travelling. Then I did not hear from him. I requested the host to forget about me attending the function. His reply: No! No! Your presence is very essential—I said to myself! Essential!? To do what! Nothing! It is really strange invitation. I asked myself: why Friday-Saturday-Sunday!? It could be only a one-evening function. That is all! But still I don't know! Maybe I should not know! I should no more poke my nose into the affairs of the invitation. By the way: I had two other invitations at the same time: One in England for an International Islamic Conference, and the other in Detroit from the Shari`ah Scholars Association of North America

(SSANA). I declined from those two invitations. I said to myself: Let me also decline from this invitation. Let me hide myself and write my books instead of travelling. I had enough travelling in my life. I should concentrate the rest of my life documenting my memoirs for the benefit of the future generations. I left the matter in the Hands of Allah (swt). I prayed and said: O Allah! If this trip is good for me in this world and in the hereafter let me go, otherwise let me not go. The travel agent could not make a regular ticket, because it was too late. It was very expensive. Finally he made the ticket on Wednesday Nov 17, 1999 to be mailed to me. My trip was on Thursday Nov. 18, 1999. He sent it by Federal Express. I got the ticket on the same day of my departure. I had to call the Airline and find out if everything was fine.

The same day we were also invited by the Sheriff Department for their Annual Recognition Day. We attended their function. Later I had to prepare my notes, books, suitcase, and briefcase for this trip from LAX to Dulles Airport. The plane left at midnight and arrived at 8:00 a.m. eastern time zone. Al-Hamdu-Lillah!. I made it. I took a taxi to the Hotel. I tried to relax, and then went to join the Muslims in performing Friday Salat at the Institute. Everything was fine. I asked the host about the functions. They told me you will get it. I went to the main office of the Institute in order to find out about the program. Finally I had a copy, and it was a big surprise to find out the detail information about the program, the list of the speakers, and the abstract of all the speakers. It was well prepared and well organized. I could not believe myself what I was reading and seeing!. Then I started asking myself:

1. Since the organizers have already planned the seminar so well, how come they could not send me a copy of it?! or at least to

send a copy by fax?! After all I requested them to do so but it was in vain!!
2. I asked myself: I am a member of the Board of Trustees of that Institute! How come they invited me the last minute, and I could not know what is going on.
3. I recognized that a good number of speakers have been invited from overseas and from the whole country of USA. Am I the only one who does not know what is going on, or what is the program for!
4. I asked myself: What is my role in attending this celebration and this program? I really don't know!. May be I should not know!! And maybe I should not ask why I was invited.
5. I had to leave Thursday Nov. 18, and come back Sunday Nov. 21, 1999. Is it worth all these days to be spent on something that one should not know what is going on!!
6. I said to myself: May be if I had gone to England or to Detroit and attended other conferences might be better!. But by analyzing the other seminars, I had nothing to offer or to participate in them, except being among the audience sitting and listening to the speakers!. Ma-Sha-Allah!!

Therefore, I realized that I had to spend time, effort, energy, and money in order to get dizzy, jet-lag, headache, and lack of sleep!! I don't know why!! My contribution is to be part of the audience to listen to a series of papers. Some of them were dull. I tried my best to be awake as much as possible. Moreover, I tried to participate in the discussion so that the session will be alive. No more and no less. I had no choice, but to cry from the bottom of my heart! I cried to Allah! Please Ya Allah! Accept this trip, and give me credit for all what I tried to do! Please Ya Allah! Forgive me for my shortcomings. As I final remark: I really appreciated what the hosts had done. I am not criticizing them. We learned a lesson.

XLIV. MONEY ... MONEY ...MONEY

    While travelling from airport to airport, I passed through many stores of many varieties. You name it and you will find stores full with passengers; each and everyone is pre-occupied and busy in selecting the commodity that he/she wants. Even in the international airports where Duty-Free stores are available, one will see a good number of people who go to them to buy whatever is there for the sake of buying, and for the idea that the products are duty-free. There are a good number of Reflections that cross my mind, some of which are the following:

1. Prices at airports are much higher than the prices at the regular stores. Why people have to buy from airport stores?!. This needs an answer.
2. People have already spent money on airline tickets, hotels, foods, resort areas, etc, and still they want to spend money more and more.
3. People work and earn money, but how much they earn I don't know. It seems they earn too much, otherwise they cannot buy all what I see them buying.
4. The presence of the credit cards system has encouraged so many people to buy and buy beyond their needs. They are to pay monthly installments. Indeed they are paying interest much more than paying the cost of the commodity.
5. I don't know why people have to buy more than what they need. Is it a matter of convenience, or a matter of jealousy, or a matter of inferior reaction.
6. It seems people try to buy and they do enjoy buying and carrying those commodities homes. Most of the time, they don't use all what they buy. They have to store them at home somewhere. They are forgotten commodities. If one wants to make a survey, he would find out that many people have already developed a department store, a grocery store and a

drug store in their houses. They don't know what to do with them. They try to forget them as if they do not exist. The expiration dates are over!! Foods, canned foods, juices, cereal, medicine, and old fashioned clothes that might have been destroyed by moth. At that time they find a good excuse to give them to charity! What a deal to give useless and dangerous food items and medicine products to innocent people. People try to feel happy that they are generous to the needy! But, they forgot that Allah will not accept from them unless they spend of the best of what they have. Allah (swt) says in the Qur'an ins Surah Al-Imran the following:

لَن تَنَالُوا۟ ٱلْبِرَّ حَتَّىٰ تُنفِقُوا۟ مِمَّا تُحِبُّونَ ۚ وَمَا تُنفِقُوا۟ مِن شَىْءٍ فَإِنَّ ٱللَّهَ بِهِۦ عَلِيمٌ ۝

By no means shall you attain righteousness unless you give (freely) of that which you love: and whatever you give, Allah knows it well. (3:92)

One has to recognize that buying for the sake of buying without need for that commodity is a sin. Those people are to be blamed in the Day of Judgement, and they are going to be charged and penalized accordingly. In Surah Al-Israa' (Night Travel), Allah (swt) says the following:

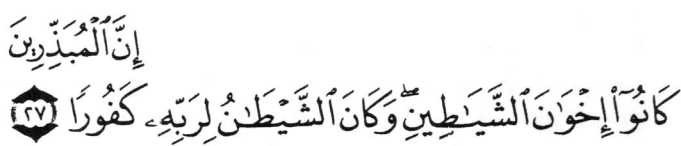

> *Verily spendthrifts are brothers of the Satans. And the Satan is to his Lord (Himself) ungrateful. (17:27)*

At the same time, Allah (swt) has subjugated the whole world for our use and for our benefits. We should benefit from the Blessings of Allah. We should not deny ourselves such benefits. We should use them properly and be grateful to Allah. In Surah Al-Israa' (Night Travel) Allah says the following:

وَلَا تَجْعَلْ يَدَكَ مَغْلُولَةً إِلَىٰ عُنُقِكَ وَلَا تَبْسُطْهَا كُلَّ ٱلْبَسْطِ فَتَقْعُدَ مَلُومًا مَّحْسُورًا ۝ إِنَّ رَبَّكَ يَبْسُطُ ٱلرِّزْقَ لِمَن يَشَآءُ وَيَقْدِرُ إِنَّهُۥ كَانَ بِعِبَادِهِۦ خَبِيرًۢا بَصِيرًا ۝

> *Make not your hand tied (like a niggard's) to your neck, nor stretch it forth to its utmost reach, so that you become blameworthy and destitute. Verily your Lord does provide sustenance in abundance for whom He pleases, and He straiten it for He does know and regard all His servants. (17:29-30)*

People have to recognize that money may not bring happiness, but surely it brings more responsibilities. Each person is going to be asked in the Day of Judgement as to how he earned the money and how he spent it. It is a tough situation. Moreover, a person who earns more money, he will be more worried as to where to save it, how to invest it, and then later how to calculate the zakat. Finally, he is responsible to find the needy, the poor, and other segments of the society to receive his zakat. It should be mentioned here that if people do know that a person is wealthy and rich, they will be jealous of him. They may have what is called `Ain-Hasood or Black eye!! He might be also a target to be robbed or killed by strangers or even by his own family members. However, one should not be too pessimistic about money. Yes! It is a blessing! But it can also be a curse. It is good to have money, and it is good to spend money for the love of Allah, and for the sake of humanity at large. Our beloved prophet had categorized people into four categories, one of whom is the one that Allah has blessed with True Knowledge, and with wealth. He uses his wealth for the love of Allah. Therefore, he is going to be in the highest level of paradise. The Hadith goes as follows:

٢٩٤ - إِنَّمَا الدُّنْيَا لأَرْبَعَةِ نَفَرٍ : عَبْدٌ رَزَقَهُ اللهُ مَالاً وَعِلْماً فَهُوَ يَتَّقِي فِيهِ رَبَّهُ وَيَصِلُ فِيهِ رَحِمَهُ وَيَعْمَلُ للهِ فِيهِ حَقًّا فَهُوَ بِأَفْضَلِ الْمَنَازِلِ ، وَعَبْدٌ رَزَقَهُ اللهُ عِلْماً وَلَمْ يَرْزُقْهُ مَالاً فَهُوَ صَادِقُ النِّيَّةِ يَقُولُ لَوْ أَنَّ لِي مَالاً لَعَمِلْتُ بِعَمَلِ فُلَانٍ فَهُوَ بِنِيَّتِهِ فَأَجْرُهُمَا سَوَاءٌ ، وَعَبْدٌ رَزَقَهُ اللهُ مَالاً وَلَمْ يَرْزُقْهُ عِلْماً يَتَخَبَّطُ فِي مَالِهِ بِغَيْرِ عِلْمٍ وَلاَ يَتَّقِي فِيهِ رَبَّهُ وَلاَ يَصِلُ فِيهِ رَحِمَهُ وَلاَ يَعْمَلُ للهِ فِيهِ حَقًّا فَهُوَ بِأَخْبَثِ الْمَنَازِلِ : وَعَبْدٌ لَمْ يَرْزُقْهُ اللهُ مَالاً وَلاَ عِلْماً فَهُوَ يَقُولُ لَوْ أَنَّ لِي مَالاً لَعَمِلْتُ فِيهِ بِعَمَلِ فُلَانٍ فَوِزْرُهُمَا سَوَاءٌ .

(الترمذي وأحمد)

...And I want to give instruction, so memorize it. He said: 'Indeed life is for four groups of individuals. A person whom Allah bestowed with wealth and knowledge. He fears his Lord in them; he spends on his relatives; he knows the right of Allah on it. He is to be in the best position. A person whom Allah bestowed with knowledge but without money. He is sincere with his intention. He says, if I were to have money, I would have done similar *to that person. He is sincere with his intention. The reward for both is similar. A person whom Allah blessed with money but without knowledge. He spends wrongly his wealth without knowing what he is doing. He does not fear Allah with it. He does not take care of his relatives; and he does not know the right of Allah on it. He is in the lowest position. A person who has not blessed with wealth and knowledge. He says if I were to have money, I would have done similar to that fellow. He is with his intention. Their penalties are the same. [Narrated by Abu Kabsha Umar Ibn Saad Al-Anmari (raa), and reported by Tarmazi.]*

It is a must that one should earn money from Halal sources, and spend them in Halal avenues. It is an excellent idea that one thinks of the following institutions: Hospitals, clinics, schools, Masajid, orphanages, cemeteries and shelters for the homeless, for battered women and for abused children. Many more projects can be supported by promoting Islamic Books and literature for the sake of Islamic Da'wah to Muslims and non-Muslims. Finally, let me remind myself and the rest of the people that Money is a Blessing and a Curse. People should look for peace and happiness rather than anguish or trouble. I pray to Allah to keep me Miskeen as the Prophet used to say:

O Allah: Let me live Miskeen, let me die Miskeen, and let me be summoned in the Day of Judgement with those who are Miskeen. Ameen

PS. Half of this article was written on Nov 14, 1999 while coming from San Francisco to Ontario. The rest of the article was completed on Nov 21, 1999 while coming from Dulles, Washington Airport to LAX, California.

XLIV. RUSH ... RUSH ...RUSH
WAIT... WAIT ... WAIT

Flying by planes is the easiest but it is the most difficult way of travelling. One may get headache, jet lag, dizziness, lack of sleeping, and delays due to weather or otherwise. There are more scary problems too! Whenever any plane crashes, and all the passengers with the crew members die in the ocean like Egypt Air 990, one will get scared more and more by trying to convince himself not to fly anymore. Da'wah necessitates travelling and flying for the love of Allah all the time till we meet Allah. Therefore, I get more spiritual support to continue travelling.

I was delayed for 1-2 hours at San Francisco Airport. While sitting and waiting I see people rushing... running...and pushing one another to reach their destinations. It is too difficult to sit watching people Rush... Rush.... Rush! I get dizzy! I had to sit somewhere there is less traffic and less crowd. I go to a different area, but I see it crowded with people waiting for their plane like myself. I wish there is a corner somewhere that I can sit down to reflect about this life. While waiting at San Francisco Airport at lunch hour without lunch on Sunday Nov. 14, 1999 I started jotting down these reflections. People are really rushing to reach on time to their destinations! But is it not true that we rush and rush to reach the end of our life on this planet earth?! Is it not true that every second of our life is counted as a loss from our life, and that we are closer and closer to our graves?! Rush... Rush... Rush... Dizzy... Dizzy... Dizzy. Right and left people go in front of me! Forward and backward going on and on. Is it not true in the Day of Judgement people are going to be over crowded, and each and everyone is rushing and rushing to his/her destination. They go like crowded butterflies going east and west, north and south; up and down!! Allah (swt) says in Surah Al-Qari`ah (The Day of Clamour) the following:

Rush ... Rush ...Rush; Wait... Wait ... Wait

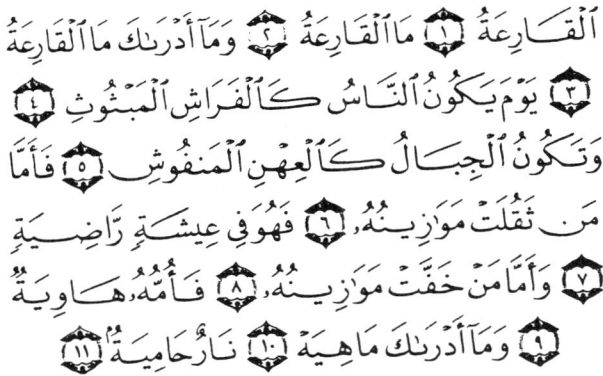

The (Day) of Clamour; what is the (Day) of Clamour? And what will explain to you what is the (Day) of Clamour is? (It is) a Day whereon people will be like moths scattered about, and the mountains will be like carded wool. Then he whose balance (of good deeds) will be (found) heavy, will be in a life of good pleasure and satisfaction. But he whose balance (of good deeds) will be (found) light,- will have his home in a (bottomless) Pit. And what will explain to you what this is? (It is) a Fire blazing fiercely! **(101: 1-11)**

I say to myself that people should take it easy even in walking, otherwise more confusion will take place. Walking slowly means that a person has planned his programs properly. Others are like those who are shocked, disturbed, baffled as to what they are supposed to do. Once I saw a big sign from a freeway on a cemetery saying: Don't Rush! We can wait for you at anytime!.. Therefore, they meant don't rush and don't drive fast otherwise you will have a car accident, and you will die soon. Take it easy, we can wait for you!. It is really a piece of wisdom to all of us. Although I get dizzy and headache when I had to sit and wait, but in the Day of Assembly one has to realize that everyone is going to be dizzy, scared, horrified, and baffled as to what is going on. The Day of Judgement is so scared that even nursing mothers will dump their infants; that expecting mothers will have miscarriages, and that all are going to be in a state of drunkenness, but none is drunk. The Qur'an explains such situation in Surah Al-Hajj (The Pilgrimage) as follows:

$$
\begin{array}{c}
\text{يَٰٓأَيُّهَا ٱلنَّاسُ ٱتَّقُوا۟ رَبَّكُمْ ۚ إِنَّ زَلْزَلَةَ ٱلسَّاعَةِ شَىْءٌ عَظِيمٌ ۝ يَوْمَ تَرَوْنَهَا تَذْهَلُ كُلُّ مُرْضِعَةٍ عَمَّآ أَرْضَعَتْ وَتَضَعُ كُلُّ ذَاتِ حَمْلٍ حَمْلَهَا وَتَرَى ٱلنَّاسَ سُكَٰرَىٰ وَمَا هُم بِسُكَٰرَىٰ وَلَٰكِنَّ عَذَابَ ٱللَّهِ شَدِيدٌ ۝}
\end{array}
$$

O Mankind ! Fear your Lord! For the convulsion of the Hour (of Judgement) will be a thing terrible! The Day you shall see it, every mother giving suck shall forget her suckling-babe, and every pregnant female shall drop her load (unformed): You shall see mankind as in a drunken riot, yet not drunk: but dreadful will be the Chastisement of Allah. (22:1-2)

It should be noted here that while I was in the plane today, everything in my mind was Blank... Blank... Blank. It was very difficult for me to write anything. I was totally absent minded. For that reason I could not write all what I wanted to do. It was a long trip of (5) hours between Toronto and San Francisco Airport. Here in one hour waiting, some hints started coming to my brain. As a result, I started writing this article. The reader is requested to read the other article: Blank... Blank...Blank.. before reading this article, to find out the difference in the thinking capacity of the Brain!!! Finally! I wish to quote Qur'an from Surah Al-Furqan (The Criterion) where Allah (swt) praised those faithful believers who walk slowly with decency and respect. The Qur'an states the following:

And the servants of (Allah) Most Gracious are those who walk on the earth in humility, and when the ignorant address them, they say "Peace!". (25:63)

Also I was able to reflect and remember another Ayah in Surah Luqman whereby he was advising his son by saying:

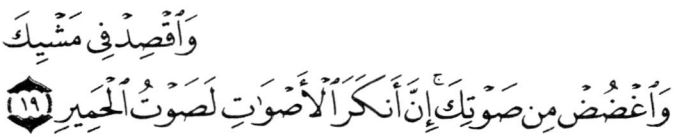

And be moderate in your pace, and lower your voice; for the harshest of sounds without doubt is the braying of the ass. (31:19)

I am very thankful and grateful to Allah for giving us the wisdom and the knowledge with peace of mind. While others are rushing and rushing to their destinations and to the end of their life, others are waiting and waiting till their turns come. May Allah forgive us for our shortcomings, and to reward us for whatever good we do. Ameen

XLVI. WE DID NOT COME TO LISTEN TO YOU

The Flying Falcon is not supposed to fly all the time. He has to walk on his feet, and also he has to drive his car to reach his destinations. Once I was invited by good friends to visit their house for a spiritual night during the month of Rabie' Al-Awwal 1420, or July 1999. They wanted me to give a talk, and at the same time to act as an M.C. for the occasion.

I went with my family to the house of our friends. They had a good dinner, with a good number of friends who were there. The Host family asked me to lead Salatul Ishaa', and I did, Al-Hamdu Lillah. The host brought all the guests to the family room and the guest room. Men by themselves and women by themselves. The host asked me in public to assume my responsibility as an M.C. Their son was to recite from Qur'an. I stood up and held the microphone in my hand. I wanted to speak, but one friend told me: please I want to say something to you before you start the session. I thought it was an emergency that somebody was sick, and that he wanted me to make Du`a' Shifaa' (Healing); or someone died, and he wanted me to make Du`a' Maghfirah (Forgiveness). I apologized to the audience, and I went with him to the other room to see what he wanted from me.

He said to me: You know I am a good friend of you! I said yes of course! He said: I can tell you on your face what others could not tell you. I said: I'll be happy to listen to you. He said: These people asked me to tell you the following: We Did Not Come Here To Hear From You. They don't want you to speak on any subject. We came here for a spiritual occasion, and not to listen to speeches or talks!. They did not come here to listen to you! It was a shock to me. He was not the host, and none of the guests has the authority over the host in his own house. I was surprised, how friends can dictate on the host what should be in the program. I did not believe that such educated people who are professionals can dictate behind the host, who should speak or not. They did not have the courtesy to tell the host in advance what they want, or what they expect.

As far as the friend who informed me about the wish of the audience is concerned, I was also surprised that he told me directly face to face the wish of the audience. He could have told the host the wish of the audience privately without embarrassing anyone. The other surprise: He did not have to wait until I got-up and held the microphone in my hand. He did not have even the right to embarrass himself or myself in this fashion and in this way.

I came back and sat with the audience as a matter of courtesy. The host asked me to assume my responsibility. I said to him that the audience are not interested to see me standing with the microphone in my hand. They don't want me to speak at all!. He was shocked! He asked me: who told you that!. I said someone. Therefore, I did not come here to make confusion or trouble to anyone. I came here because you were kind to invite us to your house. The host insisted that I should assume his request. I stood up and said to the audience: I did not come here tonight to speak, and it seems you came here for something else. I thanked the host and the audience, and I sat down. While sitting, we were told that there is a woman (a melodic chanter and religious singer) is in a hurry. She wants to present her program. She started singing (religious songs!) without the permission of the host!. It seems someone from behind the scene forced her on the host. The guests were listening to her with amusement!, One can see on men's faces how much they were happy, to the extent that some were chanting with her, and others were saying certain exclamation marks of approval about what she was singing!.

Then the host assumed the responsibility and he asked his son to recite from Qur'an. Later a good number of melodic singers chanted religious songs in a very distorted pronunciation without rules and regulations of Makhaarij or Tarteel and Tajweed. I was surprised that the audience looked as if they were in a state of drunkenness, and nodding their heads. Their eyes were closed, while their mouth were repeating with the singers. Their heads were nodding, and some used to cry or to shout: Allah!... Allah!... again and again! Seeing what we saw, we had to request the host to leave. They wanted us to stay longer, but we could not. We left about 11:00 P.M. It was already late, but we were told later, that people stayed till Fajr time!. I was also told that the youth who attended the program with their parents could not understand anything of what was going on. The songs were in a foreign language, and in singing voice. I was told later that it was not the audience, but the friend himself along with one or two who did not want me to speak!. I learned a series of lessons:

1. Not every friend is a true friend. One has to make sure who is the true Friend among all the friends that you know.
2. Wherever I go, I should expect something wrong is to take place, or someone is going to blame me for something I did not say or did not do.
3. Education does not mean degrees, or profession or money! All those who were attending were highly educated. But Education means: how to behave in a society with other people.
4. Some people think that they own a company, and that he has employees, he can dictate upon people outside his company. They should understand that none is the Boss. The True Boss is Allah alone. Even Allah does not scare us or dictate on us. He invites us in a very beautiful way. He encourages us to look around and reflect. He encourages us to use wisdom while

dealing with others. It seems that those people forgot what the Qur'an has taught us. In Surah Fussilat (Explained in Detail) Allah (swt) says:

$$\text{وَمَنْ أَحْسَنُ قَوْلًا مِّمَّن دَعَآ إِلَى ٱللَّهِ وَعَمِلَ صَٰلِحًا وَقَالَ إِنَّنِى مِنَ ٱلْمُسْلِمِينَ ۝ وَلَا تَسْتَوِى ٱلْحَسَنَةُ وَلَا ٱلسَّيِّئَةُ ٱدْفَعْ بِٱلَّتِى هِىَ أَحْسَنُ فَإِذَا ٱلَّذِى بَيْنَكَ وَبَيْنَهُۥ عَدَٰوَةٌ كَأَنَّهُۥ وَلِىٌّ حَمِيمٌ ۝ وَمَا يُلَقَّىٰهَآ إِلَّا ٱلَّذِينَ صَبَرُوا۟ وَمَا يُلَقَّىٰهَآ إِلَّا ذُو حَظٍّ عَظِيمٍ ۝}$$

Who is better in speech than one who calls (men) to Allah, works righteousness, and says, "I am of those who bow in Islam"? Nor can goodness and evil be equal. Repel (Evil) with what is better: then will he between whom and your was hatred become as it were your friend and intimate! And no one will be granted such goodness except those who exercise patience and self-restraints,-none but persons of the greatest good fortune. (41: 33-35)

One can learn so many lessons in life, but one should get wiser and wiser!. I pray to Allah to accept from us what we do for His Love, and to forgive us for our shortcomings. Ameen

PS: This article was written on Nov. 13-14, 1999 on one of my trips from California to Toronto, and was finished in the plane while coming back from Toronto to California.

XLVII. HAPPINESS THROUGH MISERIES

I. Introduction.

I started writing this article while I was in plane from Ontario, California to Chicago on my way to Toronto, Canada. Today is Saturday April 22, 2000. For a long time I was planning to write such an article as a lesson to all the new generations who wish to have good jobs in life. It is also a good lesson for those who want to be a Daiyah working for the love of Allah among Muslims and non-Muslims. I had to continue writing this article for a number of days. Sometimes I get dizzy in plane, therefore I had to stop writing. I try to read Qur'an, offer certain Salat, make Du`a', and finally take a nap. I could not find a better title than this. In this article I will try to summarize some of my miseries that I had in my life, but the results of such miseries finally turned to be good for me. Most of these occasions happened to me in North America since 1962. Some of these situations happened to me from Muslims, others took place with non-Muslims. I am being reminded by the Hadith of the Prophet when he said: Abu Yahia Suhaib Ibn Sinan narrated that the Messenger of Allah said:

٣٩ - وَعَنْ أَبِي يَحْيَى صُهَيْبِ بْنِ سِنَانٍ رضي الله عنه قال : قال رسول الله صلى الله عليه وسلم : «عَجَباً لِأَمْرِ الْمُؤْمِنِ إِنَّ أَمْرَهُ كُلَّهُ لَهُ خَيْرٌ، وَلَيْسَ ذَلِكَ لِأَحَدٍ إِلاَّ لِلْمُؤْمِنِ : إِنْ أَصَابَتْهُ سَرَّاءُ شَكَرَ فَكَانَ خَيْراً لَهُ ، وَإِنْ أَصَابَتْهُ ضَرَّاءُ صَبَرَ فَكَانَ خَيْراً لَهُ » رواه مسلم .

> *The situation of a believer is strange, but everything is good for him, no other than him is to have good credits; If and when he is having easy life, he will be grateful to Allah and therefore, it is good for him; however, when he is strucked with calamity, he is patient. It is good for him as well. (Reported by Muslim)*

I am also being reminded what Allah (swt) had said in Qur'an. In Surah Al-`Ankaboot (The Spider) Allah says the following:

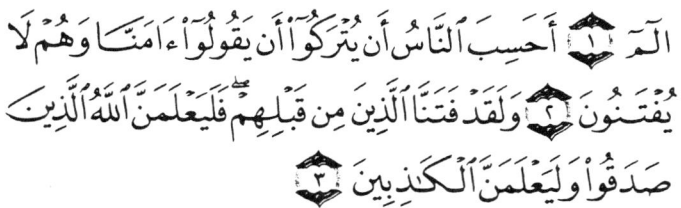

A.L.M. Do men think that they will be left alone on saying, "We believe", and that they will not be tested? We did test those before them, and Allah will certainly know those who are true from those who are false. (29:1-3)

Therefore, I will try to select very few of them, otherwise it will be too big to include them in one article.

II. Dealing with Muslims

It seems it is very difficult to deal and/or to work with Muslims. No matter what one does, the majority of the Muslims are ungrateful. They try to use you, abuse you again and again, and finally they dump you in trash. They request you to start a project. You take it seriously. You do your best to make it successful. You work hard days and nights to make it functional. Very few are those who will help you. They sit and watch! They will criticize you. After the project is functional and successful, they try their best to kick you out so that they claim that the project is successful because of them, but not you. They spread rumors locally, nationally and internationally so as to kick you out of the project with defame, insult and with false accusation. You try to give them the project. But they don't know how to handle it. They are after titles, positions, fame, reputation and even money. People were looking for the project as a success, but unfortunately most of those projects became defunct, and useless. I still recall the early days of our presence in USA 1962. Since then up until now at the year 2000, the situations have not changed very much. I wish I can write the detail information about each project or institution that Allah (swt) has blessed us with in North America.

III. Dealing with non-Muslims

What one says about Muslims, is also true about non-Muslims. The latter groups smile to you to let you feel that they are your good friends. However, they try to stab you from the back without knowing or even thinking that the so-called friend has done it for you. They find so-called legitimate excuses so that a person cannot charge them in court. After they stab you, they come to you and show their sympathy, while they are happy to dump you out in the street. They don't even write a good recommendation for you so that you will be able to find another job somewhere else. Some of the non-Muslims are blunt and do not come to tell you what is in their minds. Those are the ones who were living in the fifties and sixties. The following is a partial list of situations that I had to go through in my life in USA since 1962 till the year 2000.

1. Elgin State Hospital, Illinois

During the war between Egypt and Israel, The Chairman of the Department was a Jew. He found out that I was an Arab from Lebanon. He claimed there is no grant for my research. He fired me from my job. I recognized from other employees that there was plenty of money, but he was biased and prejudiced.

2. Loyola Medical School, Maywood, Illinois

In 1968, I had a job at Loyola Medical School. In that year I got married. I invited verbally the colleagues in the Department. They were very excited. When the Chairman received the invitations whereby there was the name of Muslim and Islam, he fired me immediately. None came to the wedding.

3. Employment Agency

I went to an employment agency in Chicago in 1968. His specially was to help academicians to find jobs at different educational institutions. When I entered the office, he looked at me, and said: Are you an Indian?! I said no! He said: But you are colored! I said I am not colored!. He said: Yes you are! We don't help colored people! They are trouble-makers. Get out of our office. I had no choice. I had to leave!.

4. A private College

I applied to different Academic institutions. I received a letter from a college. It happened that the college was a Christian Institution. I had no problem teaching Biological Sciences anywhere. To my surprise: they wanted me to be a Christian following their own denomination. They wanted me to go with them daily to their own church, and pray with them early morning before going to the classes.

5. National College of Chiropractic (NCC)

I was appointed as a Professor at NCC in the year 1970. I was promoted to be full professor and chairman of

Department of Chemistry and Nutrition. I received a certificate of Award from Washington, D.C. as an outstanding Professor. All these because I worked hard. After the college got a Jew administrator, he tried to destroy everyone in the college. We were three Muslim professors. All three of us had to leave in one way or the other.

IV. Final Remarks

One has to recognize that life on this planet earth is a life of tests. No one is exempted from trials and turmoil. The winners are those who accept such challenges and try to overcome them. During the process of trials a person gets good experience how to deal with people. He will have better immunity and better health. He will be wiser than before. He learns from the bad experiences that he had to go through, in order to build a better future.

By changing places and jobs one will recognize that this life is a life of a traveler. He has to go from place to place. He should realize that finally he is to leave this life on this planet earth and go back to Allah. Allah's Mercy makes people not to stick their necks to any place or to any type of a job. They should move from place to place, and from one city to another city.

I for one I enjoyed losing jobs and losing properties, titles and income. I realize how life is insignificant. One should plan for the hereafter much more than this life.

PS: This article was finished on Monday July 3, 2000.

ولله الحمد　　　　　　　　الله اكبر

PRAISE BE TO GOD　　　　　　　　ALLAHU AKBAR

XLVIII. A PLANE OF MY OWN

I. Introduction

I travel quite often. It is not my decision, but the decision of Allah. Whatever Allah wants me to do, I will be very happy indeed. Many times I am being asked to go to 2-3 places at the same time. It is impossible for me to jump from one state to another in the same day so as to assume certain responsibilities. Moreover, if I want to go to a particular group, one has to transfer from one airport to another in order to arrive there on time. Sometimes due to weather or mechanical problems the plane is late and many of us may lose our commitments. Yes, there are many airlines, and more facilities are at our disposal. Most of the time one cannot please more than one group in one trip. One will be extremely lucky if he can do two functions in one day in two cities. Once I was lucky in 1997. I was visiting South Africa, and I was able to travel to three (3) different cities by car, and I was able to give six (6) lectures in only one day! That was a unique incident in my life. The number of Muslims has increased tremendously in every corner of the world. In USA in the year 2000, their number has reached (10) ten millions. Their needs have also increased tremendously. It is impossible to please every group.

On Saturday, May 20, 2000 I was able to go from Ontario Airport in California to Hartford, Connecticut through Chicago Airport. I had to leave 5:00 a.m. to reach my destination 5:00 p.m. I was invited by two other groups at the same time. They wanted me on Sunday. One of them is in West Virginia, while the other is in Montreal, Canada. Each of them was insisting that they need me desperately to raise money for their schools. They recommended me to jump from one area to the other on Sunday. I said "I wish I could do it."

II. My wish

My family's name is Sakr (saqr). It means a flying falcon or eagle. I usually say I wish I could fly by myself so that I will be able to help as many groups as possible. This wish is next to impossible. I don't know if in the future scientists will develop special wings for human beings to fly by themselves or not. The other practical wish is to have personal plane for myself. Either that I act as a pilot, and I can fly to any place I want to, or I should have also a pilot. The last choice is better. However, one has to have a jet plane, and more than one pilot. One has to have a minimum of 2-3 private planes. In case one is in trouble, he will shift to the other without delay. Moreover, one has to have a minimum of three (3) pilots to take care of the series of trips that one has to attend to. Everything in this world costs money; and to make Da'wah costs more money as well.

I could not fulfill the requests of the other two communities. Coming back to my community, I had to leave at 5:00 a.m. on Sunday, May 21, 2000 from the hotel in Hartford, CT. I had to take two planes: one to San Francisco and the other to Ontario Airport. It took me 8 hours flying. Then I had to drive my car to our community center. I had arrived late as usual, but I could not help it. However, I wish I had a private plane and a pilot so that I would be able to make better Da'wah. A wish is a wish! Action is very important. All what I can do is to pray to Allah to help me achieve better results for His love. I wish I would lived most of my life up in the air, so that I will be able to go from one place to another in a short period of time. We wish, we pray, and we leave it up to Allah to do with us whatever He pleases. We pray to Allah to help us achieve our aims, hopes, visions, and aspirations for His pleasure. Ameen.

XLIX.　BLANK... BLANK... BLANK

On my way back from Toronto, Canada to San Francisco, California, the flight time was about 5 ½ hours. It was a long trip. I was tired so much so that I wanted to sleep. That was November 13, 1999. The day before, I flew from Ontario airport in California to Toronto, Canada through Denver airport. It took almost the entire day. I tried to help the local Islamic Center in Toronto to raise money for the extension of their Masjid. We finished midnight. To sleep at that time and to wake-up at 5:00 AM was not easy. So I tried to sleep in the plane, but I could not. I read Qur'an, I prayed Salatul Duha, and made many Du`a'. Still I am tired and exhausted. I tried my best to write as usual, but it was a difficult.

I have many topics on my mind, but anytime I try to write about any of them, I found out that my mind is Blank. I tried to scratch my mind, and that I should write something about my experiences in my travelling. But it was in vain. My mind was closed and all ideas were out of reach. Therefore my mind was Blank. I was unable to write anything. I don't know why. The only thing I was able to think of is Allah... Death....plane crash...Zikr, Tassbeeh... and Tilawatul Qur'an. Other than that, my mind was Blank. I could not think of any material to write about. Therefore, I gave myself a false excuse!. I could not write , and hence I had no choice but to agree that my mind is Blank... Blank... Blank... Hence I went to sleep, but in vain. I had no choice, but to agree that my mind is not functioning. It was a rare occasion in my life. I wanted to think, but I could not, because my mind was Blank, and no information was released so that I will be able to write the things I was planning to do.

My mind was Blank.. my eyes were closed. I tried at least to open my eyes, but in vain. The plane was full, and my seat was a window seat. I can't move or stretch out. My body was aching, my muscles were in pain and the seats were small, and very close to each other. The watch was moving slowly; every time I tried to look at it, I found out that as if it is lazy and did not move enough. Nothing could wake me up even when I drank coffee. I prayed to Allah not to scare me!. Not to have air turbulence! Not even to have plane crash!. I do know that Allah is the Most Merciful. I had to learn a lesson that we are human beings. We have our strength and weaknesses. None of us is a super hero. I was grateful to Allah (swt) that my Central Nervous System (CNS) was blank temporary. I do know that a person gets old, and he may lose his memory due to old age or other diseases. I remembered an Ayah in the Qur'an in Surah Al-Room (The Romans) whereby Allah (swt) says:

اللَّهُ الَّذِى خَلَقَكُم مِّن ضَعْفٍ ثُمَّ جَعَلَ مِنۢ بَعْدِ ضَعْفٍ قُوَّةً ثُمَّ جَعَلَ مِنۢ بَعْدِ قُوَّةٍ ضَعْفًا وَشَيْبَةً يَخْلُقُ مَا يَشَآءُ وَهُوَ ٱلْعَلِيمُ ٱلْقَدِيرُ

It is Allah Who created you in a state of (helpless) weakness, then gave (you) strength, gave (you) weakness, then after strength, gave (you) weakness and a hoary head: He creates whatever He wills, and it is He Who has all knowledge and power. (30:54)

I am grateful to Allah that my mind was blank on a temporary basis. I pray to Allah not to take away my brain, my knowledge, my wisdom, my tongue, my eyes, or my hearing from me; otherwise, I will be a liability on all. To have Blank mind in the plane for a short period of time is a blessing form Allah, so that I will not exhaust myself and my Central Nervous System (CNS). To travel that long distance, and to come back to our local community with all their needs is too much! Therefore, it is good to have temporary Blank... Blank.... Blank... of mind, eyes, ears, tongue, and others. We pray to Allah (swt) to bless us, to reward us, and to forgive us for our shortcomings. Ameen.

L. ISLAMIC VS. PUBLIC SCHOOLS

I. Introduction

I was invited by the Long Island Muslim Society in New York to attend and participate in a conference. The theme was Muslims in America : Issues and Challenges. It was the Fourth Annual Seminar, and it was held on Sunday October 8, 2000. It took place from 9:00 A.M.-6:00 P.M. I had to leave my home on Saturday October 7, 2000 at 5:00 A.M. and went to Ontario Airport, CA. I had to pray Fajr Salat in the car after arriving at the Airport. My wife dropped me and she went home. I went with TWA Airlines through St. Louis Airport, Missouri. Then took another plane to La Guardia Airport, New York. I arrived at 5:00 P.M. Brother Muhammad Saleh from the local community picked me from the airport, and took me to Marriott Hotel in their neighborhood. Later at 7:00 P.M. Dr. Muhammad Hussain, Chairman of the Seminar took me with the other guest speaker from the hotel to the Islamic Center where we are able to meet with the leaders of that community along with their families. We had dinner and social session. Then we prayed Isha salat and it was Dr. Muzaffar Partomah who led the Salat.

I was asked few weeks ago to prepare two lectures: (1) Islamic vs Public Schools for better character building (2) Living by Islam in Present Day America. I prepared a synopsis for each to be distributed to the audience. After arriving I was told that the topic for schools have been changed to: The Role of Islamic Education in Character Building. I did not mind what has been decided. Therefore I prepared an outline for that session. Al-Hamdu Lillah, I was able with the help of Allah to present that topic. However, since I already wrote the synopsis about the school, I thought it will be a good idea to present here what has been written. It maybe of some benefits to the readers. Therefore, the following is the synopsis about:

II. Islamic vs. Public Schools

Islamic schools are as important as Masajid if not more. In schools there will be places for worship. Children will be able to build their characters and behaviors under an Islamic atmosphere. They can practice the teachings of Islam. They will learn Qur'an, Hadith, Sirah, and Islamic civilization properly. They will behave properly and they will be safe from drugs, mixing, alcohol, and pornography. They will dress with modesty and they will learn and practice the Halal individually and collectively. They will learn and enjoy the feasts and festivities of Islam far better than being in non-Muslim schools. All what is needed would be to have better physical facilities such as classrooms, gym, courtyard, science labs, library, computer labs and so on. They need to be accredited, and the teachers need to be certified. There should be a system of employment with fairness and justice to all the teachers and other staff members.

The local communities should support the Islamic schools even if they don't have children, or even if their children are already grown up. The rich people have to help the poor families so that they will receive scholarships, and therefore, they will be able to send their children to Muslim schools. The local communities have to develop a Waqf (Trust) through which the schools will have enough money to support their existence. The local communities have to know how to get financial help from the local government by having charter school systems, or student vouchers. They should know how to get financial support from local companies by receiving either cash money or in kind such as computers and etc. Many American non-Muslim families will be happy to send their children to Muslim schools because of the moral values that are being taught there. Through the Islamic schools, Muslims should produce leaders. Our children of today are the future leaders of America and the world. Therefore we should focus our attention on how to produce such leaders. Our ancestors were the leaders of the world. Therefore, why not our children will be the future leaders of the world. In so doing we will be able to bring peace and harmony in every corner of the world. We pray to Allah to guide us all to the Sirat Al-Mustaqeem. Ameen.

III. Final Remarks

I had to come back on Sunday October 8, 2000 at 8:20 P.M. from JFK Airport to LAX airport with a non-stop flight. We had to reach at 11:30 P.M. Pacific Time or 2:30 A.M. New York time. A friend of ours is to pick me up and take me home, Al-Hamdu Lillah. He was late, and we arrived home safe at 1:00 A.M. Monday. The wisdom behind all this article is that a Da`iyah should not feel bad if anything had changed. He should be prepared for any situation. He should be courteous to the host group and work within the situation accordingly. He should recognize that Allah does test us in different ways, but He gives us moral support as long as we do things for His love and pleasure. One would ask: Is it worth that I had to spend two complete days for the sake of a small seminar for a small community. The answer is yes indeed. One should go wherever it may be for the love of Allah. It is worth going if only one person is to benefit from the Da`iyah. By the way, I gave two lectures and a session of questions/answers with the other two speakers. Of course it was worth going. The only negative feeling in my heart was that I had to leave my community on Sunday, October 8, 2000. But Allah knows best. We pray to Allah to accept from us. Ameen

PS. This article was written while I was in the plane on my way back from JFK to LAX airport on Sunday October 8, 2000.

LI. LIVING BY ISLAM
Issues And Challenges

I. Introduction

This is the second topic that was assigned to me to be delivered at the seminar in Long Island, New York. It was on Sunday October 8, 2000. In the previous article, I explained something about my trip from California to New York. It was not easy any more that a person like me and at this age to continue to travel frequently long distance for a short period of time without relaxing. One gets dizzy with lack of sleep, jet lag, headache, stomach trouble and other biological problems. But faith in Allah gives a person strength to continue to travel for serving the Muslim communities in different places on this planet earth. The credit and rewards from Allah are according to the degree of sacrificing our time, efforts, energies, knowledge, money, and our own selves for the love of Allah (swt). Moreover, one has to recognize that there is no Retirement or Rest for a believer, till he/she meets Allah. Since I wrote the synopsis about this subject, I felt it would be a good idea to include this article in this book. We pray to Allah to accept our humble efforts, and to reward all the brothers and sisters who are involved in such activity.

II. Synopsis: Living by Islam

Immigrant Muslims to America should be grateful to Allah that He inspired them to migrate to this part of the world. There is a wisdom and a reason behind that. It is only Allah Who knows that. However, we should recognize that Allah selected us to deliver His Message all over the world. There are about 80 million Americans who are agnostic. They are looking for a better religion than their own. Allah brought us as a Mercy for them, and as a challenge for us. If we practice the teachings of Islam, and if we deliver that Message to the Americans, they will accept Islam. Muslims will get the credit from Allah. Muslims of America have to integrate themselves into one Muslim community. They have to dissolve their barriers. They have to absorb one another, irrespective of country of origin, school of thought, and language. They should recognize that their identity is: Muslims first, last and forever. They are all together under the umbrella of Islam (Islamistan). We have too many issues that face us to overcome here in America. Some of these are the following:

1. We have to build more institutions such as: clinics, hospitals, schools, colleges, universities, Masajid, orphanages, senior citizens homes, cemeteries, farmlands, radio and TV stations, mass media, La Riba Banks and so on.
2. We should establish Islamic Court system with a Mufti, and Muslim judges.
3. We should demand from the American government to appoint a Secretary of Muslim Affairs, as well as to appoint American Muslim Ambassadors to some Muslim Countries.
4. The Muslim world has lost a large number of intellectual scholars. Therefore, they had Brain Drain. We the American Muslims have to reverse the cycle and start doing: Brain Regain. We should make agreement with some Muslim Countries by sending "Peace Corps" groups to help them solve their problems in the field of science, medicine, technology, industry, etc.
5. We are losing some of our children in this society. Some efforts should be made to have special tours to send some of them to visit the Muslims world, especially to make Umrah and Hajj.
6. The Muslim Relief organizations have to work together and they should have a Majlis Shura among themselves to coordinate their services to the Muslim World.

7. The other National organizations should also work together for the benefits of all Muslims and non-Muslims as well.
8. Muslims have to develop a Waqf endowment to help the Islamic institutions to succeed in their efforts.
9. Scholarships should be given to Muslim students to pursue their academic achievements in the fields of Islamic studies.
10. Grants should be given to Muslim professors to do their research in the fields of Islamic studies.
11. Da'wah to Muslims and non-Muslims is a Must. We should recruit Muslim Da'iyah to assume such responsibilities.
12. Family values are important. We should encourage our children to marry among themselves as they are Muslims.
13. Counseling is a must for families and for business to solve problems in a friendly and amicable way.
14. The inmates should be rehabilitated, especially after they come out of incarcerations.
15. Islamic Literature and books written by Muslim scholars should be distributed regularly to everyone.
16. Halal foods, and pharmaceutical supplies should be enforced on the industry.
17. Many more challenges are facing the American Muslims. Even they are to establish Muslims villages, and Muslims towns bearing Muslims streets and so on.
18. There should be follow up seminars, workshop on a regular basis.
19. Other organizations should be invited to share with the local society: Some of their vision, hopes, aspirations and dreams.

The most important is <u>Who</u> is going to do all those projects? <u>When</u> are they to be done? <u>Where</u> are we going to start? <u>Why</u> should we take these challenges into consideration? <u>Which</u> of those project is the most important among all? These and other questions should be discussed and answers should be given.

III. Final Remarks

This particular topic is so important to Muslims in America. They should take it seriously and they should find solutions to these challenges. At the same time they should not lose hope at all. Nothing can come all of a sudden. We have to plan strategies and systematic efforts step-by-step in order to reach our aims. While writing this article, an Ayah came to my mind. This Ayah is in Surah Al-Anbiyaa' (The Prophets). It goes as follows:

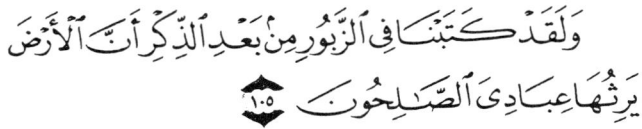

Before this We wrote in the Psalms, after the Message (Given to Moses): "My servants the righteous, shall inherit the earth." (21: 105)

Our ancestors have done a good job in different parts of the world, and we are the bi-products of their efforts and achievements. Therefore, we should take the initiative and plant the seeds of Islam in America for the future generations to benefit from us. May Allah bless us all. Ameen

PS. This article was written while I was in the plane on my way back from JFK to LAX airport on Sunday, October 8, 2000.

And it is He Who has power over all things. [Qur'an, 5:120]

LII.   AT THE AGE OF FORTY

I.   Introduction

The more I travel and fly from place to place, the more inspirations, contemplation, and reflections cross my mind. I also get scared while I am in the airplane. However, the only consolation is that I am traveling to help others helping themselves. I try my best that my intentions should be for the love of Allah (swt). This article has been written when I went from California to Chicago. I had to give Friday Khutbah at O'Hare Airport on Friday, March 12 1999. I was taken to Schaumburg City to meet the local executives in their Masjid, and discuss their activities and services. In the same night we went to Mt. Prospect to raise money for the construction of the local Masjid. At midnight, we went back to Schaumburg City and stayed in a hotel. In the morning the leader of Islamic Food and Nutrition Council of America picked me up, and went to the Headquarters in Chicago. We stayed till four o'clock in the afternoon, discussing their conference and other pertinent issues about Halal Foods. We were to go to Sound Vision Studios to do some recording, but it was not possible. We came to Lombard and stayed at my brother's house. Sunday morning, March 14, 1999, I had to leave at 5:30 a.m. from Chicago through Denver to California. During this trip, the article was written in partial segments at different places, including the plane. I pray to Allah (swt) to accept my Reflections.

II.   General Information

Allah (swt) created us without our knowledge, our opinion or even without our permission. He is the Creator, and it is He Who knows the best for us. He knows well why we have to be created. I am sure there is a purpose for us to be created on this planet earth. Some may die while they are still fetuses in the tummies of their mothers. Others may die immediately after birth; and still others may live long enough. They get married, have children, grandchildren, and great-grandchildren. The beauty of life is when a person lives long enough to see his grandchildren: A life cycle on this planet earth has been given by Allah (swt) to those who reach the age of grandparents.

Some people may grow-up in age, but they are attacked with neurological diseases such as Parkinson's disease or Alzheimer disease. They may lose their concentration, their thinking capacity, their wisdom, their mind, and their knowledge of what is going on around them, etc. This type of malfunction of the central nervous system and mainly the brain, is called in the Qur'an as Arzalil 'Umur. That is the age of senility. The Qur'an talks about senility as well as the whole processes of creation of human beings. In Surah Al-Mu'minoon (The Believers) Allah (swt), talks about the creation of people from soil till they come out as human beings. The Ayat go as follows:

وَلَقَدْ خَلَقْنَا ٱلْإِنسَٰنَ مِن سُلَٰلَةٍ مِّن طِينٍ ۝ ثُمَّ جَعَلْنَٰهُ نُطْفَةً فِى قَرَارٍ مَّكِينٍ ۝ ثُمَّ خَلَقْنَا ٱلنُّطْفَةَ عَلَقَةً فَخَلَقْنَا ٱلْعَلَقَةَ مُضْغَةً فَخَلَقْنَا ٱلْمُضْغَةَ عِظَٰمًا فَكَسَوْنَا ٱلْعِظَٰمَ لَحْمًا ثُمَّ أَنشَأْنَٰهُ خَلْقًا ءَاخَرَ فَتَبَارَكَ ٱللَّهُ أَحْسَنُ ٱلْخَٰلِقِينَ ۝ ثُمَّ إِنَّكُم بَعْدَ ذَٰلِكَ لَمَيِّتُونَ ۝ ثُمَّ إِنَّكُمْ يَوْمَ ٱلْقِيَٰمَةِ تُبْعَثُونَ ۝

Man, We did create from a quintessence (of clay); then We placed him as (a drop of) sperm in a place of rest, firmly fixed; then We made the sperm into a clot of congealed blood; then of that clot We made a (fetus) lump; then We made out of that lump bones and clothed the bones with flesh; then We developed out of it another creature. So blessed be God, the Best to create! After that, at length you will die. Again, on the Day of Judgment, you will be raised up. (23:12-16)

However, in Surah Al-Hajj (The Pilgrimage) Allah (swt), says the following:

يَٰٓأَيُّهَا ٱلنَّاسُ إِن كُنتُمْ فِى رَيْبٍ مِّنَ ٱلْبَعْثِ فَإِنَّا خَلَقْنَٰكُم مِّن تُرَابٍ ثُمَّ مِن نُّطْفَةٍ ثُمَّ مِنْ عَلَقَةٍ ثُمَّ مِن مُّضْغَةٍ مُّخَلَّقَةٍ وَغَيْرِ مُخَلَّقَةٍ لِّنُبَيِّنَ لَكُمْ ۚ وَنُقِرُّ فِى ٱلْأَرْحَامِ مَا نَشَآءُ إِلَىٰٓ أَجَلٍ مُّسَمًّى ثُمَّ نُخْرِجُكُمْ طِفْلًا ثُمَّ لِتَبْلُغُوٓا۟ أَشُدَّكُمْ ۖ وَمِنكُم مَّن يُتَوَفَّىٰ وَمِنكُم مَّن يُرَدُّ إِلَىٰٓ أَرْذَلِ ٱلْعُمُرِ لِكَيْلَا يَعْلَمَ مِنۢ بَعْدِ عِلْمٍ شَيْـًٔا وَتَرَى ٱلْأَرْضَ هَامِدَةً فَإِذَآ أَنزَلْنَا عَلَيْهَا ٱلْمَآءَ ٱهْتَزَّتْ وَرَبَتْ وَأَنۢبَتَتْ مِن كُلِّ زَوْجٍۭ بَهِيجٍ ۝ ذَٰلِكَ بِأَنَّ ٱللَّهَ هُوَ ٱلْحَقُّ وَأَنَّهُۥ يُحْىِ ٱلْمَوْتَىٰ وَأَنَّهُۥ عَلَىٰ كُلِّ شَىْءٍ قَدِيرٌ ۝ وَأَنَّ ٱلسَّاعَةَ ءَاتِيَةٌ لَّا رَيْبَ فِيهَا وَأَنَّ ٱللَّهَ يَبْعَثُ مَن فِى ٱلْقُبُورِ ۝

O mankind! If you have a doubt about the Resurrection, (consider) that We created you out of dust, then out of sperm, then out of a leech-like clot, then out of a morsel of flesh, partly formed and partly *unformed, in order that We may manifest (Our power) to you; and We cause whom We will to rest in the wombs for an appointed term, then do We bring you out as babes, then (foster you) that you may reach your age of full strength; and some of you are called to die, and some are sent back to the feeblest old age, so that they know nothing after having known (much) and (further), you see the earth barren and lifeless, but when We pour down rain on it, it is stirred (to life), it swells, and it puts forth every kind of beautiful growth (in pairs). This is so because God is the Reality: it is He Who gives life to the dead, and it is He Who has power over all things. And verily the Hour will come: there can be no doubt about it, or about (the fact) that God will raise up all who are in the graves. (22:5-7)*

III General Reflections

One has to recognize that the age of senility can come to any person at any age. One should pray to Allah (swt) not to be attacked with this type of sickness. Ameen. However, one has also to recognize that the age of forty is the age of maturity, wisdom, and preparation for departure from this planet earth.

At the age of forty, our Prophet (pbuh) received the Message of Allah (swt) and became Prophet and Messenger. Accordingly, he assumed the responsibility as it should be, and we, Muslims, are the products of his efforts.

Allah (swt) has informed us how He created us, and how He made us to grow to reach the age of forty. He also advised us what to say and what to do after we reach that age. In Surah Al-Ahqaf (Winding Sand Tracts), Allah (swt) says the following:

$$\text{وَوَصَّيْنَا ٱلْإِنسَـٰنَ بِوَٰلِدَيْهِ إِحْسَـٰنًا ۖ حَمَلَتْهُ أُمُّهُۥ كُرْهًا وَوَضَعَتْهُ كُرْهًا ۖ وَحَمْلُهُۥ وَفِصَـٰلُهُۥ ثَلَـٰثُونَ شَهْرًا ۚ حَتَّىٰٓ إِذَا بَلَغَ أَشُدَّهُۥ وَبَلَغَ أَرْبَعِينَ سَنَةً قَالَ رَبِّ أَوْزِعْنِىٓ أَنْ أَشْكُرَ نِعْمَتَكَ ٱلَّتِىٓ أَنْعَمْتَ عَلَىَّ وَعَلَىٰ وَٰلِدَىَّ وَأَنْ أَعْمَلَ صَـٰلِحًا تَرْضَىٰهُ وَأَصْلِحْ لِى فِى ذُرِّيَّتِىٓ ۖ إِنِّى تُبْتُ إِلَيْكَ وَإِنِّى مِنَ ٱلْمُسْلِمِينَ ۝ أُو۟لَـٰٓئِكَ ٱلَّذِينَ نَتَقَبَّلُ عَنْهُمْ أَحْسَنَ مَا عَمِلُوا۟ وَنَتَجَاوَزُ عَن سَيِّـَٔاتِهِمْ فِىٓ أَصْحَـٰبِ ٱلْجَنَّةِ ۖ وَعْدَ ٱلصِّدْقِ ٱلَّذِى كَانُوا۟ يُوعَدُونَ ۝}$$

> *We have enjoined on man kindness to his parents: in pain did his mother bear him, and in pain did she give birth. The carrying of the (child) to his weaning is (a period of) thirty months. At length, when he reaches the age of full strength and attains forty years, He says, "O my Lord! Grant me that I may be grateful for Your favour which You have bestowed upon me, and upon both my parents, and that I may work righteousness such as You may approve; and be gracious to me in my issue. Truly have I turned to You and truly do I bow (to You) in Islam." Such are they from whom We shall accept the best of their deeds and pass by their ill deeds: (they shall be) among the Companions of the Garden: a*

promise   truth, which was made to them (in this life). (46:15-16)

To summarize, the meaning of these two Ayat would be the following:

1. We should make a Du`a' thanking Allah and be grateful to Him for all the Blessings that He has bestowed upon us, and upon our parents.
2. We should keep ourselves busy doing good for us and for others. Such types of deeds should be for the love of Allah (swt).
3. We should make Du`a' requesting Allah (swt) to make our children good, honest and sincere Muslims.
4. We should make Salat Tawbah. We should shun away from any attractions toward this life. We should concentrate and focus our attention toward Allah and Allah alone. The Tawbah (Repentance) should be with honesty and sincerity.
5. We should make sure that our life is for Allah. We obey Him, follow His rules and regulations as being stipulated in the Qur'an, and explained by Prophet Muhammad. By obeying Allah, we proclaim that we are His servants, and we are Muslims.

If we really do these activities, Allah (swt) will accept the best of what we have achieved in life. He also will wipe our mistakes, and will send us to heaven and paradise, Insha-Allah.

It should be stated here that many people at the age of forty, are totally busy in life. They want to improve their life style and acquire more and more from this world. They want better housing, better jobs, more money, better cars, and many more. They start eating more, and become lazy in life. They can't walk or jog, and they can't do physical activities as before. They can't climb the stairways as easy as before. Moreover, their daily Salat becomes too hard on them. They may have to pray while they are sitting on chairs. This type of life style may bring diseases to such individuals beyond their control.

IV. General Recommendations

In order to live a happy life and to receive the Blessings of Allah (swt) the following is a partial list of recommendations:

1. At the age of Forty, our Basal Metabolic Rate (BMR) goes down to a minimum. This means that we should eat less, and exercise more.
2. Exercise could include walking, performing more Salat, less riding cars, using stairways instead of elevators, etc.
3. While we are to eat less, we have to include fresh fruits and vegetables to improve our blood circulation. They help our basal metabolic rate to improve. With the presence of fresh enzymes in those items, the rate of metabolism will be increased. The presence of fibers will improve digestion, the peristaltic movement will be better, and defecation will be easier. The presence of fiber, reduces the amount of cholesterol in the body as well.
4. At the age of Forty, a person should make sure that he is fasting Mondays and Thursday so as to improve his health and be close to Allah. Fasting will purify the body from toxins, and teaches the person how to have self-control, self-restraint, and self-obedient to Allah.
5. A Muslim should train himself to read Qur'an daily. He should read one volume every day. By doing so, he will finish reading the whole Qur'an every lunar month.

6. At the age of Forty, a Muslim has to train himself to perform more Salat Nafilah, Tahajjud and Quiyam Al-Lail. Among the extra Nafilah could be Salat Duha, Salat Tawbah, Salat Haajah, Salat Istikharah, Salat Sunnat Al-Wudoo', Salat Tahiyat Al Masjid, etc.
7. A person at the age of Forty should try to hibernate and make a retreat inside a Masjid. He should make I'tikaf quite often and especially in the last ten days of Ramadan.
8. A Muslim should visit the cemetery quite often so as to take a lesson, and to prepare himself/herself for departure from this world.
9. At the age of Forty, a Muslim should try to visit hospitals, and give comfort to the patients. He makes Du'a' Shifaa' for them as well.
10. A Muslim at that age should try to visit prisons and see the miserable situations of others.
11. A wise Muslim should take the initiative and make more Sadaqaat (charities). There are many orphans, widows, divorced women, refugees, homeless, and jobless people. We should try to help them directly and indirectly.
12. A sincere Muslim should allocate certain times for Da'wah. He should deliver the Message of Islam to all those who are in need of it. He should pray to Allah that at least one person will be guided by Allah through his personal efforts.
13. It is not enough to read and recite Qur'an daily, but he should listen to the recitation of Qur'an as well.
14. A Muslim has to perform Hajj to fulfill his faith and to complete the requirements as a Muslim. He should try his best to reduce his daily expenses, and save as much as possible so that he will be able to perform Hajj.

IV. Final Remarks

Every person should recognize that life on this planet earth is not eternal, but a temporary one. Our houses are not even permanent for us. Our real bedroom is not in our houses, but inside the Grave in the cemetery. We will live there till the Day of Judgment. We should remember that the value of this life comparing it with the hereafter is next to zero. The same thing applies to its duration. Therefore, X over infinity reaches zero. The happiness and the pleasure that we may get here is a zero. The sorrows that we may receive comparing them to life in Hell are zero. Therefore, we should prepare ourselves for the hereafter much more than for this life.

Allah (swt) advised us not to stick ourselves to this life, rather than to prepare ourselves for the better one. We should not allow Satan to overrule us. In Surah Fatir (The Originator of Creation) Allah (swt) says the following:

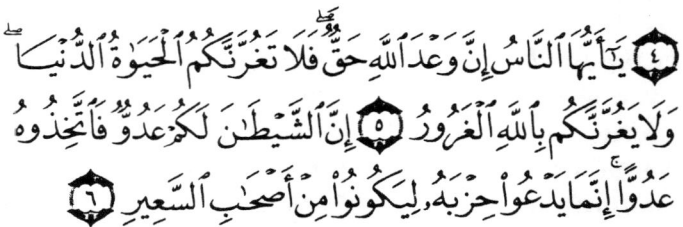

O people! Certainly the promise of God is true. Let not then this present life deceive you, nor let the Chief Deceiver deceive you about God." Verily Satan is an enemy to you: so treat him as an enemy. He only invites his adherents, that they may become companions of the Blazing Fire. (35:5-6)

Finally, let me remind myself and the reader, that we should not attach ourselves with this life and its allurements. The life-after is much better than this one. Therefore, at the age of Forty, every person should invest his time, efforts, energy, money, and wisdom for the life-after. If we do not do that we are the losers on both levels. Let me end this Reflection Paper with Ayah from Qur'an in Surah Yunus. Allah (swt) says the following:

إِنَّمَا مَثَلُ ٱلْحَيَوٰةِ ٱلدُّنْيَا كَمَاءٍ أَنزَلْنَٰهُ مِنَ ٱلسَّمَاءِ فَٱخْتَلَطَ بِهِۦ نَبَاتُ ٱلْأَرْضِ مِمَّا يَأْكُلُ ٱلنَّاسُ وَٱلْأَنْعَٰمُ حَتَّىٰٓ إِذَآ أَخَذَتِ ٱلْأَرْضُ زُخْرُفَهَا وَٱزَّيَّنَتْ وَظَنَّ أَهْلُهَآ أَنَّهُمْ قَٰدِرُونَ عَلَيْهَآ أَتَىٰهَآ أَمْرُنَا لَيْلًا أَوْ نَهَارًا فَجَعَلْنَٰهَا حَصِيدًا كَأَن لَّمْ تَغْنَ بِٱلْأَمْسِ كَذَٰلِكَ نُفَصِّلُ ٱلْءَايَٰتِ لِقَوْمٍ يَتَفَكَّرُونَ ﴿٢٤﴾

The likeness of this life of the present is as the rain which We send down from the skies: by its mingling arises the produce of the earth which provides food for men and animals: (it grows) till the earth is clad with its golden ornaments and is decked out (in beauty): the people to whom it belongs think they have all powers of disposal over it: there reaches it our command by night or by day and We make it like a harvest cleanmown, as if it had flourished only the day before! Thus do We explain the Signs in detail for those who reflect. (10:24)

We pray to Allah to help us to stay Muslims. When we die, we hope we will die as Mu'mins. We pray also that in the Day of Judgment, we will be with the Prophet and all other Prophets as well. Ameen

LIII. RETIREMENT

    This subject crossed my mind when I was coming back from my visit to Austin, Texas. I went to that city on June 12, 1999 from Ontario, California, through Dallas, Texas. We tried to raise money for their Masjid and school an average of $ 160,000.00, Al-Hamdu Lillah. We finished 1:00 a.m. I went to sleep, and woke up at 5:00 A.M. to come back through Dallas, Texas, to Ontario, California. While being in the plane, I asked myself: I am now at the age of Retirement. Why can't I retire and enjoy the rest of my life like many people do!! I had to reflect on this subject while I was still in the plane. I tried to collect my thoughts together and find out the answer.

    Yes! At the age of 66, I should relax and enjoy the rest of my life!. I should no more travel quite often as before! I am no more a young man who wants to explore life, geography, navigation or flying. I should no more get physical fatigue going from one place to another without eating and without sleeping properly. I should no more be worried about Air turbulence and jet-lag. I should no more worry too much about helping others at this age as much as I used to do before! I should isolate myself to continue writing my books that have been pending for a number of years. I should go and live in Madina, the City of the Prophet, and enjoy the rest of my life being close to our beloved Prophet. I should live there, die there, and be buried in Jannatul Baqee'. If I live there, I can pray daily five times in Jama'ah in the Masjid of the Prophet. I can meet many Muslim scholars from every corner of the world. There, I can prepare myself better for my departure from this world to the better one, namely to the hereafter.

Every time I fly, I experience that such a trip is going to be the last. I might end up in having plane crash, and my life is going to be over. But I don't know why I should accept all these trips from place to place, and especially at this age! Is it not enough for me what I was doing all my life?! Is it not time for me to relax, and take life easy?! The more I reflect, and the more I ask myself these and similar questions, the more I feel I should continue to work more and more. There are many inherent reasons why I should continue to work hard till I meet Allah. Among the many answers I recall the following:

1. Our beloved Prophet taught us that there is no rest to a believer till he meets Allah.
2. Another teaching he taught us that indeed the works and actions of the individual are counted by the last of his life. Allah (swt) tells us in Surah Al-Mutaffifeen (Those who deal with fraud), the following:

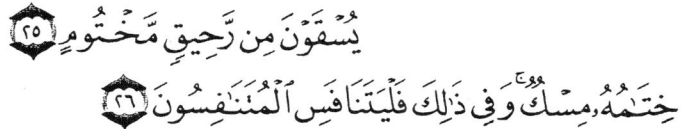

Their thirst will be slaked with pure wine sealed: the seal thereof will be Musk: and for this let those aspire, who have aspirations. (Qur'an 83: 25-26)

3. Our Prophet never retired to rest or to enjoy life. He continued working till he met Allah (swt) . Since he is the best role model to all of us, therefore, we should continue striving days and nights till we meet Allah (swt).
4. The more active life we stay, the more the metabolic rate stays high. This means that we will continue to stay active and dynamic. Therefore, a person will stay healthy and strong.
5. The more active and dynamic life a person follows, the more he feels that he is still young. He will not feel he is old or he is a senior citizen. To feel young is an excellent psychological feeling to that person who continues to be active.

6. To go from place to place, and to help others, a person will feel happy that the whole Muslims of the world are indeed his community and his Ummah. By doing so, one will remember the teachings of our beloved Prophet when he said: Indeed the whole people of the world are the family members who depend on Allah (swt). The most liked to Allah are those who help those people.
7. One more reflection that keeps me to continue travelling and flying is the teachings of Islam that says to us: indeed the credit is according to the level of hardship. The harder the life is, the more the credit, reward, and blessings are from Allah. Finally, I tried to convince myself to continue helping people anywhere in the world, hoping and praying that Allah (swt) will accept what I am doing. I do pray to Allah (swt) to forgive me for my shortcomings, and to reward me for whatever good I am doing. Therefore, I have to improve my intention, and make sure that I am doing all these activities for the love and the pleasure of Allah. I do pray to Allah to make me a good example to others. I do request Allah (swt) that I will continue to live as a practicing Muslim; and when I am going to die, I will die as a faithful believer. I do submit to Allah to guide me to do whatever He pleases. Most of these reflections came to me while I was still flying (in the plane) between Dallas, Texas, to Ontario, California, on Sunday June 13, 1999. It seems most of my reflections come to me when I am isolated peacefully in the plane. I don't talk to anyone. I look through the window to receive inspirations, and I am grateful to Allah Who inspires me to write down these Reflections.

Finally, there is no Retirement for me as long as I live on this planet earth. I did not save any money for retirement as well. The only retirement for me will be in the Hereafter, Insha-Allah. Ameen.

LIV. HAPPY... HAPPY... HAPPY

This article was written very late. Hence, instead of leaving it aside we thought it should be inserted along with the other chapters. But it was late to put it in the right sequential order. Therefore it is included at the end of this book. We pray to Allah (swt) to accept from us all. As a flying falcon, I had to travel regularly from place to place and from one country to the other. My trips are mainly to help others: Friday Khutbah, Lectures, Seminars, Workshops, Conferences, Dialogues with non-Muslims, Family Counseling, Deposits in Courts defending inmates or settle problems between two parties etc... While I am in one area or the other, happy news is brought to my attention. That good and happy news is that a lady or gentleman is interested to become Muslim. I asked the friend who brought this information to me whether this is true or what. He reconfirmed the good news. We announce that good news by telling the audience to stay for few minutes and to observe the declaration of Faith (shahadah) for a new comer to Islam. We wanted them to be witnesses (shuhadaa') for him in the Book of Allah.

The person to declare the Pledge of Allegiance to Allah is brought to the front. Every person is looking at him, with shining eyes and smiling faces. They are waiting to see the Happy news of that person. They are excited to know how he accepted Islam in a non-Muslim society. It is really a big challenge for any non-Muslim to become Muslim in a society whereby the mass media is talking bad about Islam and Muslims. Moreover, Muslims don't have missionaries to go from place to place to preach and to convert people. Islam is against Conversion, Proselytization, Baptization, or even Debate. One gets astonished as to how these well to do Americans are accepting Islam as a faith and as a total way of life.

America is a super power. The Americans were able to land on the moon. America is controlling the policy of many countries by force and ammunition. However, America is unable to give Peace, Tranquility, Serenity and Happiness to its own people. Many Americans are fed up with the economic, religious, political, social and educational systems. They are looking for a better way of life. They read and they do research. They attended different places of worships, but they were not satisfied. In one way or the other, they are finding the True Religion of Allah to all humanity at-large. That Religion is Islam. When a person wants to become a Muslims, we asked him a series of questions such as:

1. **Are you sure you want to become Muslim?** Yes
2. **Has anyone pressured you?** No
3. **Could it be that you want to become a Muslim because you want to marry a Muslim girl?** No, not at all
4. **To become a Muslim, you have to believe in One God (Allah). He is the Creator of the whole universe. He has no son and no partner.** Yes, I do believe that
5. **To become a Muslim, one has to believe in all the Prophets and Messengers of Allah. At the same time, one has to believe that Prophet Muhammad is the Last Prophet and Last Messenger of Allah to all human beings.** Yes indeed I do believe in them all. I also believe that Muhammad is the last Prophet and Messenger.
6. **One has to pray five times a day, as well as to pray Congregational Prayer on Fridays at noon.** Yes, I will do my best to start practicing Salat as of today.
7. **One has to Fast the whole month of Ramadan from dawn to sunset.** Yes, Indeed
8. **One has to give charity (Zakat) 2.5%.** I will do my best.

9. **One has to perform Hajj (Pilgrimage) to Makkah once in a lifetime if means allow.** I pray to Allah to give me that golden opportunity to perform Hajj.
10. **One has to abstain from eating pork or drinking alcohol.** I stopped such habits a long time ago.
11. **One has to live with modesty and moral life privately and publicly.** I do believe in that.

If you are ready then we will give you the shahadah or Declaration of Faith. After giving him the Shahadah in Arabic and English, everyone in the congregation says Allahu Akbar in one loud voice. The new comer to Islam feels shivering: bodily and spiritually. Then everyone comes to him and either shakes his hand or hugs him. They say to him: Happy...Happy...Happy. Allah loves you, and He showed you the Best Way. The young man is so happy that tears of happiness come out of his eyes. That person is a Revertee. He was born Muslim, but his parents and society raised him on different systems. But Allah (swt) brought him back to Islam. That Happy moment was the best moment of his life. We pray for all to come back to Allah, and make a Pledge of Allegiance to Him.

This article was written in the plane between Las Vegas and Ontario Airport after giving Friday Khutbah there. It was written on Friday June 22, 2001 and finished in my office in Walnut, CA on Sunday June 24, 2001. I pray to Allah to accept my humble contribution to the new generations. Ameen.

THERE IS NO DEITY EXCEPT ALLAH

LV. FINAL REMARKS

In the past history of mankind, flying was a dream. Only Prophet Sulaiman was given the power from Allah to fly and to send people by flying on Red Carpets. He was able to bring the Palace of Queen Saba in a twinkling of an eye from Yemen to Jerusalem. During the history of Muslims in Morocco, Abbas Ibn Firnas was the first man who tried to fly by himself with man-made wings. Later, people learned step-by-step how to fly with planes. Allah (swt) tells us in Surah Al-'Alaq (The Clot) that it is He Who is teaching people something that they knew not:

ٱلَّذِى عَلَّمَ بِٱلْقَلَمِ ۞ عَلَّمَ ٱلْإِنسَٰنَ مَا لَمْ يَعْلَمْ ۞

He Who taught the Pen, taught man that which he knew not. (96:4-5)

As far as flying birds are concerned, they constitute a community among themselves similar to us as human beings. In Surah Al-An'am (The cattle), Allah (swt) informs us that animals and birds are indeed communities and nations like us as human beings. The Ayah goes as follows:

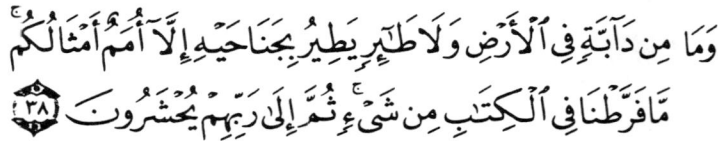

There is not an animal on the earth, Nor a being that flies on its wings, but communities like you. Nothing have We omitted from the Book, and they shall be gathered to their Lord in the end. (6:38)

Then Allah informs us that birds are usually flying in the sky. No one can stop them from this type of a life-style except Allah (swt) Himself. They are meant to fly most of the time. In Surah Al-Nahl (The Bees), Allah (swt) says the following:

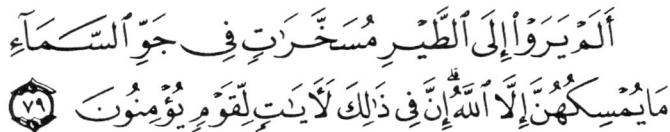

Do they not look at the birds, help poised in the midst of the sky? Nothing holds them up but Allah. Verily in this are signs for those who believe. (16:79)

Moreover, Allah is teaching people to look at the birds how they fly: They spread their wings and fold them up. No one can stop them except Allah. In Surah Al-Mulk (The Domain), Allah Says:

Do they not observe the birds above them, spreading the wings and folding them in? None can uphold them except the Most Gracious: Truly it is He that watches over all things. (67:19)

One may read more in the Qur'an and find out that those birds do glorify Allah (Tassbeeh). They do pray also. Therefore, we should not be surprised. In Surah Al-Noor (The Lights), Allah (swt) says the following:

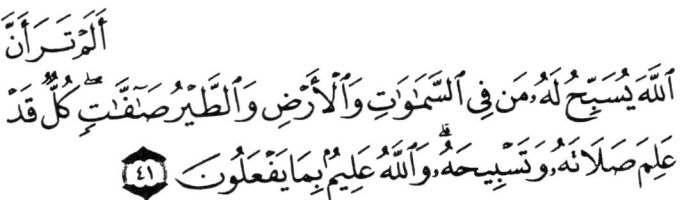

> *Seest you not that it is Allah whose praises all beings in the heavens and on earth do celebrate, and the birds with wings outspread? Each one knows its own prayer and praise. And Allah knows well all that they do. (24:41)*

After reading these Ayat, and many more from the Qur'an, as well as reading Hadith, and Seerah, one will be grateful to Allah. It is He Who made it easy for us to fly from place to place in a short period of time. Therefore, as a Flying Falcon (Assaqr Al-Taa`ir), I am also very thankful and grateful to Allah because He gave me a Golden Opportunity to travel from place to place. I was also able to fly from one country to another. I am very thankful to Allah that my trips were mainly to help others, and to spread the Message of Allah. All what I plead my case to Allah is to use my days and nights for His Love and Pleasure. I also pray to Allah to give me credit so that they will be in my Book in the Day of Judgement.

The previous chapters are nothing but Reflections. If Allah wants me to live longer, I am hoping to write My Memories. It is meant only as a lesson to any Da`iyah who wants to get involved in Da'wah. By learning the experience of others, and by reading the mistakes and/or achievements of others, one will be a better Da`iyah. May Allah (swt) bless us all, and forgive us for our shortcomings. Ameen Ya Rabbal `Alameen.

Finally, by mentioning names, cities, centers and others, I mean good to all. Never in my heart has any hate or ill feelings towards anyone at all. I had to mention sometimes such stories and reflections as a lesson for future generations to benefit from us. Allah knows the best and He is the Only One Who knows our intentions.

ADDENDUM A

COUNTRIES VISITED

The following is a partial list of countries that Allah (swt) has blessed me to visit. They are categorized according to continents. In many countries I visited a large number of cities. There is no time or space to mention the names of the cities, and how often I visited them. The most important is to demonstrate to the readers how much I am grateful to Allah (swt) for allowing me to visit those countries. By the way! I had no choice in planning any visit by myself. Almost all of those trips were designed and executed by Allah (swt) alone through some individuals or groups of individuals.

I. AFRICA

Algeria, Egypt, Ghana, Libya, Morocco, Nigeria, S. Africa, Senegal, Sudan, Tunisia

II. AUSTRALIA

Melbourne

III. ASIA

India: Bombay, Singapore, Hong Kong, Mauritius, Malaysia: Kuala Lumpur, Penang, Sarawak

IV. MIDDLE EAST

Lebanon, Jordan, Saudi Arabia, Syria

V. EUROPE

Belgium, Denmark, England, France, Germany, Greece, Italy, Slevonia

VI. WEST INDIES

Trinidad, Surinam and Jamaica

VII. CANADA

Calgary, Edmonton, Fort Mac Murray, Hamilton, Kingston, Lac La Beach, London, Mississaga, Montreal, Ottawa, Regina, Saskatchewan, Toronto, Vancouver, Windsor and Winnipeg.

VIII. UNITED STATES

Alabama, Arizona, Arkansas, California, Colorado, Connecticut, Delaware, District of Colombia, Florida, Georgia, Illinois, Indiana, Iowa, Kansas, Kentucky, Louisiana, Maine, Maryland, Massachusetts, Michigan, Minnesota, Mississippi, Missouri, Nebraska, Nevada, New Hampshire, New Jersey, New Mexico, New York, North Carolina, Ohio, Oklahoma, Oregon, Pennsylvania, Rhode Island, South Carolina, South Dakota, Tennessee, Texas, Utah, Vermont, Virginia, Washington, West Virginia, Wisconsin, Wyoming

THERE IS NO DEITY EXCEPT ALLAH; AND MUHAMMAD IS THE MESSENGER OF ALLAH

ADDENDUM B

أَدْعِيَةُ السَّفَرِ

SUPPLICATIONS OF TRAVELING

٦٣- عن أبي هريرة ﷺ قال: قَالَ رَسُولُ اللهِ ﷺ: «ثَلَاثُ دَعَوَاتٍ مُسْتَجَابَاتٍ لَا شَكَّ فِيهِنَّ: دَعْوَةُ الْمَظْلُومِ، وَدَعْوَةُ الْمُسَافِرِ، وَدَعْوَةُ الْوَالِدِ عَلَى وَلَدِهِ» حسن. رواه الترمذي (٢٧٤١).

63. Narrated Abū Hurairah, the Messenger of Allāh (Ṣ) said, «There is no doubt that three supplications are surely answered: the supplication of an oppressed person, a traveler, and the supplication of a father about his son.» *Ḥasan*. Tirmidhī (2741).

عِنْدَ رُكُوبِ الدَّابَّةِ

٦٧- عن عبد اللهِ بنِ عُمَرَ رضي اللهُ عنهما أَنْ رَسُولَ اللهِ ﷺ كَانَ إذا اسْتَوَى عَلَى بَعِيرِهِ خَارِجاً إلى سَفَرٍ كَبَّرَ ثلاثاً ثُمَّ قَالَ: ﴿ سُبْحَانَ الَّذِي سَخَّرَ لَنَا هَذَا وَمَا كُنَّا لَهُ مُقْرِنِينَ ۞ وَإِنَّا إِلَى رَبِّنَا لَمُنْقَلِبُونَ ﴾ اللَّهُمَّ إِنَّا نَسْأَلُكَ فِي سَفَرِنَا هَذَا الْبِرَّ وَالتَّقْوَى، وَمِنَ الْعَمَلِ مَا تَرْضَى، اللَّهُمَّ هَوِّنْ عَلَيْنَا سَفَرَنَا هَذَا وَاطْوِ عَنَّا بُعْدَهُ، اللَّهُمَّ أَنْتَ الصَّاحِبُ فِي السَّفَرِ، وَالْخَلِيفَةُ فِي الْأَهْلِ، اللَّهُمَّ إِنِّي أَعُوذُ بِكَ مِنْ وَعْثَاءِ السَّفَرِ، وَكَآبَةِ الْمَنْظَرِ، وَسُوءِ الْمُنْقَلَبِ، فِي الْمَالِ وَالْأَهْلِ، وَإِذَا رَجَعَ قَالَهُنَّ وَزَادَ فِيهِنَّ: «آيِبُونَ، تَائِبُونَ، عَابِدُونَ، لِرَبِّنَا حَامِدُونَ» رواه مسلم (٣٢٦٢/٩/١١٤).

When Riding An Animal, Car, Airplane, etc.

67. Narrated ʿAbdullāh ibn ʿUmar, when the Messenger of Allāh (Ṣ) mounted his camel leaving for a journey he said, « *Allāhu akbar*» thrice,

and then he recite, «Glory be to Him Who has subjected this to us, and we could never have it (by our effort), and verily, to our Lord we indeed are to return. O Allāh! we ask You virtue and piety and such deed in this journey as may please You. O Allāh! make this journey easy for us, and shorten its distance. O Allāh! You are the Companion in (our) journey, and the Guardian over (our) families. O Allāh! we seek refuge with You from the hardship of traveling, from the grief of the scenery, and evil occurring among wealth and family.» And on his return, he (Ṣ) used to repeat the same supplication and then say, «We are returning with safety; repenting, submitting, praising our Lord.» Muslim (3262, vol.9, p.114).

إِذَا عَلا مُرْتَفَعاً أَوْ هَبَطَ وَادِياً

٦٨- عن جابر ﷺ قال: كُنَّا إِذَا صَعِدْنَا كَبَّرْنَا، وَإِذَا نَزَلْنَا سَبَّحْنَا. رواه البخاري (الفتح ٢٩٩٣/٦/١٥٧).

When Ascending A Mound Or Descending Into A Valley

68. Narrated Jābir ibn `Abdullāh, we use to say « *Allāhu akbar* » when we ascended a height, and «*subḥana-llāh*» when we descended. Bukhārī (al-Fatḥ, 2993, vol.6, p.157).

إِذَا نَزَلَ مَنْزِلاً

٦٩- عن خَوْلَةَ بنتِ حَكِيم رضي اللهُ عنها قالتْ: سَمِعْتُ رسولَ اللهِ ﷺ يقولُ: «مَنْ نَزَلَ مَنْزِلاً ثُمَّ قال: أَعُوذُ بِكَلِمَاتِ اللهِ التَّامَّاتِ مِنْ شَرِّ ما خَلَقَ، لَمْ يَضُرُّهُ شَيْءٌ، حَتَّى يَرْتَحِلَ مِنْ مَنْزِلِهِ ذَلِكَ». رواه مسلم (٦٨١٧/١٧/٣٣).

Addendum B — Supplications Of Traveling

When Resting Somewhere While Traveling

69. Narrated Khawlah bint Hakīm, I heard the Messenger of Allāh (Ṣ) saying, «Whoever says, when he stops for a rest period while traveling, ‹I seek refuge with the perfect words of Allāh from the evil of whatever he has created,› nothing will harm him, till he depart from that place.» Muslim, (6817, vol.17, p.33).

Transliteration:

عِنْدَ الرُّجُوعِ مِنَ السَّفَرِ

٧٠- عن أنس ﷺ قال: أَقْبَلْنَا مَعَ النَّبِيِّ ﷺ أنا وأبو طَلْحَةَ، وَصَفِيَّةُ رَدِيفَتُهُ عَلَى نَاقَتِهِ، حَتَّى إِذَا كُنَّا بِظَهْرِ الْمَدِينَةِ قَالَ: «آيِبُونَ، تَائِبُونَ، عَابِدُونَ، لِرَبِّنَا حَامِدُونَ» فَلَمْ يَزَلْ يَقُولُ ذَلِكَ حَتَّى قَدِمْنَا الْمَدِينَةَ. رواه مسلم (٣٢٦٨/٩/١١٧).

When Returning From Traveling

70. Narrated Anas ibn Mālik, We, Abū Ṭalḥah and I, came back (from a journey) with the Prophet (Ṣ), while Ṣafīyah was on his camel. When we reached the outskirts of al-Madīnah, he (Ṣ) said, « We are returning with safety; repenting, submitting, praising our Lord.» (Anas added) He kept saying it, until we arrived al-Madīnah. Muslim (3268, vol.9, p.117).

Transliteration:

ADDENDUM C

Qura'nic Supplications

This section is devoted to a special group of Du'aa' from the Qur'an. The original text in Arabic is given, followed by its transliterated forms, as well as the English meaning of each Du'aa'.

Du'aa' #1

$$\rbrace\text{رَبَّنَآ ءَاتِنَا فِى ٱلدُّنْيَا حَسَنَةً وَفِى ٱلْءَاخِرَةِ حَسَنَةً وَقِنَا عَذَابَ ٱلنَّارِ}$$

Rabana atina fid-dunya hasanatan wa fil akhirati hasanatan waqina 'azaan-nar.

"Our Lord! Grant us good in this world and good in the hereafter, and save us from the chastisement of the fire." (2:201)

Du'aa' #2

$$\text{رَبَّنَآ أَفْرِغْ عَلَيْنَا صَبْرًا وَثَبِّتْ أَقْدَامَنَا وَٱنصُرْنَا عَلَى ٱلْقَوْمِ ٱلْكَٰفِرِينَ}$$

Rabbana afrigh 'alayna sabran wa thabbit aqdamana wansurna 'alalqawmil-karifin.

"Our Lord! Pour down upon us patience, and make our steps firm and assist us against the unbelieving people." (2:250)

Du'aa' #3

$$\text{رَبَّنَا لَا تُؤَاخِذْنَا إِن نَّسِينَا أَوْ أَخْطَأْنَا رَبَّنَا وَلَا تَحْمِلْ عَلَيْنَا إِصْرًا كَمَا حَمَلْتَهُ عَلَى الَّذِينَ مِن قَبْلِنَا رَبَّنَا وَلَا تُحَمِّلْنَا مَا لَا طَاقَةَ لَنَا بِهِ وَاعْفُ عَنَّا وَاغْفِرْ لَنَا وَارْحَمْنَا أَنتَ مَوْلَانَا فَانصُرْنَا عَلَى الْقَوْمِ الْكَافِرِينَ}$$

Rabbana la tu' akhizna in-nasina aw akh-ta'na. Rab-bana wa la tahmil 'alayna isran kam hamaltahu 'alallazina min qablina, Rabbana wa la tuhammilna ma la taqata lana bih, wa'fu'anna, waghfir Lana warhamna, anta Maulana fansurna'alal-qamil kafirin.

Our Lord! Do not punish us if we forget or make a mistake. Our Lord! Do not lay on us a burden as You did lay on those before us. Our Lord! Do not impose upon us that which we have not strength to bear; and pardon us and grant us protection and have mercy on us; You are our Patron; so help us against the unbelieving people. (2:286)

Du'aa' #4

رَبَّنَا مَا خَلَقْتَ هَذَا بَاطِلًا سُبْحَانَكَ فَقِنَا عَذَابَ النَّارِ ۝ رَبَّنَا إِنَّكَ مَن تُدْخِلِ النَّارَ فَقَدْ أَخْزَيْتَهُ وَمَا لِلظَّالِمِينَ مِنْ أَنصَارٍ ۝ رَبَّنَا إِنَّنَا سَمِعْنَا مُنَادِيًا يُنَادِي لِلْإِيمَانِ أَنْ آمِنُوا بِرَبِّكُمْ فَآمَنَّا رَبَّنَا فَاغْفِرْ لَنَا ذُنُوبَنَا وَكَفِّرْ عَنَّا سَيِّئَاتِنَا وَتَوَفَّنَا مَعَ الْأَبْرَارِ ۝ رَبَّنَا وَآتِنَا مَا وَعَدتَّنَا عَلَى رُسُلِكَ وَلَا تُخْزِنَا يَوْمَ الْقِيَامَةِ إِنَّكَ لَا تُخْلِفُ الْمِيعَادَ ۝

Rabba-na ma khalaqta hadha batilan, subhanaka fa-qina 'adhabannar. Rabba-na innaka man tudkhilin-nara fa qad akhzaytahu, wa ma liz-zalimina min ansar. Rababana innana sami'na munadiyan yunadi lil imani an aminu bi-Rabbikum fa-amanna, Rabba-na faghfir lana dhunubana wa kaffir 'anna wa'adta-na 'ala russuli-ka wa la tukhzi-na yaumal qiyammati innaka la tukhliful mi'ad.

"Our Lord! You have not created this in vain; glory be to You! Save us from the chastisement of the fire. Our Lord! Surely whomsoever You make to enter fire, You have indeed brought to disgrace, and there shall be no helpers for the unjust. Our Lord! We have heard a Preacher calling to the faith, saying, believe in your Lord; so we do believe. Our Lord! Forgive us our faults and cover our evil deeds and make us die with the righteous. Our Lord! And grant us what You have promised us by Your messengers and disgrace us not on the day of resurrection; surely You would not fail to perform the promise." (3:192-193)

Du'aa' #5

رَبِّ اجْعَلْنِي مُقِيمَ ٱلصَّلَوٰةِ وَمِن ذُرِّيَّتِي رَبَّنَا وَتَقَبَّلْ دُعَاءِ ۞ رَبَّنَا ٱغْفِرْ لِي وَلِوَالِدَيَّ وَلِلْمُؤْمِنِينَ يَوْمَ يَقُومُ ٱلْحِسَابُ

Rabb 'j'alni muqimas-Salati wa min Thurriyati Rabba-na a taqabbal du'aa', Rabbana'ghrili wa li walidayy walil-Mu'minina yawma yaqumul-Hisab.

"My Lord! Make me keep up prayer, and my offspring too. Our Lord! Accept the prayer. Our Lord! Grant protection to me and to my parents and to the faithful on the Day that the Reckoning will be taken." (14:40-41)

Addendum C — Qura'nic Supplications

Du'aa' #6

رَبَّنَآ ءَاتِنَا مِن لَّدُنكَ رَحْمَةً وَهَيِّئْ لَنَا مِنْ أَمْرِنَا رَشَدًا

Rabbana atina min ladunka rahmatan wa hayy' lana min amrina rashada.

"Our Lord! Give us mercy from Your presence, and shape for us right conduct in our plight." (18:10)

Du'aa' #7

رَبِّ ٱشْرَحْ لِى صَدْرِى ۝ وَيَسِّرْ لِىٓ أَمْرِى ۝ وَٱحْلُلْ عُقْدَةً مِّن لِّسَانِى ۝ يَفْقَهُوا۟ قَوْلِى

Rabbi-'shrah li sadri wa yassir li amri wa-hlul uqdatan min lisani yafqahu qawli.

O my Lord! expand my breast for me. And ease my task for me and loose a knot from my tongue, (that) they may understand my saying. (20:25-28)

Du'aa' #8

رَبَّنَا ٱصْرِفْ عَنَّا عَذَابَ جَهَنَّمَ إِنَّ عَذَابَهَا كَانَ غَرَامًا ۝ إِنَّهَا سَآءَتْ مُسْتَقَرًّا وَمُقَامًا

Rabbana Isrif 'anna 'Adhaba jahannama, inna 'adhabaha kana gharama, innaha sa'at mustaqarran wa muqama.

"Our Lord! Avert from us the torment of Hell. Verily! Its torment is ever an inseparable, permanent punishment." (25:65-66)

Du'aa' #9

$$\rbrace\text{رَبَّنَا هَبْ لَنَا مِنْ أَزْوَاجِنَا وَذُرِّيَّاتِنَا قُرَّةَ أَعْيُنٍ وَاجْعَلْنَا لِلْمُتَّقِينَ إِمَامًا}$$

Rabbana hab lana min azwajina wa dhurriyyatina qurrata A'yunin waj'alna lil-muttaqina imama.

Our Lord! Grant us in our mates and offsprings the joy of our eyes and make us patterns for those who guard against evil. (25:74)

Du'aa' #10

$$\text{رَبِّ أَوْزِعْنِي أَنْ أَشْكُرَ نِعْمَتَكَ الَّتِي أَنْعَمْتَ عَلَيَّ وَعَلَىٰ وَالِدَيَّ وَأَنْ أَعْمَلَ صَالِحًا تَرْضَاهُ وَأَصْلِحْ لِي فِي ذُرِّيَّتِي إِنِّي تُبْتُ إِلَيْكَ وَإِنِّي مِنَ الْمُسْلِمِينَ}$$

Rabbi awzi'ni an ashkura ni'mataka-llati an'amta alayya wa 'ala walidayya; wa an a'mala salihan tardahu; wa aslih li fi dhurriyaati, inni tubtu ilaika wa inni minal-muslimin.

My Lord! Grant me that I should be grateful for Your favor which You have bestowed on me and on my parents, and that I should do good such as You are pleased with; and do good to me in respect of my offspring; surely I turn to You, and I am of those who submit. (46:15)

ADDENDUM D

INVOCATION

In this section we wish to present a sample of a series of Invocations that were given to the City Council and the Mayor of Diamond Bar, California. It seems every three months they invite us to read the invocation before their official meeting. It happened that even the Mayor of the City of Buena Park has invited us to read the invocation at their official meeting.

Every time we go as a group to learn from each other how to make Da'wah. Moreso, every time, we take Islamic gifts to them and to their staff members. All what we wish that Allah (swt) will accept from us our efforts. Here is a sample of invocation.

Your Honor the Mayor Mr. Wen Chang
Your Excellencies the Members of the City Council of Diamond Bar
The Honorable Religious Leaders
The respected Delegates and Representatives of the Community Leaders.
Ladies and Gentlemen

I wish to greet you with the greeting of Islam and that greeting is the Greeting of Peace.

Assalamu' Alaikum
Peace Be Upon You

With this concept of Peace, we came all here tonight to share the happiness with the respected leaders of our city of Diamond Bar.

Ladies and Gentleman

Let me share with you all the following:

The Muslims of the world are 1.9 billions, while in USA 8 million Muslims, and in California 1 million Muslims. Here in Diamond Bar there are minimum 450 families along with their children. They try to live in Peace and harmony, with God (Allah), with themselves, with their families, and with the society. Part of their teachings is to respect parents and especially mothers. They are to respect the leaders, the elders, the teachers and the religious scholars.

Muslims do believe in all the Prophets and Messengers of Allah including Abraham, David, Isaac, Ishmael, Moses, Jesus and Muhammad. Muslims do believe in the originality of the Revelations from God including Torah, Bible, Psalms, and Qur'an.

We came here tonight to pray for the success of our Leaders: We ask God, The Most Beneficent and Most Merciful, to grant success to our Mayor and the Members of the Council of the City of Diamond Bar. We pray to God to give them strength and the wisdom to fulfill their goals and aspirations. We pray to God to reward them and to bless them for their genuine efforts to beautify the city.

We do pray also for the success of all our leaders in USA, and those who are in the Congress. After all, when we pray for them, we are praying for all.

While we are gathering here in peace and harmony we pray to God, the Creator of the whole universe, to protect us all from any calamity whether it may be an earthquake, tornado, hurricane, flood, brush fire, drought, or otherwise. We pray for the sick to be healed, we pray for the dead to be forgiven, we pray for the homeless for good housing, we pray for those who are out of work to have good jobs, and we pray for the refugees anywhere in the world to go back to their homes with peace, justice and fairness.

Ladies and Gentlemen

We should try to work together to protect our neighborhood from gangs, drug dealers, graffiti, taggers, shooting, killing, and drunk drivers, so that we all can live happily altogether as one family. We should try to work together to improve the life style in our schools whereby the children and the youth will respect the teachers, the administrators, the elders, their parents and the official personnel in the City and in the Government. Members of the Sheriff and Fire Departments are working very hard to protect us all, and to bring peace and happiness in our community. We are grateful to them all, and we pray for their safety and happiness.

With this prayer let me read to you the first chapter in the Qur'an. It is called Al-Fatiha or the Opening Chapter, or the Chapter of Thanks and Appreciation to God.

Surah 1. (Chapter 1)

Al-Fatiha (The Opening)

In the name of Allah, Most Gracious, Most Merciful. Praise be to Allah The Cherisher and Sustainer of the Worlds; Most Gracious, Most Merciful. Master of the Day of Judgement. You do we worship, and Your aid we seek. Show us the straight way, the way of those on whom You had bestowed Your Grace, those whose portion is not wrath, and who go not astray.

On behalf of the Muslim community in this City and the neighboring cities, we wish the members of the City Council the best. We also wish that the citizens of this city will work together to bring peace, happiness and success to all, irrespective of color, ethnic background, language or religion.

God bless you all, and God bless America.

And He (Allah) has power over all things.
(Qur'an, 11.4)

ADDENDUM E

REFLECTIONS ON THE 4TH OF JULY

The month of July in USA is the month of Independence of Americans from the European Colonialism mainly that of UK, France, and Spain. Americans became independent since 1776, and they enjoyed Freedom of Speech, Freedom of Religion, and Freedom for a Democratic way of Life rather than Imperialism. At the same time, they became Free from the problem of Secret Evidence, and they are now proud to be Americans. As George Washington once said in 1796: "There should be no more entanglement of foreign alliances. He talked about trade and commerce, about being free and independent, and about being proud to be Americans. President Jefferson said: "We hold these truths to be self-evident; that all men are created equal…"

Americans today are celebrating the happiness of their freedom. They spend millions of dollars for the sake of fireworks. However, one has to reflect on this noble occasion the following:

While we are spending money on fireworks, we could have saved money to feed the poor, the needy, the homeless, the orphans and those who are out of jobs.

1. America was liberated from Colonialism, but they continued to practice Human Slavery till Abraham Lincoln was able to convince the Americans to stop slavery.

2. Americans had to wait till 1964 where President Lyndon B. Johnson had to sign the Civil Rights Act (P.L 88-352) on July 2nd, 1964. Before that, Black Americans did not have the right to vote and they were discriminated as second-class citizens.

Addendum E — Reflections On The Fourth Of July

3. American Foreign Policy was very much concerned about Human Rights: They were not concerned about their own citizens. They had to wait till President James Carter (1977-1988) to champion the concept of Human Rights for the Jews in the Soviet Union. He did not care much for the rest of the world or even for American people.

4. American leaders were waiting desperately again and again to find out about the treatment of the Jews in Russia. Mr. Reagan had to go all the way to Reykjavik to meet the President of Russia, Mr. Michael Gorbachev and demand from him to give freedom to Jews to migrate to Palestine and USA. It was October 11-12, 1986.

5. The Leaders of the African Americans seemingly were waiting desperately to give freedom to the Jews in Russia until Rev. Jesse Jackson had to go to Reykjavik, Iceland in 1986 and to request the president of the Soviet Union to liberate the Jews to migrate to Palestine and USA.

6. The whole world was waiting for better treatment than Colonialism and Imperialism. After the Second War was over, the champions and the winners (of the killing and controlling others) came together to protect themselves from being accused of being criminals. They helped to establish UN Charter of Human Rights. They held their meeting in San Francisco in June 26, 1945 as the League of Nations. However, they gave themselves the Right of Veto Power so that no one will be able to accuse them. They are USA, UK, Soviet Union, France and China. They are the Super Power and the Heroes of the world.

7. Americans got their Freedom, and they are still waiting to free themselves from the Secret Evidence that has been practiced on a good number of Muslim Professors in this Country.

8. Americans got their Freedom from Oppression and Colonialism and Human Slavery. They are still waiting to get rid of the Economic Slavery of Capitalism. Republicans are for the rich, while Democrats are for the poor. However, both are Bourgeoisies. Both are for titles, positions, money and leadership. The rich ones become richer and the poor ones become poorer.

9. Americans are happy that no foreign country can dictate any Foreign Policy on them. But the American Foreign policy is dictating its policy on many counties in the world. What type of a deal and of Double standard.

10. America has helped many countries to have Democratic life, but will not allow the Muslim countries to have Democratic System of Government after Colonialism and Imperialism.

11. America is helping many countries in the world by giving them billions of dollars, billions worth of Ammunitions and billions worth of military tanks, planes and other technical equipment. However, the Muslim world should be denied of everything unless they act as slaves and servants to the leaders of the Foreign policy of the States Department.

12. America up till now does not allow the people of Chechnya, Kashmir and Palestine to have independent states with Democratic Life style of government. It seems

America cannot do that; otherwise it will displease Russia, Israel, and India.

13. The only two countries that refuse to sign the proliferation treaty of Nuclear Weapons are India and Israel. Still, America is helping those two states financially and militarily. On the other hand, Iraq should not have any type of Technological, Biological, or Chemical Industries at all. Moreover, Sudan should not have any pharmaceutical Lab to produce medicine to their own people. Other Muslim countries should not have any technological industries at all. Let them die from hunger, and sickness. Let them live as beggars and homeless. They have no right to vote, to elect, and to have Freedom of Speech, religion or other types of freedom. They have to have dictators who should receive instructions from the Super-Power-Countries.

Finally America should take a lesson from the previous nations: Soviet Union is no more there. Untied Kingdom and Great Britain is no more as before. The same applies to France, Italy, Germany, Japan, Spain, Portuguese, Yugoslavia, Romans, Byzantine, Persia, Tatar, Moguls, Pharaohs, and Dutch of Apartheid Regime in South Africa. Historically, one can read more and more about other nations such as the Nations of `Aad, Thamood, Salih, Loot, and Noah etc... All were destroyed in one-way or the other. Either American Leadership should come back to their normal behavior, and be humble in front of Allah, otherwise they would be waiting for a catastrophe from God to eradicate the whole country and turn it upside down.

We Muslims wish the best for America and Americans. We pray to God (Allah) to protect us all as Americans. We Pray to

Allah to guide us and to guide our leaders to do the best before it is too late. We pray to Allah not to inflict upon us tragedies in this part of the world. We Muslims have no hate against any human beings irrespective of color, nationality, language, ethnic background, or religion. We love all, and we pray for all. Ameen.

God Bless America

On the occasion of the Fourth of July, the Nation's Independence Day, I would like to share my ideas and feelings with fellow Americans. I would like to say here that:

1. America has opened its door to all immigrants to enjoy freedom and opportunities. America is a melting pot to all people from different ethnic backgrounds. Some groups have integrated themselves with mainstream America and became part of the culture and heritage. This reminds me of Hajj when people from all over the world meet in one place so they get to know one another and be proud to be Muslims.
2. America gave chance to other cultures to establish their own culture within the American culture such as the Chinese building China Town and Hong Kong building Hong Kong Market and so on. This demonstrates to us the openness of the American people.
3. America has given freedom of religion to all people. We see many world religions enjoy practicing their religions in a free way. Churches, synagogues, temples, mosques etc… are built and established for people of all religions to enjoy practicing their religion.
4. Religious schools of all denominations have been established in this country. No one is denied the right to

establish his own private religious school. The door is open to even establishing more religious schools.
5. All religious groups have the right to open universities, colleges, hospitals and clinics. Local governments will not deny the right of establishing such facilities as long as people follow the zoning rules and regulations.
6. The beauty of America is that you can travel from coast to coast without having to stop at checkpoints to verify your I.D. or otherwise. This is a true freedom of traveling with peace and honor. This reminds me of the early Muslims who traveled from Morocco to Indonesia and nobody stopped them to verify their identities.
7. Equal opportunity employment is what makes America so great. You will get a job based on your merits and not on your ethnic or religious background.
8. Freedom of Press is what our great grandfathers gave us. Radio, T.V, internet etc.. are not controlled by the government. They are free enterprise and they are available for everyone.
9. Americans enjoy the beauty of the Freedom of Speech. This one of the Bill of Rights granted to us by the amendment to the Constitution. One can criticize the President of the U.S.A. or any other government official without being in trouble. Muslims enjoy this right because an Imam can deliver his Friday Khutbah with full liberty and freedom so long it does not libel any one. This reminds me of the days of the Prophet and the Guided Khalifas.
10. America has the freedom of ownership. If a gold mine is discovered in your property, then the gold mine belongs to you without being confiscated by the government. This is pure Islamic teaching.

11. Americans enjoy free enterprise. You can own a giant company or a small one without the government interfering in your business.
12. Education is compulsory in America. Children are sent to schools free of charge till high school. I wish other countries adopt the same system. Islam demanded from Muslims to seek knowledge even if one has to go to China.
13. The right to assemble is another right that the Muslims enjoy under the American Constitution. Muslims can organize seminars, conferences, conventions, and workshops without being controlled by the government.

Muslims in America are from different parts of the world and they are living in peace and harmony. They enjoy the religious freedom and the freedom of speech. They are not being discriminated against . They recognize that most of these values are part of the teachings of Islam. Muslims are grateful to Almighty Allah that allowed them to come to America to live here and share the American dream with other Americans.

God Bless all. God Bless America.

MUHAMMAD IS THE MESSENGER OF ALLAH

ADDENDUM F

LEGAL STATEMENTS

The following is a series of short articles that were sent to non-Muslim newspapers to be published. Also one will find some statements that were given to legal personnel for knowledge about Islam and Muslims. Accordingly it was thought it would be a good idea to include them in this book.

A. Paradise At The Feet Of Mothers

Once it was said: "Mother is an institution by herself and she is a leader-maker." She knows how to mold and train her own children in the best way. She does this better than fathers and better than baby –sitters.

While we celebrate Mother's Day, we should recognize that mother is the backbone of a stable family and a good society. Mothers in their homes keep the family together. With love, affection, sympathy, mercy, trust, patience, and sacrifice they deserve to be honored and respected by all of us.

We salute all those mothers who took care of their children, and raised them with honor and dignity, and trained them to be good leaders in America and the world. We need more mothers in our societies to take care of their own children. None should leave this noble responsibility to someone else.

No other parts of the society can do what a mother can do to her own children. Schools, law enforcement, court decisions, rehabilitation centers or any other organization cannot be equal with the institute of the Mother. It is the mother who conceived and accepted the challenge of pregnancy for nine months. She went through difficulties of morning sickness, labor and childbirth.

She nurtured her child with tender and care till he/she became a grown up.

Therefore, mothers deserved to be respected not only once a year, but every moment of existence. Every child, young or old, male or female, should salute his/her mother daily for the sacrifices that she undertakes. For these reasons and many more, mothers deserve to be in Paradise; and Paradise is humble enough to make itself at the feet of the mother. "Paradise is at the feet of Mothers".

B. Zakat: Types

1. Faqeer/ Fuqaraa' : Poor
2. Miskeen/ Masaakeen : Needy
3. 'Aamil/ 'Aamileena : Employee (s)

   a. Those who are social workers: identify needy... Rich
   b. Those who collect Zakat
   c. Those who are accountants, auditors, CPA's
   d. Those who do clerical/ secretarial/ Administration
   e. Those who invest the Zakat
   f. Those who distribute the Zakat

4. Mu-allafah Quloobuhum: sympathizers
5. Those who are Al-Riqaab: Captive... in bondage... Bail.
6. Ghaarim/ Ghaarimeen: In Debt
7. Fee Sabeel-Lillah: In the Cause of Allah

   a. Battlefield... Jihad

  b. Da'wah: To non-Muslims/ Muslims
  c. Mass Media: TV... Radio... Newspapers... Fliers... Books
  d. Schools for Islamic Shari'ah... Hifz Qur'an
  e. Students' Scholarships
  f. Grants to Teachers for Research... Publications
  g. Others... and... others

8. Ibn Ass-Sabeel: Wayfarer

C. Children Custody In Islam

The teachings of Islam are very humane. The teachings of Islamic jurisprudence are meant to help people to live in peace, harmony and with fairness and justice. As far as the family is Islam is concerned, Islam insists that people should refrain from divorce. Counseling is a must. Settling problems should be taken care by relatives, otherwise by official people in the government. However, if divorce has to take place, then legal settlement has to be enforced.

As far as the custody of the children is concerned, Islamic Jurisprudence dictates that the mother of the children has their full custody till they reach the age of puberty. The father has the visitation rights.

During the period of custody the husband is obliged to take care of the following:

1. Late dowry has to be paid to the mother of the children.
2. During the three months of 'Iddah (waiting period) he is financially responsible for his divorced wife.
3. After the waiting period, the husband is still obliged to spend on his ex-wife and his children.

4. He is to make sure that they live in a reasonable housing facility. He is to pay all their expenses: food, electricity, education, transportation, clothing, medical expenses, etc.
5. If the mother is nursing her baby, the ex-husband is to spend on the mother extra money; otherwise he is to pay for another woman to nurse the child.
6. If the mother of the children decided to get married after the waiting period ('Iddah), Islam allowed her to do so. However, she will lose her monthly alimony, but the ex-husband is still obliged to take care of the living expenses of the children till they become independent. He has the right to get back his children.
7. Visitation of the father has to be agreed upon through court order, mutual agreement, or arbitration.
8. In case the mother cannot handle raising her own children, then the grandmother from the mother side will take care of the children. If she cannot handle them, then any female relative from the mother side such as sister or aunt shall take care of them.
9. In case a female relative from the mother side of the children is to take care of them, the father of those children is still responsible to spend on the foster mother, as well as taking care of the children financially.
10. After the age of puberty, the children are given the choice to decide whether to stay with their mother, or join their father.
11. The responsibility of the father will continue towards his children till they get married, and be on their own.

D. Dowry In Islam

The Islamic terminology of Dowry is called Mahr. There are rules and regulations for a marriage to be consummated. The husband has to offer his wife two types of dowries. An advanced and a late dowry. The advanced dowry is to be given to the wife as a sign of a gift at the time of officiating the marriage. It is also considered that the man is going to be responsible for the wife financially.

The late dowry is to be given to her during their married life. However, if divorce has to take place from his side, he is to give her the promised late dowry. If the husband makes the life of his wife miserable so that she may ask for divorce, he is still obliged by law to fulfill his promise to pay the late dowry.

The advanced dowry could be money, jewelry and/or estate. The same thing is to be applied for the late dowry. In Islam, the man is responsible for all the financial needs of his wife and children. He is also responsible for her financial needs and living expenses after divorce during the waiting period ('Iddah) of three months. Even after 'Iddah period, he is still responsible to spend on her and the children as long as she does not marry.

PS. The Islamic Jurisprudence dictates that the woman if divorced has to wait at least three months before she can marry again. This is 'Iddah of divorce. However, if the husband dies, the 'Iddah for the wife is four months and ten days; after which she has the right to marry someone else. By the way! The man has no 'Iddah period whether divorce takes place or death of the wife.

E. Women's Hijab

Islam teaches: Family Values, Modesty, Decency, and Morality. As far as ladies are concerned, the Qur'an (The Revealed Book from God to Prophet Muhammad) instructs them to cover their heads with a scarf (Hijab). That cover should also extend on their chest. One may read the Qur'an chapter (24), verse

(31). Moreover, Islam instructs women to wear lose dresses. They should extend those dresses till their ankles, Qur'an chapter (33), verse (59). To achieve the maximum modesty, Islam demanded from Muslim ladies not to wear in their feet or legs, any items that attract the attention of others. One may read the Qur'an chapter (24), verse (31).

Therefore, Muslim women are to cover their heads in public places. If they want to take pictures for immigration, for Driver's licenses, and for other government requirements, they should keep their Heads Covers on. They cannot be obliged to take it off, otherwise, the curse of God (Allah) will fall upon those who try to oblige them. Even if they are to be obliged, they will never follow any rules except what had been prescribed by God, Almighty. It is a religious duty, and Muslim ladies are to follow the orders of God.

And it is He Who has power over all things. [Qur'an, 5:120]

ADDENDUM G

SOCIAL SUPPORT IN HEALING

As usual, I am invited by many friends in different parts of the world. In one invitation to a hospital in a Muslim country in the Middle East, I was requested to present a paper on Healing. I selected: Social Support in Healing. I wrote the abstract and then I worked on the topic more in details. Then I was asked to write on Medical Ethics in Healing of terminally ill patients. Accordingly I tried my best. However, in this section one will find out that abstract of Social Support in Healing. We pray to Allah (swt) to accept from all of us; and we pray to Him to keep us on the Siraat Al-Mustaqeem. Ameen.

Life on this planet earth, is a life of tests with happiness and/or sorrows. Every human being has to be tested. If and when people are being tested, with what they like, they should be grateful to Allah (swt), the Creator of the universe. On the other hand, if they are being tested with what they hate, they should show patience. The rewards for both tests could be the same. Prophet Ayub was tested with what everyone hates to be tested, but he was patient (sabr). On the other hand, the Prophet Sulaiman was tested with what he liked. He was grateful (shukr). Both got similar certificates from Allah, Degree: Ni'mal 'Abd Innahu Awwab. People may be tested with a plague (Taa'oon) whereby the healing (Ash-Shafi) is Allah (swt) alone. However, our prophet (pbuh) encouraged Muslims to seek healing from doctors. At the same time, each doctor is responsible (Daamin) for any treatment he uses. For those who are attacked with a plague whereby there is no healing for them, if and when they die they will die as martyrs (shaheed). There are some different varieties and levels of shaheed in Islam. This is one of them. The healing processes have many factors, among which are the following:

| Addendum G | Social Support In Healing |

1. The doctors, the nurses, the medicines, the hospitals and the chemical diagnosis, etc... are to work together for the welfare of the sick person.
2. Family members are to visit the sick person, and giving him moral and spiritual supports. There are many supplications, Qur'anic recitations and Salat Al-Haajah that will help to heal the sick person.
3. Charity (sadaqah) is a means for healing.
4. Friends and relatives to visit the sick person, making Du'aa' (supplication) for healing, and giving him moral and spiritual supports.
5. Drinking from water of Zamzam as much as possible, because it has some healing effects.
6. Dieting and eating habits have to be adjusted accordingly.
7. For those who are Muslims, they are to be encouraged to perform 'Umrah and/or Hajj with the religious hope of being healed.
8. Each and every member of the society is to give hope of a long life to the sick person who is struck with terminal sickness.
9. One may narrate stories of the prophets and who were tested severely and bitterly with too many problems in their private and public life.
10. One of the moral support would be to uniform the patient that the more he is a faithful believer, the more the test has to inflict upon him. Accordingly, his reward is paradise, and most likely Al-Firdous Al-'Alaa (The Highest place in Paradise).
11. Some other recommendations would be that the patient should be happy that he is being tested, and that his friends, family members, doctors, and nurses are all working diligently for his well being.

ADDENDUM H

SYNOPSES

This section is devoted to some abstracts of talks and lectures that were given at different occasions, and in different parts of the world. Since it has been mentioned before that I have been invited to (40) forty different countries to attend and participate in seminars, conferences, symposia, and workshops, therefore, here is a small list of synopses that were presented. We pray to Allah (swt) to accept from all of us our contribution to the Message of Islam.

I. Code of Ethics: Halal Foods

This lecture was given at the conference held in Paris in the year 2001 under the invitation of the Islamic Food and Nutrition Council of America:

Islam came to all people of the world, irrespective of time, place, or the future generations. Islam is the last religion revealed from Almighty God (Allah); and Prophet Muhammad is the Last Prophet and Last Messenger. The Qur'an was revealed to Prophet Muhammad in a period of (23) years. It is considered to be: The Summation, Culmination, and Purification of all the Previous Books revealed from God to His Prophets. Muslims do believe in Adam and Eve, as well as in Noah, Abraham, David, Issac, Jacob, Moses, Jesus, Muhammad and all those who came before. Their teachings were the same: to obey God, to be good, and to live in peace and harmony.

Muslims are to share their Halal Foods with their neighbors whether they are Muslims, Christians, Jews, Hindus, Buddhists, or otherwise. Moreover they are to exchange Halal gifts with everybody especially during Feasts and Festivities.

| Addendum H | Synopses |

Islam has prescribed Code of Ethics in every aspect of life. It includes family, education, politics, economics, business, science, technology, industry, farming, eating, and so on. As far as the Islamic Code of Ethics related to Halal Foods, the following items are a partial list:

1. Muslims are being taught to be honest and sincere in every aspect of life
2. Islam will never tolerate cheating or lying neither in business, nor in every aspect of life, otherwise the person has to be charged accordingly.
3. To have Halal Foods the following items are to be considered:
    a. The animals should be Herbivorous
    b. The Feed should be from plants only
    c. No mixing of any blood, viscera, or other meat products
    d. No steroid hormones such as Diethylstilbestrol, nor Estrogen are to be given to the animals.
    e. Some preservatives are harmful. One has to know them.
4. Every one should release the information to the consumers as well as to the official people in the government. Hiding any information means cheating.
5. Muslims do recognize that God (Allah) knows, hears, and sees everything. We cannot hide our deeds and actions from Him. He is closer to us than our jugular veins.
6. Muslims do believe that there are angels on our shoulders. They record everything: body language, talks and our intention too.
7. Exploitation of any situation is totally unlawful (Haram) in Islam.
8. Serving people and feeding them healthy foods is more important than making money for the sake of earning money.

9. Baby animals, pregnant animals and sick animals are not to be slaughtered.
10. There are certain occasions whereby Muslims are to share the meat of animals with others:

    a. Feast of Sacrifice
    b. Feast of Fast- Breaking
    c. Waleemah: Reception after marriage
    d. 'Aqeeqah: Reception of birth of a baby
    e. Kaffarah: To wipe out a mistake

11. There are certain occasions whereby Muslims have to give foods, meat and money to needy people in the society, either as an obligation or as a charity. In so doing they will live in peace and harmony.
12. Certificates of Halal Foods have to be done by a third party, which is recognized by Muslims, as well as by the local governments.
13. Supervision has to be done on a regular basis, as well as on-and-off.
14. Muslims do believe that there is a Day of Judgment, and all of us as human beings are going to be judged by God (Allah) directly. Therefore, Muslims are to observe the rules and regulations that God has prescribed to all of us, irrespective of color, nationality or religion.

II. The 5 C's To Marriage

This lecture was given in Singapore. It was presented among other series of lectures. It should be stated here that I visited Singapore for Four (4) times. Each time was for a different purpose with different local groups. I really enjoyed all the time there. I pray to Allah (swt) to reward everyone there. May Allah bless their efforts for the good jobs they are doing. Ameen.

Marriage is a blessing and a gift from the Creator (Allah) to human beings. He created people with rules and regulations. He showed them the way, and He sent them Prophets and Messengers to lead them to the right way. If they go through such guidelines, they will be blessed, rewarded and will live in peace and happiness. Otherwise they will face troubles, problems and difficulties.

Marriage in Islam is built on solid foundations. It is a social and a religious contract between a male and a female as well as between the two families of the young couple who are planning to marry. This contract is to be witnessed in public and each has to pledge to be a good spouse to the other and to the relatives of both families. Marriage in Islam means Usrah and 'Aa-ilah. Usrah means captivity, and therefore, the young couple should recognize that they are to be captive to each other. To tie the other spouse, one has to make efforts to inspire, motivate and show his/her good qualities. 'Aa-ilah means overburden with responsibilities. To establish a family one has to accept the responsibility of being overburden with duties and obligations.

Marriage should be built on qualities that will lead to eternal peace and tranquility. If marriage is after worldly attractions, it will never be materialized; otherwise it will break-up very soon. Those who are after the C's such as Car, Credit Card, Cash, Career, Condo, or other worldly affairs, they should recognize that such a marriage will never survive. It would be worse than a business partnership. On the other hand, if marriage is built on humane qualities, the young couple will live in peace and happiness. Their relatives as well as their children will live in peace and happiness.

Some of the good C's qualities that the couples should look for are: Caring, good Character, Compassion, Communication, Conviction, Courage, Courtesy, Confidence, Coexistence, Chastity, Cheerful, Comfort, Consultation, Convey, Contribute, Concern, Compatible, Complement, Comprehend, etc. There are many more qualities that people have to look for so that they will live with respect, honor, dignity, and happiness.

Physical and material needs of life are not and should not be looked upon as essential requirements for marriage. They may bring temporary happiness, but definitely they will be catastrophe to the family and to the society at large.

Islam teaches humanity to look for a permanent solution through quality of characters and behaviors. Piety and Righteousness should be on the top of the list of qualities. People should be religiously committed without being fanatic. For those who are Muslims should follow the teachings of Allah in the Qur'an, and explained and practiced by the Sunnah of Prophet Muhammad. In so doing, they will be role models for others to imitate, emulate, and follow. The rewards are plenty in this world and the hereafter.

III. In Love But Not Married

This is another synopsis for a lecture given to the local people in Singapore. In one week I had to give a series of lectures from one group to the other. Muslims and non-Muslims were attending these series of lectures. To my surprise I was told that the local people enjoyed these series of lectures. I pray to Allah to accept from all of us our efforts, energies and contribution. We pray to Allah to reward all those sincere brothers and sisters who organized those series of lectures. Ameen.

Life is a gift from God (Allah). It has been given to us as a blessing to enjoy and to assume responsibility. Benefits without responsibilities will lead to chaos in the society and a person will act as a parasite.

Love is a general term to mean more than one level. One may love Allah, His Prophets, and Messengers. A person is to love his parents, his children, as well as his wife. Each type of love has its own definitions, terminologies, limitations, boundaries, responsibilities, and benefits. When it comes to the concept of "love but not married," it has its own terminologies, definitions and results.

If we are talking about love between the two genders, one has to stipulate rules and regulations to be followed. Anyone who transgresses the limits, he is putting himself in jeopardy. Society has rights over individuals, and government has rights over its citizens. Anyone who goes beyond the limits is to be taken to court and be charged accordingly.

Similarly, the One Who created us has legislated rules and regulations to be followed and observed. Any one who violates these laws has to be penalized in this world directly or indirectly. He may have to be penalized also in the hereafter.

Love between two genders is a natural phenomenon. Hormones are secreted and excreted from the pituitary gland under the brain and poured into the blood stream. By looking, hearing, touching, smelling, and tasting, the messenger called Acetyl-S-CoA brings the information to the brain. However, this messenger has to travel from neuron to neuron through the Central Nervous System (CNS) until it reaches the brain. The brain sends other messengers to different organs and glands to secrete their own hormones or to react accordingly. When sex hormones are secreted and excreted into the blood stream, it would be difficult for a person to control himself or herself without doing something harmful to the body or to the society.

Love between couples of two genders necessitates duties and responsibilities. Love without obligations to be assumed and to be fulfilled means a wild and loose life. The girl would be used temporarily and then abused. She is to be left all alone to search for another lover. It becomes a vicious circle. It is cheap treat to the girl who will be used as a bedmate, a mistress, or a prostitute. All these vices will undoubtedly lead to venereal diseases as well as AIDS. If pregnancy takes place, abortion is being offered to her; the taxpayers are to assume responsibility. Birth control pills are given to the girls while condoms are given to men. The industry is the beneficiary while the society is to suffer.

Islam has encouraged early marriage. Parents from both sides are to come forward and help the young couple to establish themselves. They are to help them financially, morally, culturally, socially, and spiritually so that the young couple can stand on their own in the society.

In Islam, matrimonial relationships between two genders are a matter of worship and it is a blessing and a gift from Allah. It has its beauty and happiness. However, it also has its duties and responsibilities. Both have to be informed and educated about matrimonial life by their own parents before marriage as well as during marriage. They should understand that beauty is a mater of relativity. What is beautiful before marriage, might no longer be beautiful after marriage. Financial stability today may be bankruptcy tomorrow. Position today may vanish tomorrow. Piety and Righteousness are the most stable factors for a social and stable family. Piety leads to love, affection, sympathy, concern, humbleness, and contentment. All these lead to eternal peace and happiness for the individuals as well as for the society.

AYATUL KURSI
CHAPTER (2) VERSE 255

FOUNDATION FOR ISLAMIC KNOWLEDGE

KNOWLEDGE

Islam emphasizes the importance of knowledge to all mankind. It is only through true knowledge that one can appreciate the Creator of the Universe namely Allah (swt). Muslims are ordained to seek knowledge from cradle to grave and as far as a person can to obtain it.

In as much as seeking knowledge is a must on every Muslim, dissemination of knowledge is also incumbent on Muslims to the members of the society. The methods of disseminating the information should be lawful, as well as the truth is to be released to everyone. Hiding or keeping the true knowledge away from those who seek it, is considered a sin.

The best investment for every human being is through: perpetual charity (Sadaqa Jariya), useful knowledge that people shall benefit or, and a loving child who shall make special prayers for his/her parents.

LEGALITY

The Foundation has been established and registered with the Secretary of the State of Illinois since January 8,1987 as a non-profit, charitable, educational, religious and /or scientific society within the meaning of section 501 (c) (3) of the Internal Revenue Code.

The Foundation has a tax-exempt status with the IRS, and donations are considered tax-deductible.

FINANCES

The finances of the FOUNDATION are mainly from donations and contributions in the form of cash, assets and wills.

INUMERENT OF INCOME

No part of the net earnings of the Corporation shall inure to the benefit of, or be distributed to, its members, directors, officers or other private persons except that the Corporation shall be authorized and empowered to pay reasonable compensation for services rendered.

PURPOSES

The purposes of the FOUNDATION are summarized as follows:

1. To promote Islamic Knowledge through education.
2. To create a better understanding of Islam among Muslims and non-Muslims through education and communication.
3. To publish books and other literature about Islam and its teachings
4. To disseminate Islamic Knowledge and education through TV, Radio, Video, and other means of mass communications.
5. To establish ecumenical among the religious people of America so that a better understanding will be created.

ACTIVITIES

The activities of the FOUNDATION shall include, but not be limited to the following:

1. Publishing literature pertaining to Islam.
2. Producing audio cassettes and audio-visual tapes on certain topics of Islam.
3. Giving lectures related to Islam as a religion, culture and civilization.
4. Cooperation with other societies, foundations and organizations whose aims and objectives are similar to the FOUNDATION.

KNOWLEDGE IN THE QUR'AN

The word knowledge ('ILM) is mentioned in the Qur'an more than 700 times in 87 different forms. Some of the pertinent Ayat are listed below.

1. The first Ayat revealed to Prophet Muhammad (pbuh) at Cave Hira' are in Surah Al-Alaq (The Clot) (96:1-5). They are related to knowledge of embryology through scientific investigation.

2. Allah honors all those who are knowledgeable. These people cannot be compared with the ignorant ones. See Surah Al-Zumar (The Troops) (35:28)

3. Only the knowledgeable people are those who do appreciate the creations of Allah (swt) . They are the ones who respect Him and worship Him with knowledge and humility. Please read Surah Fatir (The Creator) (35:28)

4. Knowledge is in the Hands of Allah and it is at His disposal. People are to seek the true knowledge from its source namely Allah. Read Surah Al-Mulk (The Sovereignty) (67:26).

5. People are to seek knowledge from Allah (swt) are to request Him to enrich them daily with 'ILM. Read Surah Taha (20:114).

KNOWLEDGE IN THE HADITH

Prophet Muhammad (pbuh) emphasized 'ILM tremendously and encouraged Muslims to seek knowledge in any part of the world. The following is a summary:

1. In one Hadith the Prophet says: "The Knowledgeable people ('Ulama) are the inheritors to the Prophets."

2. In another Hadith He encouraged Muslims to seek knowledge, saying: "Seeking knowledge is a must on every Muslim."

3. In another place, He demanded that knowledge is to be sought throughout lifetime, saying: "Seek knowledge from cradle to grave."

4. Knowledge is to be disseminated to all, and the best knowledge is that of the Qur'an, saying: "The best amongst you are the ones who learn Qur'an and teach it to others."

5. Knowledge is to be taught and to be carried on even after death. In His Hadith the Prophet said: "When a person dies, his deeds are over, except from three things; perpetual charity, a useful knowledge, or a good child who makes supplications for him."

The FOUNDATION will continue, with the help of Almighty God (Allah), to publish more useful literature.

Foundation For Islamic Knowledge

With the generous help of the friends, The Foundation will be able to achieve its purposes, Inshaallah.

For More Information, Please Write To:

**Foundation For Islamic Knowledge
P.O. Box 665 Lombard, Illinois 60148 U.S.A.
Phone: (630) 495-4817   Fax (630) 627-8894**

**The Return
Of The Falcon**

PUBLICATIONS

I. BOOKS ON HEALTH, FOOD AND NUTRITION:

1. Dietary Regulations & Food Habits of Muslims
2. Overeating and Behavior
3. Islam on Alcohol
4. Alcohol in Beverages, Drugs, Foods and Vitamins
5. Cheese
6. AFTO and FAO
* 7. Fasting in Islam
8. Food and Overpopulation
9. Honey: Food and a Medicine
* 10. Gelatin
11. Shortening in Foods
12. A Manual on Food Shortenings
* 13. Pork: Possible Reasons for its Prohibition
14. Food Supplementation
15. World Health Organization for Muslim Nations
* 16. A Muslim Guide to Food Ingredients
17. Natural Therapeutics of Medicine in Islam (co-authored)
18. Islamic Dietary Laws & Practices (co-authored)
19. Food and Nutrition Manual (co-authored)
20. A Handbook of Muslim Foods
* 21. Understanding Halal Foods: Fallacies and Facts

II. BOOKS ABOUT FRIDAY KHUTAB:

* 1. Book of Al-Khutab
* 2. Islamic Orations
* 3. Orations from the Pulpit
* 4. Chronicle of Khutab
* 5. Friday Khutab

* 6. A Manual of Friday Khutab
* 7. Khutab Al-Masjid
* 8. Khutab From Mihrab

III. GENERAL SUBJECTS:

* 1. Islamic Fundamentalism (co-authored)
* 2. Du 'a' After Completing the Recitation of Qur'an
* 3. Introducing Islam to non-Muslims (co-authored)
   4. Prostration – Sujood (new edition)
   5. Guidelines of Employment by Muslim Communities (co-authored)
* 6. Farewell Khutbah of the Prophet – Its Universal Values
   7. Understanding Islam and Muslims
* 8. Muslims and non-Muslims: Face to Face
* 9. Matrimonial Education in Islam (New Edition)
* 10. Life, Death and the Life After
* 11. The Golden Book of Islamic Lists
* 12. Al-Jinn
* 13. Islam and Muslims: Myth or Reality
   14. Islamic Awareness
* 15. Death and Dying
* 16. Family Values in Islam
* 17. Book of Inquiries
* 18 The Adolescent Life
* 19. Social Services and Counseling
* 20. A Course on Islamic Shari'ah
* 21. Da'wah Through Dialogue
* 22. Understanding the Qur'an
* 23. Themes of the Qur'an
* 24. Book of Knowledge
* 25. Reflections from a Flying Falcon

* 26. Feasts, Festivities and Holidays

    * These publications are available from:

Foundation for Islamic Knowledge
P.O. Box 665
Lombard, IL 60148
Phone: (630) 495-4817 / Fax: (630) 627-8894

NEWSLETTER

The Foundation has a newsletter called Perspectives, it is published bi-monthly, and distributed free. If you wish to have a copy of the newsletter, please write to the address below.

<u>Virginia Office</u>
(Newsletter/Perspectives)
P. O. Box 65250
Hampton, VA 23665

Light over Light

BOOKS TO BE PUBLISHED

1. Islamic Perspectives
2. Islamic Understanding
3. Islam vs. Muslims
4. The Book of Healing
5. Speakers Bureau Guide Book
6. Health, Hygiene and Nutrition
7. Halal – Haram book of Khutab
8. Book of Du 'a'
9. The Book of Targheeb
10. Scientific Reflections from the Qur'an
11. Biological Terms in the Qur'an
12. Educational Institutions in Islam
13. Writing an Islamic Will
14. Qur'an Commentary in Summary
15. Book of Wisdom
16. Welcome to the World of Islam
17. A Lifetime Journey
18. Arafa of the Hereafter
19. Al-Insaan: The Human Being

These and other books will not be published unless someone like you comes forward and extend a hand of help. You may sponsor any of the above books, or any number of copies of a particular book. Your help in any capacity is greatly needed even to pay the previous debts to the printers. The foundation is tax-exempt from the IRS and your donations are tax-deductible. The employer I.D. number with the I.R.S. is 36-352-8916.

For more information, or to send your donation, please contact:

Foundation for Islamic Knowledge
P.O. Box 665, Lombard, IL 60148, USA
Phone: (630) 495-4817 / Fax: (630) 627-8894

Books Available From the Foundation for Islamic Knowledge

Books Available From the Foundation for Islamic Knowledge

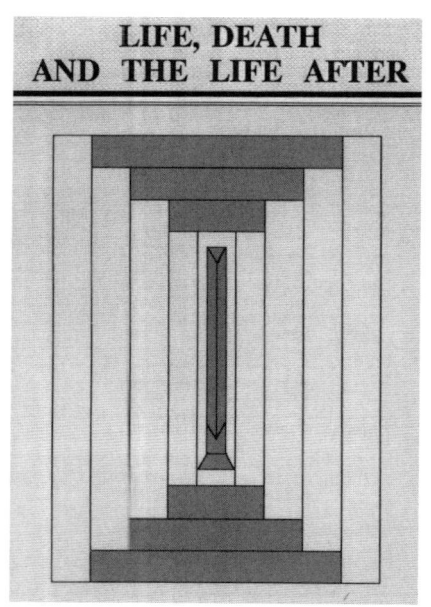

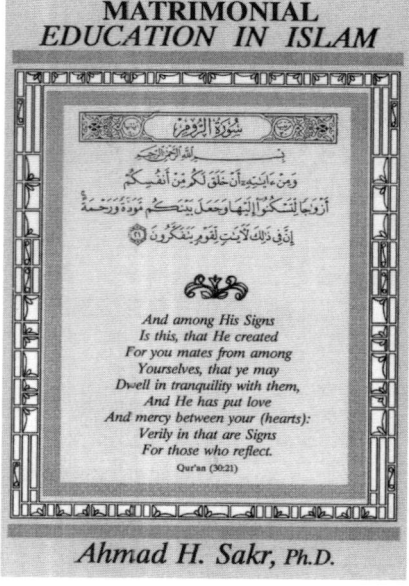

Books Available From the Foundation for Islamic Knowledge

Farewell Khutbah of The Prophet ﷺ

Its Universal Values

AL-JINN

KHUTAB AL-MASJID

AHMAD H. SAKR, Ph.D.

A Muslim Guide to Food Ingredients

AHMAD H. SAKR, Ph.D.
Professor of Nutritional Biochemistry

Books Available From the Foundation for Islamic Knowledge

FASTING
Regulations and Practices

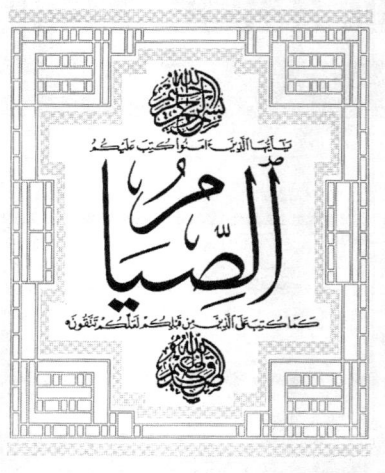

Ahmad H. Sakr, Ph.D.

Books Available From the Foundation for Islamic Knowledge

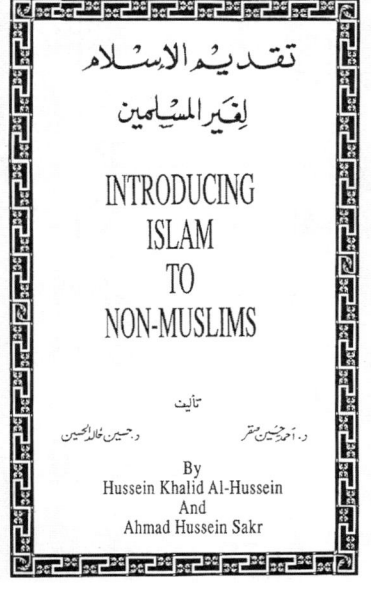

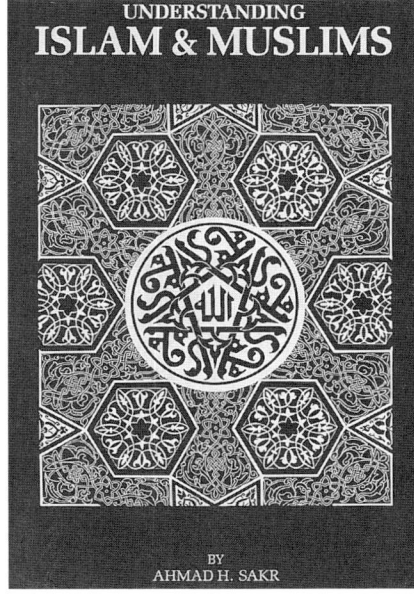

Books Available From the Foundation for Islamic Knowledge

Books Available From the Foundation for Islamic Knowledge

Books Available From the Foundation for Islamic Knowledge

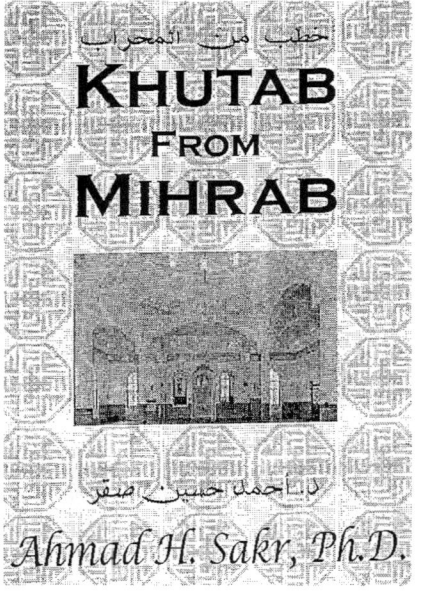

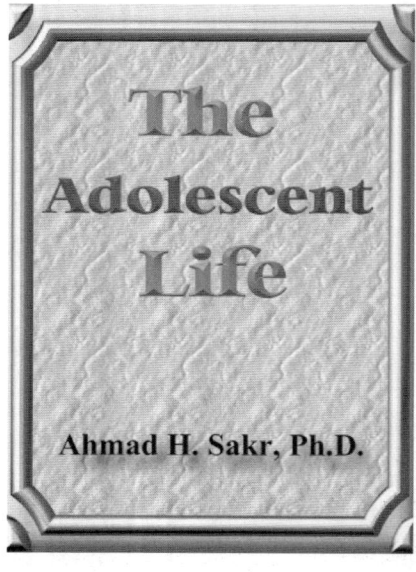

Books Available From the Foundation for Islamic Knowledge

Books Available From the Foundation for Islamic Knowledge

O mankind! We created you from a single soul, male and female, and made you into nations and tribes, so that you may come to know one another. Truly, the most honored of you in God's sight is the greatest of you in piety. God is All-Knowing, All-Aware. (Quran, 49:13)